GOD'S
MAN

A Daily Devotional Guide to Christlike Character

EDITED BY

DON M. AYCOCK

REVISED EDITION

kregel
PUBLICATIONS

Grand Rapids, MI 49501

God's Man: A Daily Devotional Guide to Christlike Character

Published by Kregel Publications, a division of Kregel, Inc., P.O. Box 2607, Grand Rapids, MI 49501. Kregel Publications provides trusted, biblical publications for Christian growth and service. Your comments and suggestions are valued.

For more information about Kregel Publications, visit our web site at: www.kregel.com

Inclusion in this collected work does not constitute an endorsement by the individual contributors or the publisher of every organization or theological position represented herein.

Cover design: Frank Gutbrod
Cover photo: Lindsey M. Gutbrod

Library of Congress Cataloging-in-Publication Data
Aycock, Don M.
  God's man: a daily devotional guide to Christlike character / edited by Don M. Aycock.
     p.   cm.
  1. Christian men—Prayer-books and devotions—English.
2. Devotional calendars.   I. Aycock, Don M.
  BV4843.G64   1998   242'.642—dc21   98-44656
                                                           CIP
ISBN 0-8254-2000-8

Printed in the United States of America

1 2 3 4 5 6 / 04 03 02 01 00

To the men in my life

My late father, Dewey Aycock. He was an oil-field man, tough but with a great sense of humor and a love of music. He found Christ in his senior years and was baptized on Father's Day in his sixty-fifth year. I still miss him.

My father-in-law, Carl Ricketts. He is a good man with a zany sense of humor and a love for his family. He's also my fishing buddy.

And my teenage sons, Ryan and Chris. I'm proud of the way they are becoming God's men.

Table of Contents

8

Week 47
A Man and His Body: Physical Fitness 290

Week 48
A Man and His Body: Sexuality 295

Week 49
A Man and His Finances: Money 301

Week 50
A Man and His Finances: Investments 307

Week 51
A Man and His Finances: Stewardship 214

Week 52
A Man and His Finances: Savings 320

Biographical Information of Contributors 326

Introduction

Unless you've been like Rip Van Winkle, who slept through a revolution, you know about the revolution that is taking place with men today. Although we're inundated with possessions, we still hunger for God (see Ps. 42:1–3). This fact is evident from the phenomenal growth of the Christian men's movement in the 1990s, which many scholars have noted and documented. Groups such as Promise Keepers have tapped into this deep-seated spiritual vacuum. Such organizations realize that men want something more than money can buy. They want a personal relationship with God.

This book is an effort to satisfy the spiritual hunger that we all have as men (see John 6:35). It's been written by men for men. You'll find topics dealing with everything from our relationships, families, and work, to our time, our money, and the special problems we have. In all, fifty-two different subjects are covered, one for each week of the year. Each topic has a number of devotions, which enables us to cover thoroughly an entire year.

I do not pretend that these subjects are everything a man needs to know. In selecting them, I have been intentionally broad and suggestive of areas we need to consider. For example, under the section titled "A Man and His Emotions," the four chapters hardly scratch the surface of our emotions. But that shouldn't be a problem, for most men I know have trouble dealing with their feelings of anger, loneliness, and despair. We also have trouble dealing with joy and other happy emotions.

The authors in this book come from a variety of backgrounds. You'll find their names and some information about each of them (including their addresses) at the end of the book. These men include pastors and laymen, professors and professionals, experts on various subjects and ordinary men with insights to share. Some of them are retired, and some of them are middle-aged; others are just beginning their careers. Some of them are seasoned writers whereas others had published little before writing for this book.

But all of the writers have one characteristic in common—we all want to be men of God (see 1 Tim. 6:11). And we're trying to do the best we can for ourselves, our families, and our Lord. If you feel especially helped by something we wrote, feel free to contact us.

Here's a word about how to use this book. Set aside time each day to read the suggested biblical text in your own preferred translation of Scripture. Remember that if you skip reading the Bible text, you won't get the full spiritual impact.

Next, read the devotional for each day. Spend time with it, and let the message sink in. Roll it around in your mind, and then ask yourself, "How does this truth apply to me?" On some days the devotion may seem to slide right off, while on other days you might think, "Hey! How did this guy know so much about me?"

Each devotion ends with a prayer. Use it as a guide for your own prayer. The devotion and suggested Scripture texts are brief, so you can easily read everything in fifteen minutes or less.

Be serious about your spiritual life, but have fun, too. Enjoy the experience of moving through this book. Accept God's "Yes!" to your life (2 Cor. 1:20). Now let's get started on the journey! Blessings on your spiritual quest!

—*Don M. Aycock*

A Man and His Relationships: God

DAY ONE

FIRST THINGS FIRST
Matthew 6:33

In Matthew 6:33, Jesus declared, "Seek first the kingdom of God and his righteousness, and all else you need shall be provided as well." Jesus made this a statement about priorities in response to the worries people had about material possessions. "What shall we eat? What shall we drink? What shall we wear?" they typically asked. Jesus never denied the importance of the things we own. He simply said that they should not be our first priority.

A stunned husband whose wife had filed for divorce said to me, "I gave her everything a woman could want." Wrong! It's true that he gave her *possessions* in abundance. But what she wanted was *him*. She wanted attention from and a relationship with a husband who, unfortunately, was so immersed in his business that he had no time for his family. He learned too late the penalty of misplaced priorities.

So what's first in your life? Jesus said that when God is first and others are second, He will give us all we need from day to day (see Phil. 4:19). But if our priorities are out of order, our emotional and spiritual lives will ultimately be chaotic.

Dear Lord, please make me wise enough to know who and what matters most. Amen.

TRUST

Proverbs 3:5–6

For six years before learning to swim, our younger son relished the experience of jumping into the deep end of the pool. The water was twice as deep as he was tall. Yet he would leap off the side gleefully and giggling. Why? Because either Mom or Dad was always there waiting to catch him. He believed that a loving parent was with him in the deep waters, and we loved him too much to let him drown. He learned to trust us unconditionally.

Theologically speaking, "trust" and "faith" are almost synonymous. We cannot believe in God in any life-changing sense unless we also trust Him to do what is best for us. Unless and until we are able trust in the Lord with all our heart (Prov. 3:5–6), we will have trouble with faith. Until we can dive into the deep waters, assured of God's presence and love; until we know that our best interests are in God's heart; until we believe that God's ways for us are always best, regardless of whether we understand them; and until we trust not only our lives, loves, and labors but also our relationships, businesses, and personal decisions to our heavenly Parent, we will not find the peace that God wants for us (see John 14:27; Phil. 4:6–7).

Dear God, whatever decisions I face today, please remind me that You know best. Amen.

QUIET PRAYERS

Proverbs 8:34

One of the most moving experiences of prayer in my life came about when a friend advised me to draw near to God by seeking His presence in silence rather than through my words. She encouraged me to clear the clutter out of my mind and concentrate on the Lord Himself, to think of who He truly is rather than what I wanted to say to Him. Taking several deep breaths and letting my mind and body release the pressures of the daily routine, I began to think.

Images flashed through my mind . . . pictures from books . . . ideas about what God ought to be or how He ought to look. But at last an impression emerged that I had not expected. It was the image of open arms drawing me in and cradling me softly and safely. I lingered there without words and experienced one of the most powerful experiences of prayer I had ever known. Even now, when life is hectic and overwhelming, I sometimes retreat to a quiet place and breathe deeply and surrender wordlessly to those arms.

Proverbs 8:34 reminds us, "Happy is the person who listens to me, watching daily at my gates, waiting beside my doors." Sometimes our words get in the way of praying, and we miss what God has to say to us. Only when we are silent and still in God's presence can we hear divine whispers of peace or purpose, comfort or challenge, forgiveness or faith.

Loving God, I pause in the silence now to listen for Your voice. Amen.

ASPIRING TO GREATNESS
I Corinthians 1:26—29

In my community many years ago was a young man named Bill who was a great football running back at the former Lee Edwards High School. When game time arrived on Fridays, the crowds would pour out to watch Bill defeat the opponents almost single-handedly.

Bill's younger brother, Charlie, didn't play football. Why try? Who could ever live up to his older brother's greatness? Charlie would languish in Bill's shadow. It seemed easier not even to make the effort.

However, a wise football coach named Lee Stone went to Charlie and said, "Son, I think you have the speed and skills to play this game. Why don't you try out for the team?" After some cajoling and encouraging, the coach convinced the reticent younger brother to give it a shot. The rest is history. Charlie "Choo Choo" Justice went on to become an All-American at the University of North Carolina and one of the leading rushers and scorers in the history of the Washington Redskins.

God is still in the business of doing what seems most unlikely. Paul reminded his readers that not many of them were wise, or powerful, or even wealthy in the world's eyes (1 Cor. 1:26). Nevertheless, the Lord redeemed them for His glory.

Who is to say what God can do with unlikely folks if He so chooses? Although our dreams may seem foolish to the world (v. 27), in God's hands they can become tomorrow's realities. Don't give up on yourself or on God's power to make something exciting of your life (v. 28).

Dear God, please remind me never to give up on either my dreams or Your power to make them come true. Amen.

THE LAW AND THE PROPHETS
Matthew 22:35–40

The Jewish law was not merely the Ten Commandments. It also contained hundreds of decrees and regulations that determined everything from traditional "biggies" (for example, "do not commit murder" and "do not steal") to such matters as how to go about washing one's hands. In the Gospel of Matthew, Jesus said that all of the laws could be summarized in two great commandments—love God and love people. In 22:40, He declared, "On these two commandments depend all the law and the prophets."

Upon his return from Vietnam, a soldier was questioned by his wife. "I have read about 'the meat market' in Saigon," she said, referring to the section of town notorious for prostitution. "Although I can forgive, I need to know. Did you ever go there?"

With obvious disappointment at even being asked, he answered, "I love you. That love made the decision for me long before I ever knew there was a place called 'the meat market.'" The husband's love for his wife dictated his actions.

Jesus said that what we love will dictate our actions. If we truly love God, we will serve Him and the church. (For example, we will witness and work faithfully.) And if we truly love people, we will treat them kindly, graciously, and honestly. All the Old Testament laws will be fulfilled with integrity if we simply love God and people. And dealing with others from that base of integrity and kindness will enable us to look at ourselves in the mirror and like what we see. This adds meaning to Jesus' words, "You shall love your neighbor as yourself" (v. 39).

Father, as Your Son loved and served You,
so may I. And as You love me, so enable me
to love others. Amen.

DAY SIX

FIRST GOD LOVES US

1 John 4:19

I'll never forget a dramatic moment I witnessed while worshiping at Riverside Church in New York City several years ago. A baby was being baptized. I recall little of the day's service—the music, the liturgy, or even the sermon. But I will never forget that moment of baptism. The pastor poured water on the child's head and then lifted the baby in full view of the congregation. "Here," he said, "is living proof of the text, 'We love God because He first loved us.'"

The pastor's statement was true. That child had no awareness of God or Christian theology. The child also had no idea where he was or why his head had just become wet. Moreover, the child understood nothing about the concept of God. But in that place at that time, a pastor, parents, and a congregation celebrated the fact that God loved that baby and wanted to see him raised to become a person of faith.

A friend told me about a boy who was the apple of his parents' eyes. Tragically, in his mid-teens, the boy's life went awry. He dropped out of school and began associating with the worst kind of crowds. One night he staggered into his house at 3:00 A.M., completely drunk. His mother slipped out of bed and left her room. The father followed, assuming that his wife was in the kitchen, perhaps crying. Instead he found her at her son's bedside, softly stroking his matted hair as he lay passed out drunk on the covers. "What are you doing?," the father asked, and the mother simply answered, "He won't let me love him when he's awake."

The mother stepped into her son's darkness with a love that existed even though he did not yet love her back. So it is with God and us. He loves us often in spite of ourselves, even when we would reject Him. But in time, the knowledge of that wonderful, searching, forgiving, cleansing love sinks in. And once we are gripped by it, what can we do but love God in return? As 1 John 4:19 says, "We love God because He first loved us."

*O Lord of unconditional love, thank You for
caring about me, even when I did not care about
You or myself. I love You, too, and want to
demonstrate it by loving other people. Amen.*

KEEPING YOUR WORD
Numbers 30:1–2

Historically Quakers have resisted being sworn in before testifying in court. Their rationale is simple. If they have to promise to be honest for the next few minutes, the obvious implication is that they are dishonest the rest of the time. And if such is the case, why should anyone trust the oath they make? A person's integrity should be such that no one would ever ask whether she or he will speak "the truth, the whole truth, and nothing but the truth." Indeed, it would never occur to anyone to suspect that the person would do otherwise. In this way, the Quakers make a strong point about character and integrity.

Jesus made the same point in Matthew 5:37 when He told His listeners, "But let your statement be, 'Yes, yes' or 'No, no.'" In other words, be a person of such integrity that when you speak, the community will never have reason to doubt what you say. In Numbers 30, Moses emphasized the same truth to "the heads of the tribes of the people of Israel" (v. 1). "When a person vows a vow to the Lord, or swears an oath to bind himself by a pledge, he shall not break his word" (v. 2).

Jesus, Moses, and the Quakers are all talking about the importance of having integrity, honesty, and trustworthiness. Whatever else we have, we remain impoverished if we lose any of these virtues. An adage says, "Reputation is what people think you are; character is what God knows you to be" (see Prov. 22:1).

*O God, let me so value my integrity that I will
endeavor to live faithfully and truthfully with
You and with my neighbors in the world. Amen.*

JIM NEAL

A Man and His Relationships: Wife

A WIFE'S BEAUTY

Song of Solomon 1:12–15

When it comes to identifying flowers, I am a blooming idiot (pun intended). For example, I can't tell a daisy from a daffodil. I must rely on experts to tell me that a henna blossom from the vineyards of En-geddi is the source of a popular reddish-brown, sweet-smelling hair dye used in the Middle East. But I don't need an expert to let me know that my wife loves flowers. Even more than the bouquet is the sentiment behind it that captivates her (Song 1:12–15).

I am attracted by pleasant perfume whereas I am repelled by a putrid scent. Just as we prepare ourselves for our wives by ensuring that we are clean and smelling good, so too our lives should be lived in such a way that we do not "stink" before our blessed Lord (see Eccl. 10:1). He is pleased when we give off the fragrant aroma of moral purity (2 Cor. 2:14, 16). The faithfulness we demonstrate before both the Lord and our wives is indeed a sweet smell!

Father, each day I confess what has soiled my life
so that You might make me clean and
presentable to You. May the aroma of my life be
such that it draws, rather than repels,
people to You. Amen.

WATCH IT!

Proverbs 6:20–35

No woman in the world is worth committing the sin of adultery (Prov. 6:20–35). Sadly, this truth is often forgotten or ignored when a man is overcome by lust. As the body screams for sexual gratification, he can hardly contain himself. But what looks so good and seems so pleasurable in the heat of passion can leave one feeling empty and broken-hearted.

Sexual immorality can ruin not only us as men but also our marriages. But we can save ourselves a lot of grief by pausing to think before we act. Here are some key questions you should ask before doing something that might make you feel terrific but that you know is downright sinful:

- How will I feel in the morning after doing this?
- Is this God's best for me?
- If I had to announce on Sunday morning what I had done, would I feel good about this action?
- When I stand before God, will I be filled with sorrow for having done this?

Father, please help me to run from sexual sin rather than embrace it. Amen.

THANK GOD FOR SEX

Genesis 4:1–2

Sex was not man's idea but God's. It is pleasurable and productive. What a great gift He has provided!

However, we sometimes think that it is one-dimensional, involving only our body. In reality it is three dimensional, involving our body, mind, and spirit. Often the mind and spirit play an even greater role than the body in sexual fulfillment.

Eve recognized that procreation occurred with the help of God. This fact made the whole process holy. With the birth of Cain and

Abel, the first branches on our family tree sprouted. Eve may have even glimpsed the promise of a line to the Messiah, as some scholars have suggested. She at least knew that something special had occurred and that the birth of her sons was a gift from God (Gen. 4:1–2).

One of the ways we can honor our wives is by respecting their role as mothers. When we make them and the children they've borne a priority over our careers and recreation, we say to them that they are important to us.

Father, please help me to be a sensitive husband and lover to my wife. Amen.

Wow!

Genesis 29:16–20

Every man is a person of vision—at least when it comes to seeing a beautiful woman! That ability can be wonderful or terrible, depending on our "linger factor." For example, when my eyes linger too long upon a woman other than my wife, the stare leads to lust.

When Jacob fell in love with Rachel, it wasn't lust. He loved her so deeply that he was willing to serve her father seven years to marry her (Gen. 29:16–20). How different this is from our "instant" society! We have microwave food and readi-mix concrete to give us instant gratification. There is little in life for which we have to wait.

For Jacob, those seven years seemed as though they were only a few days. But such a span of time would have seemed like an eternity to me. That's why I'm encouraged by the question "What do I love enough to wait for?" Jacob's love was not just a romantic fantasy. He wanted to commit himself in marriage to Rachel for the rest of his life. That's why he was willing to wait so long to be with her.

Marriages today need more than just romance to survive. They need the kind of commitment that Jacob displayed. Because I love my wife so much and am committed to her so deeply, I will look to her to fulfill my sexual desires.

Lord, please help me to remain faithful to both You and my wife. Amen.

BE A MAN—FOR YOUR WIFE'S SAKE

Ephesians 5:22—23

Love alone is never a good enough reason to get married. A man needs to be alert to a woman who is committed to the same ultimate values he holds. The problem in our society today is not in finding women who are willing to be submissive but in finding men who are wise and winsome servant leaders (Eph. 5:22–23).

Leadership has two minimum requirements: vision and followers. If you don't have both qualities, you are not a leader. Vision means that you are a pilgrim, not a settler. It also means that you have determined a direction to follow and have communicated that vision to your wife. Many men today haven't figured out that they need a big vision to motivate them for the rest of their lives and to share in common with their wife. As you and your wife are drawn toward achieving the vision, you are also drawn closer to each other.

What is your highest goal? What do you claim as your ultimate purpose? If you and your wife don't share the same basic desires, your relationship will eventually grow apart, regardless of how noble your aims might be. If becoming Christlike is your ultimate objective, ensure that you have a like-minded woman to share it with you. The issue of submission will then fall into place, especially as you help each other submit to Christ.

Lord, help me to be united with a woman who shares my desire to live in a godly manner. May the loving leadership I display earn my wife's willingness to follow me with enthusiasm. Amen.

AT LAST!

Genesis 2:20—24

The assignment was one of the most emotionally charged tasks I would ever have. Although I hadn't sung in public for a long time, I was to escort my daughter down the wedding aisle while singing, "This is the day that the Lord has made . . . and I'm so glad

He made you." We stopped halfway, and I continued singing, "with each rising sun you were there by our side; you're more than a dream come true."

Genesis 2:20–24 reminds us that God brought the woman He had created to the man. In a sense, the Father of life walked the first bride down the garden aisle to present to her man. When Adam awoke from his deep sleep, he saw "more than a dream come true." Now he was complete. Eve had arrived, and she became his helpmate (in other words, his lifelong companion).

The little girls we raise are helpmates-in-training. One day we will present them to their future husbands. One of the greatest resources we have to train our future brides and grooms is our own helpmates—our wives. They were once someone's daughters whom God appointed to be united to us in marriage. Let us never forget this wonderful truth!

Lord, please help me to show my wife how much
I treasure her by the way I treat her. Amen.

DAY SEVEN

YOU'RE THE BEST!
Proverbs 31:10–31

Now that I am getting older, I am often asked, "If you could start over again, what would you do differently as a father?" A long list comes to my mind, but one change finds its way to the top: "I would praise my kids more." Another item is that I would praise my wife more in front of my kids. The good news is that I *still* have the opportunity to praise her and the kids!

In the past when I read Proverbs 31:10–31, I missed an important point. The standards set here for the virtuous woman were not simply the musings of King Lemuel (v. 1); they were an "oracle his mother taught him."

The job description of the wife in vv. 10–31 is overwhelming. A virtuous woman contributes to her family emotionally, economically, educationally, and spiritually. The character traits described are challenging. But the most important quality mentioned in this passage is noble character, for all other affirmations spring from this virtue.

The final command of the passage is given not to women but to men: "Give her the reward she has earned, and let her works bring her praise at the city gate" (v. 31). Every day I need to ask a few important questions, such as "Have I given my wife her due? Do my kids know how much I appreciate her? Can others readily see the respect and honor I have for her?"

Lord, please help me to say to my wife, "You're the best, sweetheart!" Amen.

JIM   BURTON

A Man and His Relationships: Children

DAY ONE

BOOT CAMP

Psalm 127:3-5

Warfare is a recurring theme in the Old Testament, and so are large families, particularly families that include many sons. In ancient times, men wanted to have many sons so they would have more help with the family business. Many sons meant more hands to till the soil and to harvest the crop. In wartime, more sons meant more hands to defend the family property.

Unless your last name is Hatfield or McCoy, warfare and feuds may seem foreign. Nevertheless, Psalm 127:3–5 applies to you, for you are in the midst of a spiritual battle (Eph. 6:10–12). This war does not involve charging horses and flaming arrows. Evil doesn't always have to dress in army fatigues and wave a flag to announce its charge (1 Peter 5:8).

America is in a fight for its soul. As the West continues to become more pagan, the army of the Lord needs more "soldiers" to win the spiritual battle that rages. Our families perpetuate the Christian heritage best when we dads are seen as men of faith. Remember, you're not raising just kids; you're raising the next generation of God's soldiers, whom He will use to "contend earnestly for the faith" (Jude 1:3).

Father, thank You for the blessing of children.
Please teach me how to prepare them for the
spiritual battles of their generation so that they
might stand strong against the evil one. Amen.

FAITHFUL FAMILY

1 John 2:12–14

For years, you could always count on singing the hymn "Faith of Our Fathers" during the Father's Day recognition at church. The song celebrates the positive influence of a faithful father on his family. Sadly, I don't hear this hymn sung as often these days. Perhaps it's because faithful fathers are becoming rare.

Faithful fathers are a blessing. Children raised in a home where dad leads them in Christian spiritual development are more likely to become believers themselves. Of course, this is not always true. As faithful as a father might be, his belief cannot save his children. His decision to follow Christ is not a package deal that ushers the family into heaven. But the father's faith can create a predisposition within the family toward believing in Christ. In the families of most faithful fathers, it is natural for the children and grandchildren to become believers (1 John 2:12–14).

Although the Christian faith is lived within a community of believers (i.e., the local church), other crucial issues are worth remembering. For instance, every individual must decide whether to reject or accept Christ. And everyone must deal with the sin issues in his life. Although the faith of a father can unite his family spiritually, the children remain accountable to God for their actions.

Lord, please teach me how to be faithful and accountable to You in such a way that my family also will be encouraged to commit their lives to Your Son in faith. Amen.

LIFE'S LABORATORY

Deuteronomy 4:9–10

Every home that's blessed with children has this common trait—it's a laboratory for life. Students (children) get practical, hands-on experience under the tutelage of professors (their parents). The home is where they learn behavior, values, and convictions. They learn whether it's proper for a man to hit a woman. They learn appropriate and inappropriate ways to express affection. The syllabus also includes lessons on sharing versus selfishness. From this example, we see that education is not just an institutional process. All of life is a school where every person is both a student and a teacher (Deut. 4:9–10).

By God's design, religious instruction is primarily a function of the home. Oddly enough, local churches carry the weight of formal spiritual instruction today in part because Christian fathers surrender their role of leadership to the church. However good a church education program might be, what a child learns about Christ in the home will be far more influential than what he learns in church.

God uses local congregations to reach the unchurched and to convert entire families. And He also uses committed fathers to bring their children to faith in Christ. Is your lesson plan current?

Father, please teach me how to teach my children about You. Amen.

DAY FOUR

GOD'S GOOD GIFTS

Matthew 7:9–12

Some folks have major hang-ups about God. They say that He's mean, hateful, and vindictive. And they warn others that God's out to get them.

It's true. God is out to get you. But His hunt isn't vindictive. The first desire of God's heart is to bless you spiritually. His blessings are His good gifts to you (James 1:17). If you have not experienced His abundance, perhaps it's because you haven't asked for it (James 4:2).

Most likely your children are not hesitant to ask you for what they want. In the early years of a child's life, asking for things is one of the few things that she or he knows how to do well. And children typically communicate their desires in one way—by crying.

When was the last time you cried out to God for help? Don't be surprised by the idea. After all, you are God's creation, and He takes great joy in you, just as you derive great joy from your children. The relationship between you and God is grounded in His love. His compassion builds up instead of tears down; it affirms rather than condemns.

This day make every effort to love and provide for your children as your heavenly Father has loved and provided for you (Matt. 7:9–12).

Father, please teach me to show unconditional love through my actions toward my children. Amen.

WHEN I GROW UP. . . .

1 Chronicles 22:6

For many generations, a common practice, particularly in the Orient, has been for sons to enter their father's vocation. If dad is a carpenter, the son also becomes a carpenter. Vocational choice seems to be almost nonexistent. A boy is expected to follow in his father's path.

Practical reasons exist for this practice. In the centuries before public higher education was available to the masses and before the industrial revolution, dad was about the only teacher a son had. Home was like a technical school. Truancy didn't happen often. The son learned the trade whether or not he liked it.

Can you imagine a father's joy to have his son work beside him? The son becomes a mirror of the father's skills. If the son takes the vocation to heart, he may even take the skill to a higher level of expertise.

David's vocation included politics and military service. He accomplished much in his life, but he could not complete the building of a temple to the Lord. But David had a son named Solomon whose life's training was designed to make him a leader. He would take his father's accomplishments to the next level (1 Chron. 22:6).

Instead of building strength through bloodshed, as his dad had done, Solomon would build the infrastructure of the nation peacefully through wisdom. Like his dad, Solomon's obedience to God would ensure the prosperity of the Israelites. At the heart of David's request to Solomon was the hope that his son had learned from his mistakes, which would help Solomon accomplish his God-given task.

Father, please help me to teach my children something that's more important than a mere vocation. Enable me to teach them to trust and obey You. Amen.

BOYS AND BASEBALL

Colossians 3:21

When I was young, baseball was important to me. I loved the game so much that I studied it and played it every day. I hustled when I played, for baseball was my life.

You can imagine the excitement I felt when my oldest son began playing baseball. This game would be one of our main bonding mechanisms. I didn't know beans about soccer, so baseball would be a mentoring vehicle. He also has more talent than I ever had. My love for the game has far exceeded my ability.

If my son would just listen to me, I could help him be a great baseball player. Learning to read curve balls, shift his body weight with the swing, steal bases, turn double plays—these are the little things that separate the amateurs from the professionals.

A pattern developed in our relationship. Because of my familiarity with the game, I saw every mistake that my son made. In addition, I knew how to correct them. So post-game drives home became a critique of how to improve his game. It soon got old for my son. One night he finally said, "Dad, could you not start by telling me everything I did wrong. Tell me what I did right first."

My mobile coaching clinic wasn't helping. My son had become discouraged. I was anxious to help, but I had become a hindrance. He was becoming bitter toward me. It caused me to think. Was my childhood obsession with baseball worth risking a relationship with my son? It was time to de-emphasize a game and refocus on the person (Col. 3:21).

*Lord, please help me to guard my emotions
and agendas toward my family so that I might
not impose unrealistic, burdensome
expectations on them. Amen.*

A CHILD'S FAITH

Luke 10:21

Some years ago, I was sharing my faith in Christ with a former high school friend. She had become financially successful after college, and she was self-sufficient.

This person had many intellectual questions. After trying to answer them, I finally explained that no matter how much one tries to understand God, he or she still must have simple faith to become a Christian. That statement stunned her. "I don't think there is such a thing as simple faith," she replied.

A child comes to Christ the same way as an adult—by grace through faith. Few children understand deep theological issues. They've not experienced all of the complexities of life. They simply take God at His word.

Trusting Christ represents two sides of a fence. Each side gives us a different perspective. One side is a worldly and intellectual view; the other side is a new, Christ-transformed worldview. Hope replaces hopelessness. Possibilities replace impossibilities. Love replaces hate. Trust replaces mistrust. Faith replaces skepticism. It's a world a child could love.

Do you have an intellectual pursuit of God? If so, that pleases Him. After all, asking questions about Him is better than ignoring Him. Nevertheless, the issue comes down to this: Can you take God at His word? Chances are your child can (Luke 10:21). Why not take a cue from him or her?

Lord, please help me not to forget how to love You
with the simple faith of a child. Amen.

C . T H O M A S   H I L T O N

A Man and His Relationships: Others

BROTHERLY LOVE

1 Samuel 18:1

Many men see *love* as a "sex-saturated" word that involves two people of the opposite gender in an intimate relationship. One man said, "If it isn't genital, it isn't love." Women might agree that love involves intimacy, but they also know that it entails much more than that. Love isn't limited to a man and woman having intercourse in bed. Love is also expressed by holding hands, showing kindness, being tender, displaying sympathy, choosing to listen, and having compassion.

A husband and wife were reading separate books while sitting together in their living room. They spoke not a word for an hour. Then one of them broke the silence by saying, "You know, I just love being in your presence." This couple truly enjoyed each other's company.

First Samuel 18:1 says that Jonathan and David had a brotherly love for one another. Chapters 18–20 suggest that they were kind and considerate to each other. They evidently had qualities that encouraged one another to be better people. They undoubtedly respected each other's minds, ideas, bravery, and discipline. Their friendship is one of the closest and deepest between two men ever recorded in the Bible.

Men can show brotherly love to other men when they offer mutual assistance in time of need, give encouragement, and show a willingness to help. Does the idea of brotherly love surprise you or make you feel uncomfortable? It shouldn't. Think of Jonathan and David as one example of two godly men who had a close relationship.

The brotherly love between these two endured some tough times. Even when it became clear that David would be Israel's next king, Jonathan remained committed to him as a friend (23:17). Jonathan was willing to lay aside any personal desires he might have had so that his friend could prosper (Prov. 18:24). Now this is brotherly love at its best!

O Lord, please help me to show brotherly love to other men I know. Amen.

THE FONZ GOT IT RIGHT

Proverbs 22:24–25

One of my favorite television programs is "Happy Days," and one of my favorite characters is the Fonz. He was able to remain calm and control his temper in any crisis. Perhaps he understood the truth that when you lose your temper, you also lose self-control.

Different translations render Proverbs 22:24–25 in distinct ways, giving it a variety of shades of meaning. But regardless of which version you prefer, they all make the same point. People tend to become like the people with whom they spend a lot of time. Even such negative characteristics as being angry and short-tempered can rub off on us.

From this passage we learn two reasons to avoid people who are out of control. First, their unchecked lives can be dangerous. Second, their rampaging emotions can affect you adversely. These observations agree with the adage that says we are influenced by the company we keep (see 1 Cor. 15:33).

For example, if I were to tell you that some of my grandfather's best friends were "Machine-Gun" Kelly, Ma Barker, John Dillinger, and Frank Nitti (all of whom were notorious criminals), you would know something about my grandfather.

So who are your friends? How would you describe them to someone who doesn't know you? Are you ever out of control? Are they?

O Lord, please help me to give control of my emotions to You. Amen.

I DON'T LIKE CRITICISM

Proverbs 25:12

Some people welcome criticism. In fact, they seem to thrive on it. They are always open for other people to comment on their behavior, lifestyle, dress, vocabulary, children, wife, skills, abilities, and job performance. They might thank you for sharing your critical words with them because they think that this is how they grow. They believe that if others didn't share their feelings, they would not become the full person God has called them to be.

I am not one of those people, mainly because I don't like criticism. If you have something negative to say about me, I don't want to hear it. If you really have to make a comment, please sugarcoat it. A spoonful of sweetness helps the criticism to go down. Better yet, how about giving me three words of praise with every word of criticism?

I don't tend to grow when I hear criticism. I feel diminished, especially as I mull over the comment and wonder what it means. In fact, I lie awake at night worrying about what you said. So the next time you get a chance to criticize me, please don't do it.

Despite what I've said, I know that some criticism can be good for me. Proverbs 25:12 reveals that just as some people value jewelry made from the finest gold, so we should treasure valid criticism. In fact, a "wise man's rebuke to a listening ear" will enhance the beauty of our Christian character.

The Bible tells me that I should be open to the insightful, godly feedback of fellow Christians. I'm reminded of Proverbs 27:17, which says that as iron sharpens iron, so a friend sharpens a friend. One of the ways God communicates with me is through other Christians. I need to open my ears to their comments so that I can adorn myself with Christlike graces. I'm trying, and with God's help I'm making progress.

Dear Lord, please help me to hear You speak
to me through other believers. Amen.

BEING TRUSTWORTHY

Proverbs 25:9

Proverbs 25:9 assumes that one is having a personal quarrel with his neighbor. The point is that if in arguing your case, you betray another man's confidence, you will be considered a gossip and lose your good reputation (v. 10). Thus, it is always better to keep a sensitive matter private and avoid being publicly disgraced.

One of the givens in life is that we will get into arguments with others. You can count on it. Therefore, when it happens, do not let it destroy your Christian life or your relationship with your friends. Deal with it directly rather than run from it. Don't ignore the problem or pretend that it isn't happening.

I met someone who, when her children were small and had to be disciplined, would feel guilty. She said, "My mother never raised her voice to me. She never had to give me a 'time out.' She never had to spank me." Now when this person disciplines one of her children, she feels worse than the wayward child. Clearly, this parent and her mother are quite different and deal with life in their own ways.

When you find yourself disagreeing with someone, try to do so directly with him. Make every effort to be understood. Also, when you disagree, keep confidences that have previously been shared with you.

Our temptation in a heated argument is to use all that we know to make our point. But winning is not everything. Who you are now and who you are becoming is much more important. Therefore, resist the temptation to win an argument by betraying confidences. You may not get the upper hand in the dispute by being trustworthy, but you will preserve your good reputation.

Lord, please help me to remain trustworthy
even during a heated argument. Amen.

FRIENDSHIP

Proverbs 27:9–10

A song from yesteryear stated, "Friendship, friendship such a perfect blendship. When other friendships have been 'forgot,' ours will still be hot."

How many friends do you have? Try counting and naming them individually. When I do this, I don't come up with a big number. I'm not surprised, for most men have trouble making close friends. They might have many acquaintances but only a few real friends.

Proverbs 27:9–10 refers to the "pleasantness of one's friends." It is a good thing to have a number of others who know you and still want to be with you. This is the benefit of longtime friends. New friends are nice, too, for that's an affirmation of who we are today, but old friends know where we're coming from.

This passage encourages us to be loyal to our friends. They have invested time and energy in us, and we should assume the best about them. They should receive our prayers and our words of encouragement. There are times when they can use a telephone call, a note, a visit, or a gift.

Scripture says that a close friend is better than a brother far away. My brother lives in Minnesota, and I'm in Florida. I love my brother and value his friendship. But I realize that a neighbor who is near and a good friend can be of more immediate help to me than my far-away brother.

Men need to be open to making new friends. Yes, there's a risk involved. Even if someone takes advantage of us, we shouldn't stop trying to be a friend and to make friends with others. Life is too short to be friendless. So try to make and keep a few good friends.

Dear Lord, please help me to be friendly to others and thus make more friends. Amen.

LONE RANGERS

Ecclesiastes 4:9−12

I was once a member of a church in south Florida where almost all of the men were aggressive, hard-driving, adversarial, and successful entrepreneurs. As "up-and-outers," they had left their former communities and retired to Florida. But being retired didn't change their basic personalities. Despite their financial success, they were bankrupt when it came to having good relational skills.

Some men who have found success in business think they got there on their own. They are self-made men who worship their independence. Sadly, they are like the Lone Ranger, that famous radio hero of yesteryear, who, with his faithful horse Silver, single-handedly rode the range for justice.

If a day like that ever existed, it is long gone. Today we all need each other, for life is too complicated to live in isolation. We all need the encouragement, insights, and constructive criticism that others can give (Eccl. 4:9–12).

Genesis 1:18 tells us, "It is not good for man to be alone. I will make a helper suitable for him." In this instance, God was providing Eve for Adam. But a broader truth is that no human being is meant to be a Lone Ranger and to run roughshod over other people. With God's help, we can learn to be loving, good-hearted, and considerate of others.

O Lord, please help me to be kinder, gentler, and
more caring toward others. Amen.

YES, SIR!

John 15:12

John 15:12 says, "My command is this: Love each other as I have loved you. Greater love has no one than this, that he lay down his life for his friends." Although Jesus would rather persuade us to follow Him, He also issued commands. And as followers of Christ, we are to say "Yes, Sir!" to His directives.

Just how are we to love each other? Jesus said, "As I have loved you." The Savior's compassion for us was so great that He gave His life for us. We may not have to die for someone, but we can practice sacrificial love in other ways. For example, we can give of ourselves unconditionally by listening, helping, encouraging, and caring.

Jesus said that we demonstrate the reality of our friendship with Him when we obey Him. For example, we are to follow His command to love other people more than we love ourselves. It sounds hard, doesn't it? That's because it *is* hard. In fact, believing in Christ and living for Him is immensely difficult. That's why there are so few of us (by percentage) in the world.

Being a true Christian is more than what say we believe or claim about ourselves. A true follower says "Yes, Sir!" to what the risen Lord has commanded. We do not bluff our way into faith but rather act positively upon its directives.

If you want to be known as a Christian, act like one. Be willing to give your life in service to another in need, just as your Lord and Savior did for you and me at Calvary.

Dear Lord, please help me to serve others
unconditionally and sacrificially, just as
Your Son did for me. Amen.

ROBERT LESLIE HOLMES

A Man and His Relationships: Home

CHOSEN TO DIRECT

Genesis 18:19

Adam caught our attention as we watched the seals in San Francisco Bay. We estimated the child to be about six years old. His mother repeatedly begged him to leave the slimy sand in which he was digging. I remember thinking that the child was appropriately named. *Adam* literally means "mud," which reminds us that God made the first Adam from the ground. This little boy named Adam was muddy from head to toe.

Finally, his mother threatened, "Come now! Or Dad will get you." Sure enough, Dad soon arrived. "Okay, Adam," he whimpered, "please come." Adam, digging and filthy, paid no heed. Dad's second approach demonstrated what was really wrong: "Okay, Adam, let's negotiate. What will it take to make you leave?"

Negotiate! That scene was a far cry from the role God originally intended for fathers. Dad's are not negotiators with but directors of their children. The Lord has called fathers to demonstrate godly leadership. Negotiation gives children executive equivalency, whereas direction teaches them to respect authority and to be responsible in their actions (Gen. 18:19).

A father and son on a mountain climb came to a particularly treacherous place. The father paused to consider which way to go, and the lad called out trustingly, "Choose the right path, Daddy. I'm following right behind you." God calls us to be stewards of our own souls and the souls of our families. May we do it well for both Christ's sake and theirs.

Gracious God, please make me a father whose children know that I belong to You. Crown me with wisdom and strength for this sacred task. Amen.

A GOOD HUSBAND MAKES A GOOD WIFE!

Ephesians 5:25

A man accompanying his friend home for dinner one evening was impressed by the way the husband entered his house, asked his wife how her day went, and told her she looked pretty. Then, when they had embraced and kissed, she served dinner. After they ate, the husband complimented his wife on the meal and thanked her for it. When the two fellows were alone, the visitor asked, "Why do you treat your wife so well?" "Because she deserves it, and it makes our marriage happier," replied the host.

Greatly impressed, the visitor decided to adopt the idea. Arriving home that evening, he embraced his wife and exclaimed, "You look wonderful!" For good measure he added, "Sweetheart, I'm the luckiest guy in the world."

His wife, amazed, burst into tears. Bewildered, he asked her, "What in the world's the matter?" She wept, "What a day! Billy fought at school. The refrigerator broke and spoiled the groceries. And now you come home drunk!"

It's natural for us to chuckle when we read this story. Yet, tragically, that sometimes reflects the way things really are in some homes.

Paul calls us to a marital love standard that reflects Christ's sacrificial love (Eph. 5:25). Pain and suffering are not necessarily part of it, but consistency and caring are. Faithfully demonstrating that my primary interest is to help my beloved become everything God wants her to be will almost always result in a better partner for both of us. Think about it—and do it!

O Lord, by the power of your Spirit, please enable me to demonstrate consistently to my dear wife the love that proves Your presence in my life. May we together be drawn nearer to both each other and You. Amen.

WINNING ON WALL STREET BUT LOSING ON MAIN STREET?

Acts 10:1—2

A well-dressed executive grabbed his briefcase and sped out the door as usual one morning. As he left, his wife called out, "Remember, dear, this is moving day." He mumbled a response and hurried on. After a full day in the city, he drove home as usual. Parking in the same driveway, he turned the handle on the same back door. He immediately discovered that it was locked!

The executive knocked and looked through a window. The walls were bare. Scratching his head, he walked to the front and spotted a boy riding a bicycle. "Hey, kid," he called, "any idea where the family that lived here went?" The boy replied, "Sure, Dad. Remember Mom told you we were moving today?"

Cornelius, the centurion, led a regiment of Roman soldiers. More importantly, however, he led his family in their life with God (Acts 10:1–2).

It takes more than a house to make a home and more than a dad, a mom, and kids to make a family. Godliness, love, devotion, and involved leadership are necessary, too. This reminds us that the most important investment we will ever make will not be on Wall Street but on Main Street—namely, in our home.

At your funeral, no one will ask how many deals you closed, how many verdicts you won, or how many promotions you received. They will almost certainly inquire about your family. Nothing you leave will compare with your relationship with the people whom God has called you to lead.

Dear God, please help me to put life's riches in their proper perspective and to go after that which is really valuable, especially as I lead my family in their relationship with You. Amen.

BE SURE TO BRING THE FAMILY!

Acts 16:31

The God of the Bible takes families seriously. All the way from "It is not good for the man to be alone. I will make a helper suitable for him" (Gen. 2:18) until today each of us is instructed to bring our family to faith. The Bible's covenant promises are always family oriented. Yet, it often seems harder to speak of salvation to loved ones than to strangers.

In Acts 16, two conversion accounts are set in juxtaposition. One account is of a woman named Lydia whereas the other account is of a man who guarded the jail in Philippi. Both of them came to faith in Christ under different circumstances—one through gradual prayer and teaching, the other through startling suicidal fear.

Despite these differences, however, they have an exciting similarity—they both brought their families to faith in Christ. The faith of neither Lydia nor the jailer saved their families, for each person had to come to Christ individually. What their stories tell us is that the Lord often uses us as the means of bringing our entire family to Him in faith. Their testimonies help us to see that God has different ways of calling us (v. 31).

A wise, old country preacher once said, "God calls some of us with a kiss and others with a knock up the side of the head." The Lord has different methods but a similar goal. He wants our entire family saved. Our challenge is to partner with God's Spirit to win them to Christ.

Dear God, please keep my witness strong and consistent, and help me to be useful to You in bringing my whole family to the Savior. Amen.

CHOOSE TODAY!

Joshua 24:15

The slave-making ant of the Amazon provides a striking illustration of the predicament in which many people live their lives. Hundreds of these crafty creatures periodically storm neighboring colonies of weaker ants and seize all the cocoons of working ant larvae. When these captured offspring hatch, they assume themselves to be part of a family and work with gusto, never realizing that they are nothing more than forced laborers of their enemy.

Joshua could see that until the Israelites resolved to serve the Lord, they, too, were unwitting forced laborers of their greatest enemy. At a vital crossroads in their wilderness journey, Joshua challenged them to make up their minds. Would they follow the Lord, who had repeatedly proved His faithfulness, or would they serve a pagan god and become like enslaved ants? They had to choose (Josh. 24:15).

A church visitor asked a pastor, "How many of your members are active?" Without hesitation the pastor replied, "They are all active. Some are active for Christ and the rest are active for the Devil!" Never a truer word was spoken!

Your life each day, and the life of each member of your family, advances the cause of Christ or the cause of the one the Bible repeatedly calls the prince of this world (see Eph. 2:1–3). Each of us, often without realizing it, chooses daily to be a servant of either Christ or Satan. Remember that not to choose is always to choose!

Glorious God, I reaffirm my choice to lead my family in serving You this day. By your Spirit's power, please help me to remember to do so. Amen.

DAY SIX

WHAT IS GOD DOING AT YOUR HOUSE?

Acts 18:8

The Christian faith is a family matter. John and Janet Paton believed that. In an inconspicuous thatched-roof cottage in Scotland, they reared eleven children. We would never have heard their name, except that their son, John Gibson Paton, became one of Christendom's great missionary statesmen and evangelists. Behind the walls of that simple cottage, God molded a child to become His spokesman in the New Hebrides and Australia.

J. G. Paton often recalled what life was like in that humble home. As a boy, he often pressed his ear against the door of a tiny room where his father prayed. In his later years, J. G. testified, "Never in temple or cathedral, on mountain or in glen, can I hope to feel that the Lord God is more near, more visibly walking and talking with a man, than under that humble cottage roof. Eleven of us were brought up there. All of us came to regard the church as the dearest spot on earth and the Lord's day the brightest day of the week."

From this example we see that the Christian faith is a family matter. Crispus became a leader in God's church. Even more importantly, Crispus became God's leader in his home (Acts 18:8). Who knows what God is doing at your house through your Christlike example? Ultimately only God knows. Take courage, friend, and remain faithful. Eternity alone counts the full results of your steadfast walk with the Lord.

O Lord, please help me to be faithful at home so that my entire household might see Your glory and that my children may be especially fruitful in Your service. Amen.

HEAD LINES!
1 Corinthians 11:3

In an ancient European city stands a statue of a Greek maiden with exquisite face, elegant figure, and gracious expression. Her alluring form one day caught the eye of a young maiden who was passing by. For a while she stood admiring, wishing she could look like that. Then and there she determined to emulate the beauty.

Rushing home with a mission, the woman bathed and combed her hair. She then ran back to the statue. Staring into its face, she observed the model's smile and tried to imitate it. In time, she had it just right. But her tattered clothes made her different from the model, so she rushed home to mend them. The next day, she was back before the statue comparing once more. Day after day she returned, each time observing something new that she must improve. In time, more than her appearance changed. Her whole life was transformed by emulating the splendor of her model.

That maiden's transformation has a message for all of us who are called to be "the head" of our wife (1 Cor. 11:3). We, too, have a model. Our headship ideal is Jesus, who sacrificed His life for us.

Will we look closely at Him, making all the necessary changes so that we might mirror His headship for those whom we are called to lead and love? May we be so for Christ's sake.

Almighty God, please open my heart to those
areas in my life that need to change so that
I might be more like the Savior. Amen.

H .   R A Y   N E W M A N

A Man and His Relationships: Friends

DAY ONE

A FRIEND LOVES AT ALL TIMES
Proverbs 17:17

The rain had been pouring down from black clouds for several days. The springs were full, the river was near flood stage, and the town had received the evacuation order. Boats were quickly filling with people who were trying to escape the rising waters. The low area on the south side of the railroad already had several feet of water, and it was rising higher by the hour.

When the order was given to evacuate, no one thought about the elderly couple who had no television or radio. They had no way of knowing about how to escape unless someone went to their home.

In the same town, John was now in his eighties and looking after a bedridden wife who could not walk without help. His son, who lived many miles away in the next town, had helped him to leave. As they were making their way to safety, John suddenly remembered his friend who was of another race and who would not know about the order to leave unless someone went to his home.

Upon John's relentless urging, he and his son went in a borrowed boat to the old house. John then moved his friends many miles away to his son's home and safety. Doesn't John's kind action serve as a sterling example of Proverbs 17:17?

Lord, thank You for friends who love at all times, and please help me to be like them. Amen.

AGREEING TO AGREE

Amos 3:3

Jim and Jack had known each other all their lives. They were from the same town, and they went to the same schools, sporting events, and social circles. They dated the same girls, and eventually they married sisters. Although they were related by marriage, they remained lifelong friends. They built next door to each other, reared their families together, and attended the same church. Jim and Jack were always together.

One day, Jim became sick, and the doctor said that it would not be long before Jim would die. Jack stayed with his friend. In those last days, Jim and Jack talked often about what would happen after Jim was gone, and Jack agreed to look after Jim's family and property as long he was able to do so. Jim and Jack had never disagreed about anything they had done in life, and now they were planning for the continued agreement even after Jim was no longer living. All the remaining days of Jack's life, he fulfilled the promises he had made to Jim upon his deathbed.

Jack lived a long and successful life. Upon being questioned about his unique relationship with his departed friend, Jack said that they had agreed that their friendship meant more than some petty difference of opinion they may have over any one issue or event. Jack said, "Long ago Jim and I agreed to agree" (see Amos 3:3).

Dear Lord, please teach me the lesson of agreeing and working together with others to have a successful life in You. Amen.

DEVOTED FRIENDS

Job 6:14−15

Job is the classic example of someone who has friends who turn against him when he is experiencing trouble. At the moment when Job's friends should have been standing by him, they brought charges against him. They assumed that God was punishing him for some secret sin he had committed. Tragically, Job found no help or hope from his friends (Job 6:14–15).

A friend will stand by a person in times of need without becoming part of the problem. Many times the easy way is to accuse or to assume guilt before all of the facts are known. But a true friend will reach out to support and help in a time of need and not join in the chorus of "nay sayers."

Jumping to a false conclusion can ruin lifelong friendships. Joe and Paul had known each other all their lives. As adults, they found themselves on opposite sides of an issue facing their town. It was an honest difference of opinion. Joe refused even to speak to Paul, but Paul continued to pray for Joe and to treat him as he always had—as a friend. Years passed, and Joe came to Paul to seek restoration of the friendship, admitting that he had been wrong. Paul was forgiving, and the friendship was restored. Devoted friends never hold a grudge, even though the times or issues might divide them.

Lord, please give me understanding as I deal with a close friend who is going through a time of struggle. Also, please forgive me for the times that I have failed to be a friend to those in need. Amen.

DAY FOUR

FRIENDS/BROTHERS
1 Samuel 20:17

Two boys were born in the same town to different parents. One set of parents lived on the wealthy side of town whereas the other set of parents lived in the factory village. The two boys grew up in separate social circles, although they attended the same school. As young teens, the two boys became friends and went into the military together on the "buddy system."

With the influence of the father, one of the boys could have received special treatment. This young man, however, wanted to stay near his friend. No special treatment was accepted. When the orders came for this young man to go into a combat zone, he went with the knowledge that his friend would not be going with him on this duty. He was on patrol, and came upon another unit that was pinned down by enemy fire.

Upon surveying the scene, this first young man saw that his best friend was in the unit under enemy attack. Without regard for his personal safety, he fought back the enemy with great fervor.

After hours of carrying on this fight, the soldier collapsed. He later woke up in a field hospital with his best friend beside him. The soldier learned that his friend's unit was almost totally destroyed. The other man, though wounded, had fought with unusual courage, as he knew his friend needed him to carry on the battle. Both men received medals for their bravery.

In 1 Samuel 20:17, Jonathan, the son of King Saul, loved David, the shepherd boy, as he loved himself. As men, we need friends with whom to share our life.

Lord, thank You for the friends You have given me. Amen.

DAY FIVE

FRIENDS ARE NOT TO BE FORSAKEN
Proverbs 27:10

In a time of adversity or disaster, it is good to have friends. During these difficult moments, they are willing to do whatever they can to help. Oddly enough, many friendships that survive times of crisis fall apart when things are going well. For example, jealously can creep in when one friend is given a promotion, receives a raise, or wins special recognition. The resentment that the other person feels can eventually destroy their friendship.

A true friend will stick with a person whether times are good or bad (Prov. 27:10). For example, Ernest and Jerry were best friends in Vietnam. After being discharged from the military, each man went to work at a factory and remained friends for several years.

One day Jerry was given a promotion that placed him as a supervisor over his friend Ernest. Jerry sought to be fair, honest, and objective in his new position as supervisor. Ernest, however, was not happy having his best friend in the new role. This predicament almost caused the friendship to end.

One day Ernest was injured on the job, and Jerry risked his life to pull Ernest to safety and get help for him. While in the hospital, Ernest came to understand the depth of the feelings that Jerry had for him as a friend, and this realization caused Ernest to change his attitude about Jerry. From that point, the friendship was restored.

Heavenly Father, thank You for the true friends
that You have given me. Please help me never to
abandon my friends in their time of need. Amen.

UNCONDITIONAL LOVE

1 John 4:11–12

It was a clear, sunny day, and the swimming party would be a success—or so all the attendees thought. Several boyhood friends, now in their late teens, had been looking forward to this day at the end of a school term as a sign of their freedom for the summer. They did not know that their fun day would soon turn into a nightmare that no one could have ever imagined.

One of the boys jumped into the water and hit his head on a rock at the bottom of the shallow lake. Another friend jumped in to save him, only to be overcome by the struggle to lift his unconscious friend to safety. A third boy was able to bring both friends to safety, and then get help. The third boy was seen as a hero, but he quickly said that he had done only what the other two friends would have done for him if had he been the one in trouble.

The heroism and sacrifice of the third boy is an apt illustration of what we read in 1 John 4:11–12. When we love others unconditionally, the way God has loved us, He lives in us and His love is brought to full expression through us.

Lord, please help me to see that to have friends
I must be a friend to others. Enable me to express
my love for them through my actions. Amen.

NO ONE TO HELP

Ecclesiastes 4:9–12

Several years ago there was a television commercial that had an elderly person acting out this line, "I have fallen and I can't get up." This stirring line was intended to remind us that we all need someone to help us in times of need. For example, in many areas of the country where senior adults reside, they have a "friend call" program. It's designed to have someone check daily on the elderly citizens to account for all of them.

Men need friends who will check on them and to whom they are accountable for their daily actions. Ecclesiastes 4:9–12 reminds us that "two are better than one." When one must make a decision or keep a commitment, two men can hold each other accountable for their actions. Men also need other men as friends with whom they can discuss the concerns and issues of life. Remember that even the Lone Ranger had a partner who traveled with him and with whom he worked to fight the outlaws of their day.

Father, please help me to be a friend to other men I know. May I also allow other men to befriend me. Amen.

DON M. AYCOCK

A Man and His Relationships: Accountability

TELL EACH OTHER THE TRUTH

Galatians 6:1–7

Right after the Civil War, a host of people became teachers because they thought it was an easy way of making a living. In his autobiography *Up From Slavery,* Booker T. Washington tells about such a fellow. This man went from village to village teaching a little and receiving pay for it. In one town, the people asked whether he taught that the earth is round or flat. The man replied that he was prepared to teach that the earth was either flat or round, depending on the preference of the majority of his patrons.

This represents truth by survey! But what is the truth? Is it determined by a select group of people or leaders? No. God has given us the truth revealed in Scripture, and we are to share it with others.

Paul told the Galatians to help each other be accountable to the church by telling the truth. The apostle also stressed the importance of every believer's looking out for fellow Christians. For example, if a believer is going astray, don't simply look the other way. Go to him and help restore him to the fellowship (Gal. 6:1–7).

This can be difficult. Some Christian men intentionally leave the church whereas others just wander off course. Others may resent any attempt you make to correct and restore them. Regardless of how they might respond, however, you should do whatever you can to get them to forsake their sin and return to the Lord.

Do you know a Christian brother who needs correction? Why not make it a point this week to reach out humbly and gently to that person with the love of Christ?

Lord, please help me to encourage an erring
Christian brother to return to the fold. Amen.

Sharpen the Iron (and the Man)

Proverbs 27:17

Routine and habit are powerful taskmasters. When we do something over and over again, we learn it deeply. For instance, a child plays scales up and down the piano keyboard even when she would rather tackle something with rhythm. A college student writes out foreign words again and again to make them part of him. And an athlete practices his moves on the gridiron many times so that he will not have to think consciously about them on game day. In each of these instances, habits can be helpful and positive.

But we all know that longstanding bad habits can be difficult to reverse. Lon Chaney Sr. starred as the villain in the classic movie *The Hunchback of Notre Dame*. He said that he had to strap himself in a harness to look like a genuine hunchback. But as the days of the filming stretched into weeks, Chaney found that the longer he stayed in a stooped position, the longer it took him to stand up straight after the day's filming had ended. His body was getting used to being bent over.

If you live a morally crooked life long enough, it becomes increasingly difficult to straighten out. That's why we all need to be accountable to someone. God can use our Christian friends to teach us, guide us, and, if necessary, straighten us out (Prov. 27:17). Staying bent over is fine for a question mark but not for a man of God. You are an exclamation mark, so straighten up!

O Lord, please give me the strength I need to help my Christian friends become spiritually sharper, and enable me to humbly accept their sharpening influence in my life. Amen.

You Are Your Brother's Keeper

Genesis 4:8–9

All churches have problems with members who become inactive. For example, Bill is gifted at knowing how to deal skillfully with dropouts. He takes the initiative to reach out to them. Bill is sensitive to people's hurts and patiently listens to their stories. If he can offer specific counsel or assistance, he does so. He tries not to take expressions of anger personally. He gently wins the confidence of people who drop out of church and then leads them back into the fellowship.

Not everyone wants to go back into a church where they have experienced pain or rejection. If Bill cannot get people to go back to their old church, he encourages them to find a new place to worship. He demonstrates a nonpossessive attitude when he says, "After all, these are not my people. They're God's people. If they can't worship and serve at my church, perhaps they can serve somewhere else."

May Bill's tribe increase! How we need Christian men who see themselves as their brothers' keeper, not only at church but also at work and in the community (see Gen. 4:8–9).

O Lord, please help me to love other Christian men enough to reach out to them and restore them to fellowship with You and Your people. Amen.

DAY FOUR

BE FAITHFUL TO YOUR FRIENDS

Proverbs 27:6

"Who cares?"

This is a desperate question that can be asked in a variety of ways. For example, a child acts up to get her mother's attention. It is her way of asking, "Do you really care about me?" A teenager from a stable Christian home steals a car and ends up in the county jail. He is asking his father, "Do you truly love me?" A member of a warm, friendly church stops attending for a while. She just wants to know whether anyone genuinely misses her.

In a day of overloaded senses and enormous demands on time, energy, and resources, it's tough to care for other people. But just exactly what is *care*? It is putting yourself in the shoes of someone else and trying to feel their pain. The "self-made man" is a pure myth. No one makes himself. Whatever we are and whatever we have is the result of others helping us along the way.

I remember a conversation I once had with an insurance agent. He noted how he had made his business into a million-dollar corporation. He bellowed, "I did it all by myself!" I silently thought, *That's nonsense! You received help from all of your customers and from the national office.*

We need to remember that we are called by God to care for each other. If one part of the body of Christ is hurting, the rest of us are adversely affected. I cannot say, for example, "Well, I have lung cancer, but I won't worry about it because it's just my lungs. That doesn't affect the rest of me!" Similarly, if a believer in your church is grieving, you have a responsibility to care for him (see Prov. 27:6).

O Father, please teach me to care for my hurting Christian brothers. Amen.

DON'T BE JEALOUS OF YOUR CHRISTIAN BROTHERS
Galatians 5:20

The Devil once decided to have a yard sale. He had too many devices and techniques with which to defeat people. Up went hatred on the dealer's table. Rebellion and drunkenness next followed. Then vice after vice was put on the table to be sold. But as one of the Devil's minions placed jealousy on the table, Satan quickly snatched it away. "I can't sell this," he exclaimed. "It's my most valuable weapon!"

There's a lot of truth in that statement. Jealousy is indeed one the Devil's most valuable weapons (see Gal. 5:20). He uses it to discourage people. He gets them to focus on what others have rather than being content with their own possessions.

Jealousy is envy's twin and hostility's first cousin. Jealousy gets people to think thus: *Just look at Jim there. He has everything, and he didn't even have to work very hard to get it! But look at me. I've worked hard all my life. And what do I have to show for it? Nothing! I should have what Jim has.*

Don't fall into this trap. Life is not fair, and the world does not owe you anything. Some people have more than we do, and they can do more than we can. But remember, others and their possessions are not your primary concern. Rather, becoming more godly should be your foremost priority (see 1 Tim. 4:8). Therefore, don't make a bid on jealousy at the Devil's yard sale.

Dear Lord, please help me not to be jealous of others, especially my fellow Christian brothers. Amen.

DAY SIX

CULTIVATING GOODNESS
Galatians 5:22

Two men moved to the desert to devote themselves to holy living and prayer. Although they lived together in the same hut, they never had the slightest disagreement.

One hermit said to the other, "Let us have just one quarrel the way other men do." The second answered, "But I don't know how one starts a quarrel." The first replied, "Look, I'll set a tile between us and say, 'That is mine,' and you say, 'It's mine,' and in this way trouble and contention will arise between us. They agreed to do this. They set the tile between them, and the first holy man said, "It's mine." The second replied, "I hope that it's mine." To which the first responded, "If it's yours, take it." After that, they could find no other way to quarrel.

Holy men living as hermits in the desert may not be able to find much to quarrel about, but the rest of us are not so fortunate! Strife seems to be our middle name. Yet most people want to get along with others. Sadly, the inability to do so has wreaked havoc on both personal and international levels. On the personal level, it has stunted and even ended the careers of many talented people.

Goodness is one of the fruits of the Spirit (Gal. 5:22). Why not commit yourself to cultivating this character quality for both your sake and the sake of your Christian brothers? You'd be surprised how the presence of this one virtue can make a profound difference in your relationship with others.

O God, please help me to be a man of goodness, especially in the way I relate to my Christian brothers. Amen.

TAKE THE RISK

Genesis 12:1–4

The acclaimed author of *Roots*, Alex Haley, once said about taking risks, "Nothing is more important. Too often we are taught how *not* to take risks. When we are children in school . . . we are told to respect our heroes. . . . What we are not told is that these leaders . . . were in fact rule-*breakers*. They were risk-takers in the best sense of the word; they dared to be different."[1]

God calls Christian men to be risk-takers. I do not mean this in the sense of a reckless pursuit of excitement, such as bungie jumping. Rather, God wants us to the take the risk of being spiritually transformed. That is what Abram faced. The relative comfort of being with his people would prompt him to remain in Ur of the Chaldeans. But God called him to do something different (Gen. 12:1–4).

Abram left his "father's household," which was the source of his emotional and spiritual strength. By going out, he had to face the problems that come with separation. Physical protection was a part of it, but so was a sense of being in the right place. Because he accepted the risks of God's invitation, Abram changed his entire life.

When we read the New Testament, we also see God calling us to be spiritual risk-takers. Following the way of God is never simple. In fact, it always involved risks.

"Who Dares, Wins" is the motto of the elite Australian SAS forces. Formed in 1957, the SAS is dedicated to superior performance under the extreme demands of operating in a combat environment. These soldiers are required to push the envelope of personal limitations to develop stamina, endurance, and tenacity.

Abram had never heard of the SAS, but he knew the intent of their motto. He was willing to risk everything for God. What about you? Are you willing to do the same?

Lord, please give me the strength to take the risk
of being spiritually transformed. Amen.

Notes

1. Quoted in Walter Anderson, *The Greatest Risk of All* (Boston: Houghton Mifflin, 1988), 240.

HAROLD IVAN SMITH

A Man and His Relationships: Single Men

SINGLE FOR A SEASON OR A REASON
Matthew 19:10–12

Jesus, as a single adult, was an incredible relationalist! His relationships resemble a pyramid. He interacted with the crowds who followed Him (forming the base). He worked through a core of disciples. Of the twelve disciples, He invested significantly in Peter, James, and John. And of this trio, Jesus nurtured a strong relationship with John. Although Jesus was a single adult, He was not a relational "lone ranger." Instead, He devoted Himself to others.

Most single men spend their time "looking for Miss Right" instead of following Jesus' example and creating and maintaining a network of friends, acquaintances, and colleagues. Many men believe that if they can just find "her" life will be Kumbayic!

We smirk when widowers—particularly those from good, long marriages—quickly remarry. Yet, widowers (and many divorced men) lament their "lostness." One such person explained, "I feel like a fish out of water."

Many men have a hard time accepting the idea that singleness is a "gift" (Matt. 19:10–12). Although Jesus didn't mandate singleness, He did indicate that for some people it would be God's best. Thus, Jesus modeled manhood for both married and unmarried men. Whether we are single "for a reason" or for a "season," as the gospel hymn insists, "He, the great example, is a pattern for me."

Father, please help me to accept and enjoy my current state of singleness. Amen.

DAY TWO

WHAT'S IN IT FOR ME?

Matthew 19:27–30

Men have an obsession with "the bottom line." What's in it for me? What's the payoff that will make it "worth it someday"? Unmarried men are no exception. Many protest, "I've never been accused of being a 'swinging single.'" Custodial single fathers confess, "I'm too pooped for romance." Many noncustodial dads long for the next opportunity to actively father their children. Some of them expect God to drop the most incredible woman into their life as something of a "for all you've been through" consolation prize.

I love the gospel hymn, "When We All Get to Heaven." It reminds me, that "when we all see Jesus," single adult males will realize that most of what we labeled as problems were merely inconveniences. "When the Son of Man sits on his glorious throne," it won't matter how long you were single or even how you became single. What will matter is that you said "Yes!" to Jesus' invitation to the abundant life (see Matt. 19:27–30). Dag Hammarskjöld, a single adult and Secretary General of the United Nations from 1953–1961, journaled this prayer, "For all that has been—thanks. For all that is to be—Yes!"

> *Lord, please show me how to make the most of my singleness. Amen.*

DAY THREE

WHOLLY AVAILABLE

1 Corinthians 7:7

Who has more time to give to work of the kingdom—the single adult or the married adult? That question is difficult to answer. Perhaps Paul's thinking had been influenced by a married aide who declined an invitation to go on a particular missionary trip. Or maybe Paul had heard a married Christian say, "If I go on one more journey with you, my wife's gonna. . . ." No doubt the veteran preacher longed for more associates who were fully committed to the ministry (1 Cor. 7:7).

Obviously, Paul, as a committed and focused single adult, had no time for or interest in a social life. Nevertheless, he acknowledged that both marriage and singleness are gifts from God. One option is not morally superior to the other. In fact, both situations are valuable in accomplishing God's purposes. The apostle's intent was to encourage both singles and marrieds to accept their present situation.

Paul, of course, expressed his desire that more people were like him (i.e., unmarried). His conviction may have influenced John Powell's prayer life. As a single adult, free of marriage responsibilities, John, like Paul, became "wholly available" to God. For years Powell prayed, "Hey, God, what have You got going on today? I'd like to be part of it." That prayer will certainly prevent spiritual boredom!

Lord, please help me, as a single Christian, to
make myself wholly available to You. Amen.

DAY FOUR
WHAT DO YOU MEAN MARRIAGE IS NOT "ETERNAL"?
Mark 12:25

It's easy to forget that marriage is not an "eternal" relationship (Mark 12:25). Rather, it is temporal or, in too many cases these days, temporary. For example, when lawyer Melvin Belli died, there were four ex-Mrs. Belli's to join the current Mrs. Belli. Sadly, many people have "marital resumes" rather than a marriage.

Jesus clearly taught that marriage is a temporal matter. Marriage, like singleness, is a time of preparation for the eternal state. Thus, the kingdom of God and living for the Lord from day to day should be our primary concern (see Matt. 6:33). But tragically, many single males are desperately seeking the kingdom of marriage. They think that a spouse will be something like a spiritual "tag-team" partner. In reality, one's mate could become a spiritual impediment.

The world has been vastly influenced by unmarried men who deliberately and without distraction sought the kingdom of God. Could the great German theologian Dietrich Bonhoeffer have so boldly opposed the Nazis if he had had a wife and children, a house to paint, grass to cut, and soccer games to attend? Yet, fifty years after he was hung by the Nazis, Bonhoeffer's books are still read by many people.

Fifty years from now what will people remember about you? Will it be that you were a spiritual giant or a spiritual dwarf? The choice is yours.

O Lord, this day please help me to focus on the things that have eternal significance. Amen.

DAY FIVE

SINGLE IN THE SON!
Psalm 84:11

If the Lord doesn't "withhold one good thing," then why am I *still* single? Why can't I find someone (or someone find me)? Why am I divorced? Why am I widowed? Why *me? I* didn't volunteer to be single!

Well, because life happens. It's not so much what happens to you, but how you respond to life's surprises and ambushes that makes the eternal difference.

Many men have theological reservations about singleness. Others will never give singleness a try. We might moan (or scream), "Jesus, I want marriage!" or "These hormones are driving me crazy!" to which Jesus responds, "My grace is sufficient for you" (2 Cor. 12:8). We overlook that we have been "favored and honored" by being born in this country, and that we are rich by the economic standards of the third world. To people living in dreadful circumstances, our preoccupation with being single seems absurd.

The last phrase of Psalm 84:11 can be troublesome. If marriage is a good thing—and it is—then, many people conclude, God is "keeping" me from being married. This sort of thinking leads to spiritual defeat. I prefer to focus on the first words of the verse. When I am so anxious about doing something about my singleness, when I am in the frantic-panic, tired-of-being-single mode, I am *least* likely to make good romantic, let alone marital, decisions. The Lord *is* faithful to shield me from relationships that could ruin me spiritually, emotionally, and financially—but only if I cooperate.

In some relationships, God brings discomforting light to show us that *this* person cannot be the right one. But some single adult males walk around carrying an umbrella to shield themselves from the light of the Son. They cling to the notion that a bad relationship is better than no relationship. How sad is such thinking!

*Lord, please help me to accept and follow Your
leading in the relationships I have with women.
Amen.*

CARPE TEMPUS

1 Corinthians 7:32–35

In 1 Corinthians 7:32–35, Paul noted that "an unmarried man is concerned about the Lord's affairs" whereas a married man is more focused on "how he can please his wife." However, not every single adult male is concerned wholeheartedly about how he can better serve the Lord. Many single adults prefer "lite" faith—namely, something that is less demanding and more convenient. While they could invest more time in kingdom-oriented activities, they waste away the God-given time they have. Activities that could lay a foundation for either a life of single servanthood or potential roles as husband, father, and, perhaps grandfather, get relegated to "if I have time."

In the movie *Dead Poet's Society,* when Robin Williams uttered the phrase *Carpe diem* ("Seize the day!"), he grabbed my attention as a single male. I learned that I should make the most of *this* day's opportunities. But I've concluded that *Carpe tempus* ("Seize the season!") is more adventuresome. Singleness is an invitation to take our human experiences seriously, to allow our hearts to be broken by things that grieve the Lord, and to allow our schedules and priorities to be interrupted by God.

I browse old cemeteries. On one occasion, I was stunned by this inscription that appeared on the gravestone of political strategist Lee Atwater: "I do not choose to be a common man—it is my God-given right to be uncommon." The declaration could have described Paul's singleness as an adult. But does it describe me? I left Greenwood Cemetery determined to alter my fondness for "lite" servanthood. I do not choose to be a common single adult male, especially when God invites me to be uncommon!

*O God, please give me the strength to be an
"uncommon" single adult male for Your glory.
Amen.*

"COME ON DOWN! THE WATER'S FINE"

Acts 8:39

Today's church seems to have difficulty understanding that marital status is not a final determinant of God's plans for us. Sadly, in too many congregations, single adult males are not warmly welcomed. Supposedly church growth is by twos (i.e., married couples), not by ones (i.e., single adults).

In Acts 8, an unmarried Ethiopian official had been to Jerusalem to worship. Perhaps he was barred from the temple because he was a eunuch (see Deut. 23:1). On his way home, the official was reading from the Book of Isaiah when he encountered Philip, who answered this single adult's spiritual questions.

The Ethiopian exclaimed, "Why shouldn't I be baptized?" (Acts 8:36). I'm amazed that it was the official, not Philip, who seized the moment. This single adult, hungering for God, took the initiative to declare his faith in Christ by going through the rite of baptism (v. 39).

Although the official's circumstances had not changed, his attitude toward his situation was radically transformed after trusting in the greatest single adult who ever lived. Tradition says that the eunuch took the gospel home and launched the Ethiopian church. What might be some great things God would have *you* do as a single adult male?

*O Lord, please help me to do whatever I can as a
single adult male to share the gospel with the lost.
Amen.*

JAMES CARTER

A Man and His Birth Family: Father

DAY ONE

IF THE UNTHINKABLE HAPPENS

Psalm 27:10

The classic western movie *High Noon* had a haunting title song with the words, "Do not forsake me, O my darling." At a time when the main character in the film felt totally forsaken by others, he called on his darling, the one whom he had wed earlier that day, not to forsake him.

For many men being totally forsaken by their parents is the most frightful experience they could ever imagine. Unfortunately, many such people have been abandoned by their father or mother. Even as adults, the pain of that tragedy still lingers. Psalm 27:10 says that God can fill the void in our life and heal the hurt we feel. Regardless of the situation, His love is sufficient for all our needs.

Perhaps as a parent you have told your teenager that he can never do anything so wrong that you would stop loving him. What could a person do that would cause his parents to forsake him? Why would they give up on a son? Although some parents might give up on their children, God will never give up on you. He will never forsake you (Heb. 13:5). His love will remain with you throughout your life.

Dear God, please help me to be as faithful to You as You are to me. Amen.

FOLLOWING IN
THE FOOTSTEPS OF ANOTHER

1 Kings 9:4

The boy really wasn't big enough to play football. But his father had played football, even making All-State in high school. So his son went out for football. He practiced very hard. He followed the team disciplines rigorously. He was determined to follow in his father's footsteps.

Another boy's dad had started a business. All of his life the boy had assumed that he would be a part of the business. When his time came to manage and ultimately to own the business, he wanted to be sure that he was prepared. His college major, his summer jobs, and his after-school jobs all pointed in that one direction. He wanted to follow in his father's footsteps.

Solomon followed in his father's footsteps. He succeeded David as king of Israel. Solomon even did something his father had earnestly desired to do—build the temple in Jerusalem. After Solomon finished the project, God appeared to him and directed him to follow in his father's footsteps by being a man of integrity, uprightness, and obedience (1 Kings 9:4). What a challenge and an opportunity to leave footsteps fit for our sons to follow!

Dear Lord, please help me to be such a man
of faith that my sons will want to follow
in my footsteps. Amen.

SHOWING HONOR

Deuteronomy 5:16

"Son, you honor me," the father said when his boy called to invite him to sit on the platform with him when he received an award. Most of us would like to honor our father. But how is it done? To honor your father means to show him respect and high regard. You also honor your father by following the guidance, example, and teachings he has given you.

Paul said that the commandment recorded in Deuteronomy 5:16 is the first one "with a promise" (Eph. 6:2). This commandment presupposes two things. First, it assumes that the family unit will be stable and strong. Second, it presumes that the father will be worthy of honor. Unfortunately, neither of these two presuppositions can be taken for granted in our society.

Nevertheless, you should make every effort to honor your father. Wrapped up in the concept of honor are the ideas of prizing him highly (Prov. 4:8), providing him with care (Ps. 91:15), and obeying him (Deut. 21:18–21). Through what you think, say, and do, you can honor your father for his excellence in character and service. If you choose to do so, you will please the Lord (Col. 3:20).

Heavenly Father, please help me to honor my father and so please You by my actions. Amen.

DAY FOUR

To Whom Do You Listen?

Proverbs 23:22–24

A man once said, "When I was fifteen, my dad didn't know a thing. Then, when I became twenty-five, he seemed to know everything. It's amazing how much the old man has learned in ten years!"

Most of us would be better off if we had listened to our fathers more. Out of their wisdom and experience they have some things to share that can be beneficial to us (Prov. 23:22–24). For the most part, however, we choose to learn from our own experience rather than from their experience.

Undoubtedly, our fathers are saddened when we spurn their wise counsel. But perhaps it's not too late to change things. Why not take the opportunity to bring your father joy by asking him for some advice on an important matter in your life? When he gives it, be sure to listen to what he has to say. And make every effort to affirm his wealth of experience.

Who knows what truths your father might share with you? When you receive it, be sure to treasure it. Better still, try to do what your father has advised. You can't imagine how much satisfaction he will get from seeing you achieve your best because you heeded his wise counsel. You might be surprised by the smile on his face and the joy in his heart that results!

Dear God, please help me to seek out and apply the wise counsel of my father. Amen.

A FATHER'S PLEA
Proverbs 27:11

My father had a practice that was somewhat exasperating to me as a teenager. I would ask him whether I could do something, or go somewhere, or participate in some activity. Instead of making my decision for me, he would often answer, "Let your conscience be your guide." Although I was looking for an easy way out, my dad forced me to take personal responsibility for my actions.

My dad's response presupposed that I have a conscience. His answer also assumed that I had the training and background to know the difference between right and wrong. Moreover, his response presumed that I had the ability to apply different rules to specific situations. My dad was right, for he knew that my conscience was the voice of God in my soul (see Rom. 2:14–15).

Proverbs 27:11 records the desire of a father for his son to be a person of wisdom. In other words, the father wanted his boy to use sound judgment and good sense in the decisions he made. Doing so would not only make the father proud of his son but also enable the father to answer his critics. Whenever criticism or contempt was leveled at that father (for example, for not having achieved more financially), the father could always silence the critics by pointing to the sterling character of his son.

Dear Lord, please give to me the ability to teach my children the way of wisdom so that they might become people of integrity. Amen.

WHAT BRINGS PRIDE?

Proverbs 29:3

What did you have to do to make your father proud of you? Bring home all *A*'s on your report card? Hit home runs? Score touchdowns? Kill deer or ducks? Get a job? Perhaps your father was proud of you simply because you were his son. In this case, you easily met his every expectation.

Many men think that they have to earn their father's love. In some cases the father has been dead for years. Nevertheless, the son is still working hard to earn the respect and appreciation of his deceased parent.

Proverbs 29:3 contrasts two courses of action. The first is the son who brings joy to his father because of his love for wisdom. (Wisdom has to do with the way a person lives.) Undoubtedly, the prudent father is pleased that his son has opted to follow the path of virtue rather than vice.

The second course of action is represented by a son who spends his time in the company of prostitutes. As a result, he squanders his wealth. He loses not only his money but also his self-respect, virtue, and standing in the community. This loss brings nothing but sorrow to his godly father.

Which son best describes you—the son who is a source of pride for his father, or the son who is a source of embarrassment to the family?

Dear God, please enable me to be a source of pride to You and my family. Amen.

A WAY TO SHOW LOVE

Proverbs 13:24

My parents believed in corporal punishment, and I suspect that I needed it for the most part. My dad would often include a couple of statements when he administered a spanking. One statement was, "This is for your own good." Another was, "This is hurting me more than it hurts you." I had a hard time understanding and accepting these statements as a child. Now, as both a parent and a grandparent, I know what my father meant.

Does the counsel of Proverbs 13:24 seem strange to you? To withhold discipline from a child indicates that the father does not really love him. And to discipline a child is an indication of love. Yes, these statements are true.

Today we see the results of the lack of discipline in our society. The West has especially suffered because of it. Discipline must be imposed in some way. If a person does not have self-discipline, other forms of restraint will be forced on him (e.g., by the police or by the military).

Most fathers desire to discipline their children so they will grow up being responsible, well-behaved adults. Fathers learn how to discipline their children from the example of their parents. If the previous generation of fathers truly loved their children, they disciplined them. And if the current generation of fathers (including us) has the same compassion and concern, we will also discipline our children.

To discipline our children is to show them love. At first it might seem like tough love, but in the end it is true love. When the discipline is given in love, rather than in anger or vengeance, it will encourage our children to follow the path of righteousness and avoid the road to destruction.

Dear Lord, please help me to show my love for my children by performing the difficult but necessary task of disciplining them when they do wrong.
Amen.

ED SCOTT

A Man and His Birth Family: Mother

SETTING THE RECORD STRAIGHT

Deuteronomy 27:16

Talk about majority opinion! In ancient Israel there was no doubt about the respect children had to give to their parents. As the young nation prepared to cross the Jordan River and enter the Promised Land, Moses told the people that they needed to obey the law or suffer the dire consequences of their disobedience.

Moses told the people that, after crossing the Jordan, the tribes of Simeon, Levi, Judah, Issachar, Joseph, and Benjamin were to stand on Mount Gerizim to proclaim a blessing over the people. Similarly, the tribes of Reuben, Gad, Asher, Zebulun, Dan, and Naphtali were to stand on Mount Ebal to proclaim a curse. Then the Levites were to shout a series of statements to all the Israelites (Deut. 27:11–14). As each declaration was spoken by the Levites, the people would respond together in a thundering "Amen!"

Verse 16 is clear that God wanted the Israelites to honor their parents. For example, children were expected to obey their parents, and adult descendants were expected to listen carefully to the advice of their elders. Failure to do this was regarded as a severe violation of the law.

Nothing has changed since that time. God still blesses our lives with parents, and He still expects us to honor them. Perhaps the best way we can do so is by passing on their godly values to our children.

Lord, thank You for my parents. Please help me
to honor, rather than despise, them. Amen.

WISE UP!

Proverbs 15:20

The "foolish" man is a common topic of conversation in Proverbs. He is described, categorized, and analyzed throughout this incredible book. In 15:20 we find one of the most tragic statements in Proverbs—a foolish man despises his mother.

The foolish man is absolutely blind! That's the only explanation for his unbelievable callousness toward his mother. He has utterly failed to appreciate the wisdom, sacrifice, care, and love she has shown him. All of these resources have been placed at his disposal in one caring person, and he has turned his back on her.

The wise man is not like this. He recognizes and appreciates the wisdom, sacrifice, care, and love of his mother. He sees how much she has done for him, and he is genuinely thankful. He may not turn out to be the most successful or most famous son in the world, but he is grateful, and that's all a mother really needs to be content.

Dear God, please help me to appreciate the
wonderful gift You have given me in my mother.
Amen.

THE FAITH CONNECTION

2 Timothy 1:5

Many churches have one—the TEL Sunday school class! People who aren't familiar with 2 Timothy 1:5 generally don't understand the name of this ladies' group. But those who know the verse can readily understand the acronym. TEL stands for the "Timothy, Eunice, Lois" connection. Like Timothy's grandmother and mother, the ladies in these classes know the joy of passing their Christian faith on to the next generation.

The heritage of faith was unmistakable in Timothy's family. Trusting in the Lord was important to his grandmother, and she passed this conviction on to Timothy's mother, who then passed it on to him. There was nothing fake or temporary about this faith. It was genuine to the core.

Most likely you have experienced the TEL connection, especially if your initial exposure to Christianity came from your mother, your grandmother, or perhaps a "spiritual mother" in your church. These ladies have not only passed on the heritage of your religious tradition but have also shown how to remain a genuine believer in the rough and tumble of life.

Think about it. You have the same opportunity to show the sincerity of your faith to other people within the context of everyday, run-of-the-mill circumstances. Just remember that God initially used the TEL connection to make your faith a reality!

Lord, thank You for the women of faith You have brought into my life. Amen.

DAY FOUR

ONLY HALF THE STORY
1 Samuel 1:21–28

Hannah's praying for a child is one of my favorite Bible stories. It concerns a woman who trusted God completely for what she wanted most in life. But that is only half the story. We also find in 1 Samuel 1:21–28 the fitting conclusion of the account.

Hannah wanted not only a child but also that the child would come to know God! In her expression of this desire, Hannah became a pattern for all Christian mothers. Like Hannah, saved moms pray for their children, witness to them, live godly lives before them, and worship with them at church.

Do you, like Hannah, want more than anything else for your children to know God? Make every effort to display your faith and devotion, especially as you encourage your children to trust in Christ for salvation.

Loving God, please help me to do whatever I can to encourage my children to trust in Your Son for salvation. Amen.

DAY FIVE

MORE THAN LIP SERVICE
Matthew 15:3–9

When the Bible talks about honoring parents, it means much more than just giving "lip service." Jesus made this point well in

Matthew 15:3–9 when He reminded the Pharisees that there was no loophole in the commandment to honor one's parents.

In ancient times, people could dedicate all or a portion of their wealth to the temple with a gift-vow. It could be a pledge uttered in all sincerity, but it could also be a promise made in anger. Regardless of the motive, the people believed that once the gift-vow had been made over some piece of property, the temple retained ownership of it. This remained true even when the equity from the property would have been used for the care of the owner's parents.

Although the action of giving money to God seemed praiseworthy, it set up a situation in which parents were being dishonored. Jesus told the Pharisees that they used the vow as a handy way to permit adults to neglect the care of their destitute parents.

That commandment (like the rest of the ten) was not meant to be just a matter of lip service. A heart attitude of respect and care was also required by God. And the proof of that would be seen in the people's actions, not just in their words.

O Lord, please help me to fulfill my responsibility
to my parents, especially in their time of need.
Amen.

DAY SIX

An Ongoing Relationship
Ephesians 6:1–3

You quickly get the impression that Paul is not just talking to school-age children in Ephesians 6:1–3. For example, to obey means to do what one is told (something we would expect of children), but to honor means to respect and love (something we would increasingly expect of adults). Children must obey their parents, especially while they are under their parents' care, but the responsibility to honor parents is lifelong.

Do you see that one command is temporary whereas the other is ongoing? When we are children, we are subject to our parents. But eventually we grow up, leave home, and occasionally we might even find ourselves disagreeing with mom and dad. But although we might disagree with them about certain issues, we still continue to honor them by listening carefully, showing due respect, and offering our care and attention. That part of the relationship does not end.

Our ongoing relationship with our parents is supposed to be a hint about the way we never outgrow our relationship with God. He is not just for our trials and tribulations any more than parents are just for school-age children. Our willingness to continue loving our parents even as we grow older teaches us to continue loving God regardless of the circumstances we face in life. The relationship we have with our parents and the one we have with God will never cease to develop. They keep on growing.

Dear God, thank You for the privilege of being able to love You and my parents. Please help me to remain faithful in doing this. Amen.

DAY SEVEN

TURNABOUT TIME

Deuteronomy 4:9

You've probably heard the old saying that, "Turnabout is fair play." According to Deuteronomy 4:9, turnabout is the most proper play! Moses told the Israelites that they were to help each succeeding generation learn the lessons they had learned about God. The elder generation had been students, and now it was time for them to be teachers.

The same thing happens to us. We have already had the benefit of learning from our parents. They have taught us the practical, the emotional, and the spiritual things of life. They have given us their best, and the wonderful news is that their gift does not have to end with us! It is our privilege (and our responsibility) to teach what we have learned to future generations.

Teaching is not an automatic process. We have to devote our time and effort to the task. It requires a willingness on our part to think about what we are doing. We will have to work at it continually. But if we stay on track, we can make a real difference in future generations!

Lord, please help me to do my job of teaching future generations of children the valuable lessons about life that You enabled my parents to teach me. Amen.

Z. ALLEN ABBOTT

A Man and His Birth Family: Siblings

DAY ONE

YOU CAN CHOOSE YOUR FRIENDS, BUT . . .

John 13:35

A little bit of wisdom came my way one day. Several people were talking about family matters and some of the embarrassing things families do. One person in the group injected, "You can choose your friends, but you can't do a thing about your family."

Jesus unleashed some controversy over the concept of "family." His disciples came to Him and noted that His mother and brothers were outside and asking to see Him. What was the Savior's reply? "My mother and brothers are those who hear the word of God and do it" (Luke 8:21). This was not exactly a warm reception. For whatever reasons, Jesus defined "family" in unconventional terms. Anyone in the family of faith and love qualified. This certainly expands the family tree!

My wife and I distinguish between "family" and "relatives." While there are no intentions of exclusion, we've observed how some friends totally unrelated to us are actually closer than some of our relatives. It seems that we can select who is among our "family." But relatives are biologically or maritally attached regardless of our choosing. There's plenty of overlapping between the two groups, but not everyone we consider "family" is of any relation, and there are some relatives we know only vaguely.

In John 13:35, Jesus said that our Christlike love will show that we are His disciples. Perhaps you know some people who are hard to get along with. Why not show them the unconditional love of God? Who knows, they might be so moved by your kindness that they will want to become a Christian and thus join the family of God!

*O Lord, please help me to show Your love to
other people and thereby encourage them
to become a member of Your family. Amen.*

BROTHERLY LOVE—
YOU GOTTA PROBLEM WIT DAT?!

Genesis 37:14−36

A few years ago I moved from the Midwest to Philadelphia. The City of Brotherly Love is a beautiful and exciting place to live. But when I'm driving around town, the only "brotherly love" exhibited is more akin to what had been displayed by Joseph's brothers. Remember, these guys callously sold their brother into slavery (see Gen. 37:14–36). Philly drivers demonstrate a similar aggressive "addy-tude" that is characteristic of the big cities of the Northeast. They are swift on the horn, vicious with the accelerator, and unyielding to the poor soul trying to leave a parking lot.

Joseph's brothers added insult to injury by lying to their father about their scheme. They reported that Joseph had been killed by wild animals. Jealousy had so poisoned their relationship that they completely lost the brotherly connection.

That connection is explored in the movie *A Family Thing*. A small-town Arkansan discovers that he has a brother in Chicago who was born from an indiscretion of his father. The relationship is complicated by the fact that the father is white and the deceased mother was black. The two men, practically strangers, resent their unfortunate history but choose to become brothers. Ultimately love overcomes the greatest of evils and brotherly ties endure.

In Genesis 45, Joseph offered forgiveness, instead of vengeance, to his brothers. Has not God done even more for us? Through His Son He has shown us unconditional love and forgiveness. Are you willing to do the same for others?

*Lord, thank You for my birth family. Please help
me to love them as well the spiritual children
in Your family. Amen.*

OH, SISTER!
Ephesians 4:32

Sisters. Some guys wish they had one. Most guys who grew up with more than one sister wish they had more brothers. It seems we don't want to be outnumbered.

Unfortunately, that's a characteristic prevalent in some churches today. We often hear the term "Brother So-and-So," but less commonly spoken is "Sister So-and-So." Despite centuries of contribution to the sustenance and leadership of Christ's church, our sisters in the faith still struggle for equality.

Galatians 3:28 teaches us that "all of you are one in Christ Jesus." Our sisters in Christ, just like sisters in our birth family, help us to understand the female gender, and thus they define our own masculinity. They take us beyond stereotypical roles. They show us how God made each of us unique to reach a diverse world.

Why is it that we say, "Oh, Brother" but never "Oh, sister"? We usually say the first expression as we roll our eyes, after having learned about a frustration or loss. Maybe your team not only lost but also blew their chance to take the division. Or perhaps your candidate "mis-spoke" miserably, thus costing him the election. Maybe the saying originated in a time when news was shared only in groups of men. It's amazing how our language reveals historically embedded problems.

God knows that the bond that exists between brothers and sisters can be just as strong as that between brothers. As one who has been forgiven by God through Christ, strive to be kind, tenderhearted, and forgiving to not only your biological sisters but also your sisters in the faith (Eph. 4:32).

Lord, thank You for my Christian sisters. Please help me to show them respect and accord them the equal status they have with me in Christ. Amen.

HAND-ME-DOWNS

Mark 11:25

One current sociological trend shows that fewer parents choose to have several children, and that some choose to have no kids at all. In addition, the average family size has diminished over the decades here in America. In fact, today more families have only one child than in the days when most families worked on farms.

"Only children" miss out on one of the great traditions of growing up: hand-me-downs. In this respect, I was fortunate. I am the first-born of three, with a sister two years younger than me, and a brother two years younger than her. Like most families, we had limited resources, so there were always hand-me-downs. From baby items to toys to sweatshirts, by the time the items reached my brother, they were out of shape, out of style, or out of stock. Why should I have been the lucky one who had everything new?

During our childhood, we kids shared a lot—rooms, travel, food, even bath water. We encountered many of the same events, but we each have a different take on what happened and why. And now that we're all grown with families of our own and scattered throughout North America, we continue to share life's experiences together. Our birth order is less important now, especially as we explore who we are in Christ and where we fit in God's family.

Mark 11:25 shares this same perspective. Rather than hold grudges against others, we are to forgive them unconditionally. Instead of thinking selfishly about gratifying our own needs, we are to give unhesitatingly of ourselves to others. After all, through faith in Christ all of us can be equals in God's family.

Lord, please help me to elevate my spiritual sisters and brothers to positions of equality and to nurture mutual respect. Amen.

BROTHER VERSUS BROTHER

Genesis 4:7−8

Growing up together in Detroit, Kevin and Derian Hatcher played a lot of hockey. Now when they take to the ice, there's more at stake. Derian plays for the Dallas Stars, while Kevin skates with the Pittsburgh Penguins. Both teams are vicious NHL contenders. Both Hatchers are reputed for defensive scoring. Both of them play rough and know the penalty box well. Historical Hatcher battles are resurrected on the ice when the Penguins face off with the Stars.

Brotherhood has a way of bringing out competitiveness. In Dostoyevsky's novel *The Brothers Karamazov,* the full spectrum of human relations to God are personified. One brother is a rebel against God, one brother is consumed with earthly passions, and one brother is a Christlike servant. Over several years, the three engage in quarrels over a woman, a murdered father, and a disputed inheritance. The narrative persuasively argues that only Christian love can rescue us from our selfishness. As the author states, "We must love life more than the meaning of it."

Nowhere is this point more clear than in the biblical account of Cain and Abel. Cain's jealousy and anger drove him to murder his brother (Gen. 4:8). He failed to heed God's warning, "Sin is lurking at the door; its desire is for you, but you must master it" (v. 7).

Competition can drive us to excel beyond our perceived limits, but to value victory over everything causes us to miss life's lessons. Most of all, we can destroy our relationships with our brothers and sisters.

O Lord, please help me to focus on being more compassionate and less combative with my biological and spiritual brothers and sisters. Amen.

DAY SIX

WHY CAN'T YOU BE LIKE YOUR BROTHER?

Genesis 16:12

There's something about brothers that sometimes makes for a study in contrasts. Isaac and Ishmael were brothers with different moms. Abraham's first-born, Ishmael, apparently made his mark from day one. God said to Hagar his mother, "He shall be a wild ass of a man, with his hand against everyone, and everyone's hand against him" (Gen. 16:12). Isaac, Sarah's son, was nothing like

Ishmael. Isaac's name meant "laughter" (see 17:17; 18:12; 21:3). Ishmael was reared in the wilderness and became a hunter whereas Isaac lived a comparatively comfortable life with his parents.

Comparisons with our siblings are inevitable, especially if you stay in the same community for long, go to the same schools, work in the same jobs, and attend the same church. *A River Runs Through It* is a movie about two sons of a Presbyterian preacher who grow up together in Montana but take different approaches to life. One lives daringly on the edge, while the other chooses conservative sensibility and certainty. Neither brother wanted to be like the other; they wanted to be themselves. Each made his decisions differently and lived with the consequences.

Any man who is a brother is also a son and could also be an uncle, a dad, and a husband. When families convene and the stark differences become apparent, I can almost see God leaning back with a hearty smile and saying, *"Vive la différence!"*

> *Lord, please help me to learn from those who are closest to me things that I have not already seen. Amen.*

SOUL BROTHERS

1 Peter 2:17

First Peter 2:17 says, "Love the brotherhood." That sounds commendable, but it's not that easy when you consider the nature of your spiritual brothers. As equal members of God's family, we're like boys who must share the same room under one parent's roof.

Spike Lee's *Get On the Bus* is the story of several African American men who share a bus ride from Los Angeles to Washington, D.C., for the Million Man March. Their differences are immediately clear. While they journey across America, they find out how each complements the other, even though each man would not choose to be the other.

The business world provides plenty of examples where brothers combined their differences to achieve success—the Ringling Brothers, the Warner Brothers, the Harper Brothers, and even the Smothers Brothers. But you can bet your circus tickets that the family relations weren't always businesslike. Just consider Moses and Aaron, who were partners in what I call "Exodus Leadership Ministries."

When we as brothers place as much value on our differences as we do on our commonalties, a synergy emerges that is more powerful than the combined efforts of us all. We'll find an accountability and mutual mentoring that opens our eyes to reality. And reality is where God has called us to serve.

> *Lord, please don't let me live in an imaginary world. Show me the way things are, and let me see Your hand in it all. Amen.*

STEPHEN CLARK

A Man and His Church: Salvation

RIGHT IS NOT ALWAYS MIGHT
John 3:14−21

Men love to be right. It's a quirk that's buried deep in our genes and psyches. And it's not just that we want to be right and win arguments. We want to be right in everything from the most mundane of the myriad array of choices we confront daily to the most significant actions we might take in our lifetimes. We want to look good, always win, and never have to say the words "I'm sorry, I was wrong," or "I made a bad decision." By allowing these words to pass between our manly lips, we believe we will become less than a man. It means we're a sissy, a wimp, just another sweet nice guy, which would totally annihilate our macho self-image!

It isn't that we're never wrong, or that we never make a mistake, or that we never do anything hurtful or stupid or foolish. We're men, and it's here in rampant impulsive foolishness that we live! We just don't want to admit to this frightful truth. As a result, we expend enormous amounts of energy and engage in incredible contortions of behavior to cover up and hide the wide trail of *faux pas* (i.e., stupid mistakes) that nag our heels. The most frightening scenario we can imagine is having to look back and see the mass of tiny destructions that have accumulated in the wake of our life.

Yet that's what Jesus calls us to in John 3:14–21. He bids us to be exposed and to lay bare our whole lives before Him. His intent is not to condemn us, or to beat us up over the failures that shame us. Rather, He wants to free us from all condemnation (see Rom. 8:1). A real man is one who knows his limitations and runs to the Savior for strength, renewal, and cleansing every day.

Dear Lord, may I come to You daily in humble acknowledgment of my perpetual need of You and Your salvation. Amen.

DYING TO SELF IS NO TRICK

Romans 6:1–14

Dying to self. What a concept. What a glorious pain. When I think about the process of dying to self, or of getting rid of selfishness, an image that comes to mind is a magician pulling an endless rope of scarves out of his jacket pocket. In the beginning, it seems like such a simple act. There's only the end hanging out of his pocket. Then he gives it a yank. He continuously pulls and pulls and pulls. Soon, a multicolored pile is at his feet, and still he keeps pulling.

That's what it's like to die to self (Rom. 6:1–14). The more of your selfishness you allow to die at the cross, the more there is to die. And yet, the more you die, the more you're alive in Christ! Self-dying is a daily, even an hourly, act. Christ said to put our lives down and daily take up our crosses (see Matt. 16:24–25). Sadly, we put down our crosses continually so that we can pick back up our sinful selves. Up and down, up and down, all day and every day throughout our lives this takes place.

Some people are amazed at the concept of resurrection, that is, rising from the dead. But we actually do it all the time. We die to ourselves a million times a day, and come back from the dead almost as often! Did you ever think about that? I do. And every time I'm called on to die again, I wish I could just stay dead! But then the Lord pulls another "colored scarf" out of my pocket—in other words, the Spirit surfaces yet another issue—and I must die again so that I might live in Him more fully.

Dear Lord, please teach me through the Spirit the infinite value of dying to self. Help me to fully grasp how wonderful and liberating it is to rest in You. Amen.

TRUE BELIEVING IN SEEING THE TRUTH

John 14:6

When we are first confronted with truth—a truth that makes us look at the sinfulness in our lives—our reaction is often to lash out at the messengers. We want to wound them and beat them down with our words. We strive to make them small so that we can feel big. Yet we know that embracing God's truth is the only way to salvation. The very thing we react against is what will give us that which we desire most—spiritual strength, power, and freedom.

Truth is a Person (John 14:6). And applying truth to your life, even when it comes from a source you don't expect or respect, will lead you into true salvation. Believing the truth about yourself will kill the lies you have used to deceive yourself. Satan is the father of lies—all lies (see 8:44). You can choose to be saved and stand in truth, or foolishly cling to macho lies and be destroyed (v. 32).

Taking in truth and applying it to your life will equip you to meet all the needs of your family. You will become a source of encouragement and love to your wife and your children instead of a source of despair and defeat. Jesus is ultimate Truth. Let the truth of His saving love and presence flood your soul, give you life, and enable you to be a blessing to your family.

Dear Lord, please help me to understand that You are the Way, the Truth, and the Life. Amen.

ALL MEANS ALL, WITHOUT EXCEPTION!

Romans 3:21–24

Aren't you an exceptional guy! You're so cool and together. They love you at the office. And the people at church, when you attend, think that you're a great husband and father. Man, oh man, you've got it all! You tithe faithfully. You contribute even more to worthy causes. You donate food and clothing to a nearby homeless shelter. You volunteer your time to help out with school activities. You even remember your anniversary every year and get your wife her favorite flowers. You're one terrific guy! You're a really good person!

You're also full of sin! If all you try to stand on are the good things you do, you will remain spiritually lost and your soul will be headed for hell. On the outside you might look like the "best" guy in the world. But if you have not laid yourself at the foot of the cross and received God's grace, you are still unclean, unworthy, and unholy.

True goodness, or holiness, is found only in the righteousness of God. Only by trusting in His Son are we declared righteous (i.e., not guilty). All the good stuff in the world won't get us to heaven. We must renounce our sin and turn to Christ in faith, for only He can wipe clean the record of our misdeeds against God (Rom. 3:21–24).

When it comes to sin, no one is exceptional. We've all sinned. We all need Christ and the forgiveness He offers. You can't buy yourself a shortcut to grace. There's only one way, and it is through faith in the Son.

Dear Lord, I put my faith in Your Son.
Please cleanse me of my sins and make me
right with You. Amen.

DAY FIVE

WHO'S CHANGING YOUR CHANNELS?

Romans 6:19–23

A prominent symbol of American maleness is the TV remote control. It's generally accepted that the man holds the remote and therefore controls what's on the tube. And what you choose to watch also indicates what's in your heart. Guys love to be in control and to be free from the manipulation and bondage of others. Yet, we're all slaves, regardless of whether we acknowledge it.

There is no middle ground or neutral zone when it comes to your spirituality. You will either be enslaved to sin or controlled by the Spirit. It's your choice. And here's the real rub. If you choose slavery to sin, your behavior bears a cost that will earn you a place in hell. Have you ever thought about that? Sin is costly, and its payoff is big. On earth, sin can cost you your peace, health, marriage, and more. In the end, it brings you eternal condemnation and separation from God.

However, there is hope. By turning away from sin and accepting the free gift of righteousness through faith in Christ, you also receive eternal life. You are freed from sin so that you can serve God. Instead of reaping death, you will walk in holiness with God (Rom. 6:19–23).

Every day you have a choice to get up and go to work for the Devil and punch hell's time clock. Or you can get up and serve Christ and reap righteousness and joy. Your life through your choices and actions will motivate others to follow you wherever you are headed. Just as you control the TV shows you watch, so you can choose who controls what others watch in you.

Heavenly Father, this day I choose to serve You, not sin. Please give me the strength from day to day to abide by this decision. Amen.

IT'S MY WAY OR THE HIGHWAY!

Ephesians 2:8–9

Doesn't it feel great to accomplish something all on your own! You love that feeling of having done something your way without the help of anyone else. Standing back to admire the work of your hands—that thing that's cost your blood, sweat, and tears—fills you with immense pride and satisfaction. When it's a "thing" that you've made, then this is a good, God-ordained experience. God created, and He imparts in you a need and desire to create.

But, when the area of accomplishment is the honing of a character quality, the teaching of a spiritual truth to your children, or the acting out of a husbandly duty, you must beware of claiming credit. Apart from the grace of God, you would remain depraved in your behavior, in your caring, and in your concern for others.

We men often try to express our salvation and sense of worth by doing stuff. We love to think we can boast in our works, whether it's a word of wisdom or an act of intended kindness. But our salvation does not depend upon the quality of our deeds. Rather, the quality of our deeds depends upon our salvation. Our righteous standing before God comes through faith in Christ. Because salvation is based on God's grace, there's nothing for us to boast about (Eph. 2:8–9).

Heavenly Father, please help me to never lose sight of my intense need of You and Your grace in my life. Amen.

LIAR! LIAR! PANTS ON FIRE!

1 John 5:9–13

Have you ever thought about what salvation is? What some of the elements of salvation are? To be saved means being forgiven of *all* your sin. It means possessing in you *all* you need to live a holy and righteous life. It means that you are a new person; in other words, you're not the sinful person you used to be. It means that your life has been cleansed and reconstructed in power. It means that you are daily becoming more and more just like Christ! All of this is part of the testimony to the truth that God provided through Jesus. And this is the truth we are to believe in our hearts and live out in our lives (1 John 5:19–23).

If you don't believe even just one part of this testimony, you are calling God a liar! If at any moment of time you feel as if your sins aren't forgiven, you are calling God a liar. If you believe that you just don't have what it takes to be good in Christ, you are calling God a liar. If you think that the Spirit doesn't want anything to do with you, you are calling God a liar.

Here is where Satan tries to deceive us. The goal of our enemy is to kill, steal, and destroy us, even if he has to do it doubt by doubt. The Devil will bring situations and people across your path that will sow disbelief, discouragement, and disappointment in your heart. The testimony of others will label you a failure, a fool, and a coward. But God's testimony is greater, for He is the One who has spoken about His Son! In Christ you are more than a conqueror. You have eternal life, and you have endless access to God's grace.

Heavenly Father, thank You for the spiritual power, life, and grace that You make available through faith in Christ. Amen.

WILL POLLARD

A Man and His Church: Discipleship

DAY ONE

IS IT MY WAY OR HIS WAY?

Matthew 16:24

Peter knew Jesus pretty well, or so the disciple thought. He was involved with Jesus' earthly ministry right from the start. Peter loved Jesus and wanted to follow Him. So Peter was shocked to hear Jesus say that while in Jerusalem, He would suffer, die, and rise again on the third day (Matt. 16:21).

Verse 22 indicates that Peter had his own view about how Jesus' ministry should have progressed. The leading disciple told Christ that suffering and death would never happen to Him. In response, the Lord declared that Peter's statement reflected the plan of Satan, not the will of God.

God's plan for Jesus included the suffering and shame of the Cross. Knowing this, Christ said to His disciples, "If anyone wants to follow me, he must say 'no' to the things he wants. He must be willing even to die on a cross, and he must follow me" (v. 24).

Three key elements of Jesus' plan for us as His disciples are evident here. First, we must have a sincere desire and a true commitment to follow Christ. Second, we must say *no* to our selfish ambitions so that we can fulfill God's desires for us. Third, we must accept the possibility of becoming unpopular and even risking death, if necessary.

Lord, this day I say yes to Your will for me
as a disciple of Christ. Amen.

CAN YOU HATE YOUR FAMILY?

Luke 14:26–27

Many passages of Scripture encourage us to love our families. That is why it's startling to read Jesus' statement in Luke 14:26–27. He used the word rendered "hate" in reference to our families. In other words, we are to love Christ so much, that even our families take second place to Him. This instruction was especially relevant in Jesus' day, for deciding to become His disciple often meant rejection by family as well as persecution and possibly even death.

All of us have accumulated possessions and made relationships that are precious to us. We sometimes sacrifice time and energy to preserve them. Family members can easily win so much of our attention that they sidetrack God's call for us to be committed followers of Christ.

Here's the unspoken challenge for us as men of God. The Lord has called us to lead our families to the same level of devotion that He wants us to have. In other words, they must give Jesus first place in their lives. You and they undoubtedly will be rejected by some. As disciples, you and your family must be ready to face and accept such rejection. With God's help, you can!

Dear Lord, please give me and my family the strength to remain committed followers of Your Son, regardless of the personal cost. Amen.

ARE WE THERE YET?

Romans 8:18

Our son and daughter-in-law joined us in a four-hundred-mile drive to visit relatives. Everything went smoothly until my son and his wife began asking some questions from childhood. It made travel more complicated. We barely got off their street when one of them exclaimed, "I've got to go to the bathroom!" A little later, the other one wanted to know whether we were "there yet." Recently, they took their two preschoolers on a weekend trip. I'm sure that the difficulties of travel were well rewarded when they got to grandmother's house.

The writings of Paul remind us that the difficulties of our pilgrimage as Jesus' disciples will be well rewarded when the journey is over and we go home to be with God. In Romans 8:18, Paul declared that the sufferings we now endure for Christ are nothing compared to the glory He will one day give to us.

Jesus modeled suffering for His followers. He faced ridicule, an illegal trial, a cruel execution, and death on the cross as a criminal. We are not promised an easy way when we follow Jesus. But we are assured that He will be with us throughout our pilgrimage on earth. It is encouraging to know that we don't travel alone!

Lord, thank You that Jesus is always with me through each step of my journey through life. Amen.

DAY FOUR

BOGGED DOWN?

Luke 21:34

Our new church building was almost ready. But the guttering needed to be connected to the drainage system. Some of the men in the church decided we could handle the project. Arrangements were made to rent a trenching machine. It would be a good Saturday project.

Everything was set for the next weekend. However, during the week, we had monsoon-type rains. Because the ground around the building was barren, the mostly clay soil became soaked. The trenching machine was delivered to the site on Friday, and the messy, muddy job began on Saturday. The ground around the building was workable, but the long drain behind the building was difficult because the wet clay soil was unstable.

It was getting late. The trencher was so bogged down that we couldn't get it to move. The more we tried to lift and rotate the machine, the deeper we sank into the mud. The man in charge of the project said, "It looks like we will have to leave it here until tomorrow. I don't think anyone will be able to steal it anyway."

We left the trenching machine bogged down. Driving into the church parking area the next morning, I came upon a wrecker with a wench. He was able to pull the machine loose and take it to a better location.

In Luke 21:34, Jesus warned against being bogged down in our lives as disciples. He urged us to watch and be spiritually prepared for His return. This means remaining faithful to what God has called us to do as Jesus' disciples. We shouldn't let the cares of this world weigh us down. Instead, we should be ready at all times for Christ's return.

Lord, please help me not to get so bogged down
with life that I forget to watch and wait for
Jesus' return. Amen.

DAY FIVE

A Disciple Listens and Follows
Luke 5:27–28

Most of us have played the party game where a person shares a story with the person on his right. That person then repeats the story to the next person on his right. The process is repeated until the story makes its way around the circle and is told to the original person. It is amazing how the story changes as it travels through the group!

The person who hears the message first has the best opportunity to know exactly what was originally said. But those who don't hear or understand well might alter the story. And sometimes a person who doesn't care about the details of the message distorts what he is told.

We are not to be this way as Jesus' disciples. When Christ issues the call for us to follow Him, as He did with Levi, we must listen, understand, and obey (Luke 5:27–28). Nothing less will do.

We can be so busy with life that we do not hear Jesus summoning us to follow Him. How would you respond if Jesus came by your workplace and called you to be His disciple? Many fail to respond because they are so distracted by mundane concerns.

Are you too busy to give God the attention He deserves? Levi wasn't. When Jesus called, the tax collector immediately responded. Are you willing to leave everything to follow Jesus? Levi was. He knew that setting aside a material fortune for eternal blessings was worth it!

Lord, please enable me to listen, understand, and
obey Your call to discipleship. Amen.

SAYING NO TO OUR DESIRES

Romans 15:1

Many societal ills come from the desires that people have to please themselves. Gratifying these sinful impulses leads to all kinds of hurt for ourselves and others. The renewed mind of a disciple marches to a different drummer.

Mother Teresa, though small and bent in stature, was a giant of faith and compassion. She did not see the poor, sick, weak, and dying as persons to be viewed and pitied. As a follower of Jesus, she felt compelled to touch, encourage, and comfort those who were weak. She was willing to sacrifice her desires to bear the burdens of a multitude of hurting people. She was known around the world for her humanitarian efforts. She was truly a disciple who displayed the compassion that Jesus modeled.

Some of us are stronger than others in the faith. Paul said that we might know that certain practices make no real difference from an eternal perspective. Nevertheless, we can't just go ahead and do them to please ourselves. We must be considerate of the doubts and fears of those who think that what we are doing is wrong (Rom. 15:1).

Out of love for those who are weak in the faith, we must be willing to say *no* to our desires. This requires a lot of strength and maturity on our part. It also requires a high level of commitment from us to build up those who are struggling in their walk with Christ. By saying *no* to our desires, we demonstrate to the world that we are genuine followers of Christ.

Lord, please help me to keep my own desires in check so that I might build up, rather than tear down, the faith of others in the church. Amen.

"AM I MY BROTHER'S KEEPER?"

Genesis 4:9

All churches have problems with members who become inactive. Some people seem to take discipleship loosely. My friend Bill is gifted at knowing how to deal with dropouts skillfully. He takes the initiative in reaching out to them, is sensitive to their hurts, and patiently listens to their stories. If he can offer specific counsel or assistance he does so. He tries not to take expressions of anger personally. This man gently wins the confidence of people who have dropped out and then leads them back into the fellowship of the church. Of course, not everyone wants to go back to their old churches; he encourages them to find new places to worship. He has a nonpossessive attitude and says, "After all, these are not my people. They are God's people. If they cannot worship and serve at my church, perhaps they can serve somewhere else."

This is the antithesis of the cry of Cain in Genesis 4:9. Cain's "brotherhood" benefitted only him. He felt no responsibility toward another. Bill's approach to brotherhood is that of a servant. One response kills; the other empowers.

May Bill's tribe increase! How we need people who do see themselves as their brother's keepers, not just at church but at work and in the community. Part of our discipleship is keeping up with others, especially when they seem to fall by the wayside. Yes, each of us really is our "brother's keeper." Where is your brother?

Lord, help me to love others enough to reach out to them and restore them to fellowship. Amen

LEONARD ALBERT

A Man and His Church: Leadership

PASTORAL LEADERSHIP
Jeremiah 3:15

When many Christians think about the subject shepherding, they immediately consider pastoral leadership within a church. This is commendable. In fact, we Christians should be considerate of our pastors and give them due respect.

Nevertheless, pastoring is not the only form of valid spiritual leadership for men. As husbands and fathers, they are the priests of the home. If they are in a supervisory capacity at their job or are business owners, they must exercise leadership, especially if they want to succeed. Men who are active in their communities through civic organizations are leaders and have the possibility of influencing many. Finally, as members of their church, men serve in many kinds of leadership positions that enable them to influence the eternal destinies of others in ways that a pastor cannot. Jeremiah 3:15 is applicable to all of these forms of leadership.

Where are you today—not just with God, but with the leadership responsibilities He has given you? Do you know that you are a leader for God? Or do you just think that leadership in His name is reserved for the pastor? Are you a shepherd after God's own heart? Or are you following a worldly pattern of leadership?

Lord, please give me a clear understanding of what it means to be a biblical leader. Amen.

VIGILANCE AND PERSISTENCE

Acts 20:28

Of all the challenges facing men and the ministries to which God has called them, one of the greatest is answering the call to vigilance and persistence. It's easy in the heat of the moment, when the Spirit is moving and everyone's excited, to step forth and offer ourselves to God's service.

But what do we do when things get rough, when we have conflicts with others, or when we don't achieve our goals? Our immediate response might be to throw up our hands in despair and quit. But God wants us to persist and be vigilant in that which He has called us to do. For example, we are to guard the spiritual flock of God from the attacks of Satan (Acts 20:28).

Long ago, Leo the Great offered the following observation:

> But since the Lord says, "Blessed is he who shall persevere unto the end," whence shall come this blessed perseverance, except from the strength of patience? For as the Apostle proclaims, "All who would live godly in Christ shall suffer persecution." And it is not only to be reckoned persecution when sword or fire or other active means are used against the Christian religion; for the direst persecution is often inflicted by nonconformity of practice and persistent disobedience and the barbs of ill-natured tongues; and since all the members of the Church are always liable to these attacks, and no portion of the faithful are free from temptation, so that a life of either of these nor of labor is devoid of danger, who shall guide the ship amidst the waves of the sea, if the helmsman quit his post?

Father, please help me to remain at my post
of spiritual leadership, regardless of
the circumstances. Amen.

LEAD, DON'T PUSH

I Peter 5:2

Many men think that leadership is a "command and control" proposition. Supposedly all they need to do is take command, bark a few orders, and ride people until the job gets done. Unfortunately such men only manage to demoralize everyone around them, which does nothing to advance God's kingdom.

In 1 Peter 5:2, the apostle exhorted us to "shepherd the flock," meaning that we are to care for and lead God's people, not drive them harshly like cattle. When organizing a cattle drive, the cattlemen's task is simple. They are to "round 'em up and move 'em out!" They do this by getting behind the cattle and using a sharp prod to force the animals to go in a certain direction.

Peter also urged us not to lead the flock grudgingly, but rather to do so willingly. The Lord's army is a volunteer force, not a group of conscripts. We need to remember this as we lead God's people.

One night a pastor told his congregation, "The church doesn't need any of you to be here." One of the members observed that the pastor would have a different view if no one came to hear him preach! We often incorrectly assume that those we lead come to church only because it is their spiritual duty. In reality, they attend because it's their genuine desire to please and serve God.

Peter also reminded us not to lead the flock for what we might get out of it. Rather, we should do so because we are eager to serve God. Many people today are stuck in jobs that they absolutely hate. Often they stay because of the salary they're earning. That should not be our motivation for leading Jesus' disciples. Whatever our leadership role might be, let us do our job zealously and joyfully.

O Lord, please help me to shepherd Your people,
not to drive them crazy. Amen.

CHOSEN BY GOD
John 15:16

The idea that God chose us for eternal life is hard to understand. On one hand, we know from John 15:16 that this is true, and we are encouraged by that knowledge. On the other hand, we have a hard time grasping why the God of the universe, who is over all things and has so many important tasks to perform, would bother to choose us for any good purpose.

How wonderful it is to know that Jesus took the first step. He loved us so much that He died on the cross for our sins. He now invites us to accept His offer of salvation and to live with Him forever. If we say *yes* to eternal life, we will be able to bear spiritual fruit for God.

The question is this: Are you ready to accept the Lord's offer of eternal life? And are you also willing to serve Him faithfully? By answering *yes* to both of these questions, you are on the road to an abundant spiritual life with God. Jesus will enable you to produce fruit that will last forever. This is His will for you. So accept it and get started!

O Lord, please enable me to bear spiritual fruit
for You that will last forever. Amen.

LEADERSHIP AND SUBMISSION
Hebrews 13:17

The subject of biblical submission—whether in the church, in the marriage, or in other areas of life—is controversial. We have been so conditioned to think of our individual "rights" and what God has promised to do for us that we are uncomfortable with the idea that we have to submit to anyone.

God's idea of spiritual leadership is far different from ours. First, the leader must be willing to make sacrifices for the flock. Overseers in the church are not like worldly kings who force their subjects to do what they want. Rather, they are humble and sacrificial in the performance of their duties (Matt. 20:25–28). Jesus illustrated this concept most powerfully by washing His disciples' feet (John 13:1–17)

Second, leaders of the flock are accountable to God for their actions. In fact, He will use stricter standards to evaluate the quality of their service (James. 3:1). Your desire to become a leader in the church is commendable (1 Tim. 3:1). But remember that with the privilege comes the responsibility. What you say and how you act will affect the spiritual lives of others, so take your duties seriously.

Third, spiritual leaders should shepherd believers in love, not in fear. This starts in the home. Our model as husbands comes not from the world but from Christ, Who loved His bride, the Church, and gave His life for her (Eph. 5:25–29). If we are compassionate and caring leaders in the home, we will encourage people in the church to follow us rather than to hide from us when we appear.

Most likely you are both a leader and a follower. Hebrews 13:17 exhorts you to obey your spiritual overseers. Their task is to help you mature in your walk with Christ. Do your actions and attitude give them cause for delight or grief? Make sure that you give them reason to be joyful rather than sorrowful.

Lord, please help me to be both a better leader and a better follower. Amen.

DAY SIX

A NEW PERSPECTIVE

1 Corinthians 1:27–29

Many years ago on a television series, the main character was shown an unconventional school where people learned information in unusual ways. He noticed one person standing on her head. The tour guide explained that the student was "gaining new perspective." Although the explanation was absurd, it illustrates an important point. To look at a situation in a new light, it's often necessary to turn things upside down.

God did this for us in Christ (1 Cor. 1:27–29). It is the ultimate irony that, to transform our lives spiritually, God had to act in ways that defy conventional wisdom. The world says that only the rich, powerful, and smart are the winners. But God deliberately chooses things the world considers foolish, powerless, and ignominious to bring glory to Himself. His ways guarantee that no can ever boast about their accomplishments in His presence.

Matthew 10:39 says, "He who has found his life shall lose it, and he who has lost his life for My sake shall find it." This process starts when we are saved. We surrender our life to God, and, in return, we receive something far greater—eternal life. Conversely, if we cling to this life, we will ultimately lose it.

The decision could not be clearer. The best way to enjoy life is to loosen your grip on earthly rewards so that you can be free to follow Christ. Then, and only then, will you be most fulfilled.

O Lord, please help me not to so cling to power,
popularity, and financial security that I fail
to experience the joy of following Christ. Amen.

DAY SEVEN

NOT OURSELVES, BUT CHRIST
2 Corinthians 4:5

Being a Christian leader is a difficult task. We're not in a situation where the more impressive our title sounds, the more we can delegate to others the work of preaching the gospel. And when we witness, we must not focus on our abilities and accomplishments. Rather, we are to lead such that people see Christ and His power at work in our lives. Regardless of what our leadership role might be in the church, the Lord has called us to make Christ the cornerstone of our ministries. We present ourselves to others as His servants (2 Cor. 4:5).

Sadly, too much leadership these days is nothing more than self-promotion. It involves making people into a "legend in their own time." But from God's perspective, they are really "legends in their own mind." If someone preaches about himself or his own ideas, rather than about Christ, he could be a false teacher.

God has entrusted the supremely valuable message of salvation in Christ to frail and fallible human beings (v. 7). Although the container (i.e., us) is perishable, the contents (i.e., God's power dwelling in us) is priceless. Although we are weak, God uses us to declare the good news to others. As genuine Christian leaders, let us accept the privilege of communicating the gospel such that others may receive eternal life.

Lord, as I share the gospel, please help me to
proclaim Christ, not myself, to others. Amen.

FISHER HUMPHREYS

A Man and His Church: Mission

UNEXPECTED SUCCESSES

Jonah 3:1–10

The Lord called Jonah to preach in Nineveh. Although Jonah was reluctant, he eventually went. After Jonah preached, the king, the leaders, and the people of Nineveh turned from their sins and prayed for God's mercy. Jonah 3:10 says that because they put a stop to their evil ways, God didn't carry out the destruction He had threatened.

From the account of Jonah we learn that sometimes God uses reluctant men to do things that turn out to be more successful than what they originally had expected. Of course, it's better when men are eager to do the Lord's work and expect to succeed in their God-given task.

In America today, some Christian men feel surrounded by hostile groups. For example, some radical feminist organizations seem to hold them (indeed all men) in contempt. Thus, it is natural for Christian men to want to retreat into themselves and to put up walls to deflect the hostility of those who do not appreciate them.

An easy way to retreat from the intimidating world is to refuse to attempt to take any initiative in serving the Lord. That is how Jonah initially operated. Although retreating is an understandable response, it is not a good response. The Lord did not put us here simply to observe the unfriendly groups around us. Rather, He wants us to work for Him in this world. If we accept the challenge, that work can fill our lives with meaning. And when God's work is done in His power and for His glory, it will succeed, even if we don't expect it to.

*Lord, thank You for giving me opportunities
to serve You. Please glorify Your name by making
the work I do for You successful. Amen.*

WHERE IN THE WORLD IS GOD?

2 Kings 17:27

The Israelites believed that there is only one true God (Deut. 6:4). They also believed that He made the world and remains in absolute control of it (Job 38:1–10; Dan. 5:34–35). Israel's neighbors did not agree. They believed that there are many gods. These pagan deities supposedly were local, with each one controlling a specific territory.

This clash of beliefs led to an odd situation. In 722 B.C., Assyria conquered the northern kingdom of Israel and exiled many of its inhabitants. The conquerors then moved in a host of foreigners. The Assyrians shuffled people around to prevent them from organizing a rebellion (2 Kings 17:23–24).

When some of the foreigners who settled in Israel were killed by lions, they assumed that they needed the protection of the local deity. So the king of Assyria ordered an Israelite priest to return to Israel to teach the people how to worship the Lord (vv. 24–27).

We don't always understand why God allows certain things to happen. For example, why did He allow an imperfect situation to exist in Samaria? Although this aspect of God's will seems unfathomable, it's clear that the exiled priest whom the Assyrians returned to the region had a wonderful opportunity to teach the new residents about the Lord (v. 28).

Recently, two friends of mine went as missionaries to Albania, which is said to be the least religious nation in the world. They sensed that God was calling them there to spread the gospel among hundreds of thousands of non-Christians. But fierce fighting broke out in Albania, and my friends were forced to leave. Now they live in a neighboring country, where they minister to Albanian refugees.

My friends' ideas about God's specific will for them may have been mistaken. But the Lord graciously redirectedly them where they belonged so that He might use them greatly in the proclamation of the gospel.

*Lord, please guide me into Your perfect will
for my life. Amen.*

THE GOSPEL FOR EVERYONE

Revelation 14:6

David Barrett is the author of *World Christian Encyclopedia,* the most comprehensive study of religion ever made. He encourages the church to think about missionary work in terms of people groups, some of them with millions of members, among whom the gospel is virtually unknown.

In Revelation 14:6, John referred to people groups when he wrote about proclaiming the eternal gospel "to those who live on the earth—to every nation, tribe, language and people." The Greek word translated "tribe" is *ethnos,* from which we get our English word "ethnic." The gospel is for every ethnic group, or every people group, on the earth.

Today, many missionary strategists are taking Barrett's work seriously. Missions agencies attempt to find ways to place missionaries among each of the people groups in the world. Because some people groups have few or no Christians living among them, new strategies must be devised to get missionaries placed in these areas. Some of them go to teach English; others go as businessmen; and still others go as agriculturists, computer specialists, or medical personnel.

To practice Christian missions well today, we must think carefully, plan shrewdly, work hard, and make sacrifices. It's an undertaking that brings out the best in Christian men and women. He gives them the gifts necessary to accomplish the task. Only those who answer God's call and give missions their best effort know how fulfilling it can be.

Lord, I know that You call Christian men to take the gospel to all peoples. I am willing to do my part. Please give me the wisdom to know what that is. Amen.

A WIDENESS IN GOD'S MERCY

1 Chronicles 16:23

I subscribe to one of the national news magazines, and it's divided into several different sections. In some issues there is a section on religion, which I am inclined to read carefully. Sometimes I wonder whether that is what a Christian man should do. After all, God made the whole world, and He wants us to be interested in the things that are happening throughout it. I sometimes think that God's heart must break when He sees children starving and people being cruel to each other.

God is interested in our religious life—how we pray, how we struggle against temptation, and how we participate in church life. But God is also interested in other parts of our lives. For example, He is concerned about whether we honor our marriage vows (assuming we're married) and about how we handle being single (if that is our situation). God is interested in how we relate to our children or grandchildren. He is concerned about how we make our living and how we do our work. God is even concerned about what kind of citizens we are.

The wideness of God's interests is clear in 1 Chronicles 16:23, which is part of David's song of praise to the Lord. The king of Israel had his hands full ruling God's people. Nevertheless, David was convinced that the Lord's interests extended beyond the boundaries of Israel. That's why he declared, "Sing to the Lord, all the earth."

Lord, please teach me to share Your wider concern
for the unsaved people of the earth. Amen.

DAY FIVE

New Horizons

Acts 10:9–20

Peter had come a long way in his spiritual growth and development. He originally had been a fisherman on the Sea of Galilee. When Jesus called him, Peter followed (Luke 5:1–10) and later confessed that Jesus is the Christ. But when he urged Jesus to avoid the Cross, Christ rebuked Peter (Matt. 16:16, 21–23).

At the end of Jesus' earthly ministry, Peter was warming his hands at a fire when he swore that he was not one of Christ's followers (Mark 14:66–72). After Jesus' resurrection, He restored Peter to a place of prominent leadership as an apostle in the church (John 21:15–19).

On the Day of Pentecost, Peter boldly proclaimed the gospel of

Christ, and thousands of people became Christians (Acts 2:14, 41). Shortly thereafter, Peter (along with John) courageously accepted imprisonment and persecution for his faith (chaps. 3–4).

Despite the tremendous spiritual growth that had occurred to this point in Peter's life, he still had a long way to go. His work had been among only Jews, and God wanted him to work also among Gentiles. So when God directed Peter to go to the home of a devout Gentile named Cornelius, Peter obeyed, shared the gospel, and led the centurion and his entire household to faith in Christ (chapters 10–11).

Peter made a lot of mistakes, and he learned from them. Through it all, he continued to spiritually grow. He never said, "I have grown so much that I don't need to grow any more." God continued to show him new horizons.

God still uses Christian men who are like Peter. They don't have to be perfect; in fact, they won't be. But if they recognize their need to continue growing, God can—and will—use their lives.

Lord, thank You for the new horizons You have
in store for me as You help me to grow and
mature spiritually. Amen.

DAY SIX

HONORING THE PROTOCOLS

ACTS 13:47

Paul's parents had ensured that he received a thorough Jewish training. In fact, he later became a member of the Pharisees (Acts 26:4–5). But when Christ saved him on the road to Damascus, He intended for Paul to be an emissary to Gentiles as well as Jews (9:15). Throughout the rest of his life, Paul remained faithful to his apostolic calling (2 Tim. 4:7).

During Paul's missionary travels, he operated by a certain protocol. His customary practice upon arriving in a city was to enter the local synagogue and proclaim the gospel to the Jews (see Acts 13:14). If they rejected it, the apostle then redirected his efforts to evangelize the Gentiles (vv. 45–46). This ministry of the gospel to non-Jews was anticipated in Isaiah 49:6 (Acts 13:47).

Paul's example encourages us to be sensitive to the protocols that exist in cultures where God would have us proclaim the gospel.

Properly, we should minister the truth first to our own families, friends, and colleagues. But God also wants us to share the message of His love and grace to those outside this circle of acquaintances.

The outsiders might be the poor of our community, people of another race, or individuals who have become social outcasts. Whoever they are, we can be sure that God wants us to share the truth with them so that they might be saved (1 Tim. 2:4).

Lord, please help me to share the gospel
with people outside my immediate circle
of acquaintances. Amen.

A REASON FOR OUR HOPE

1 Peter 3:15

Does the gospel speak to our emotions or to our intellects? The answer, of course, is both. Because God created us as whole persons, we should respond to the truth with our minds as well as our emotions and will.

We have good reason to respond thus. God's boundless mercy enables us to be born again. Because Christ has risen from the dead, we have the wonderful hope of one day also being resurrected (1 Peter 1:3). The Lord is reserving this priceless inheritance in heaven for us, and He will ensure that we one day receive it (v. 4).

Because there is no doubt about our salvation, we ultimately have nothing of eternal value to lose when we boldly affirm our allegiance to Christ. And because this is such an important job, Peter urged us to be ready always to explain the nature of our faith and commitment to inquirers (3:15).

When we invite people to trust in Christ, we are not asking them to take a blind leap of faith into the dark. Rather, we are encouraging them to turn from the darkness of sin and death to the light and life of Christ. What a glorious privilege it is for us to tell the lost about the Messiah so that they might come to a knowledge of the truth and be saved!

Lord, please give me the wisdom and strength
I need to tell the lost about Your Son. Amen.

GUENTER APSEL

A Man and His Church: Service

TO SERVE: LOSS OR GAIN?

Matthew 16:24–25

Throughout the journey of my life, I have set goals. Some of them have been small, whereas others have been large. To reach these goals, I have had to invest much energy and intelligence. This affects both my job and my personal life. Sometimes I gamble everything on one opportunity. How is it possible for me to I receive everything I wanted and yet end up feeling empty inside? What really counts in the end?

These are the sorts of questions that lay at the heart of Jesus' ministry. As His disciples traveled with Him throughout Galilee, He candidly told them that suffering and death awaited Him in Jerusalem (Matt. 16:21). This information didn't sit well with them (especially Peter), and they tried to dissuade Christ from such an end (v. 22). But Jesus refused to veer from His God-appointed destiny (v. 23).

What Jesus said in verses 24–25 applies just as much to Christian men and women today as it did nearly two thousand years ago. More important than being successful is following and serving Christ faithfully. We should take a cue from our Savior. After all, He did not live for success, or happiness, or wealth, but for people. He unconditionally loved them, and He ultimately gave His life on the cross for them.

Here's the piercing question: Are you willing to serve Jesus to the same extent? Remember that if you try to keep your life for yourself, you will lose it. But if you surrender your life to Christ, you will find true life—eternal life.

*Lord, please help me to put aside my selfish
ambitions so that I might be fully committed
to serving You. Amen.*

TO SERVE:
AN UNMANAGEABLE ASSIGNMENT?

Matthew 11:28–30

A certain man had reached all the goals that he had set for himself. He had a family, a good job, and lots of money. But he noticed that something was missing in his life. After much soul-searching, he discovered that he was famished spiritually. After becoming a man of faith, he looked for and found his place of service in his church. His former colleagues were amazed that this once powerful and close-fisted man would donate his time and energy freely to religious work.

Do you find yourself anywhere in this story? Most men do. Perhaps some of the details might be different, but all of us struggle with the same ambitions and unmet needs. Like the man mentioned here, we will not find true joy and lasting satisfaction until we surrender our lives to Jesus and His service.

People at first might be shocked to learn that you are able to donate your time and energy freely to Christian work. They might even be amazed at the talents and abilities you have for serving others. Most of all, they might be moved by your willingness to unselfishly reach out to others in need. To your colleagues, this commitment might seem like an unmanageable assignment, and on the merely human level it is. But in God's power no ministry that He wants you to do is too difficult for us to handle.

Perhaps you're afraid of the possibility of serving Jesus. Take heart. As Matthew 11:28–30 reveals, ministry in the name of Christ is not meaningless, wearisome toil. Rather, Jesus' yoke fits perfectly, and the burden He gives you is light.

O Lord, please help me to realize that serving You
does not have to be a scary, dreary prospect.
Enable me to experience the joy and satisfaction
that comes from ministering in Your name. Amen.

TO SERVE:
STUPIDITY OR VOLUNTARY ABSTENTION?

Romans 14:21

Men like to come out on top. To be considerate is supposedly equal to being stupid. After all, we have to achieve! We think that showing consideration toward others is a luxury we cannot afford.

Although this is the way the world thinks, it is not how Jesus wants us to be. To serve is not stupidity but rather voluntary abstention. As followers of Christ, we belong to a religious community in which every member should seek to be helpful, friendly, and considerate. The more we Christian men strive to achieve this goal, the more attractive our faith and place of worship will be to outsiders.

It's so easy for us to think about only ourselves and to ignore the needs of those around us. Perhaps something we said or did annoyed or offended someone else. Regardless of the affront, Romans 14:21 cautions us to avoid such activity at all costs, not because it is inherently wrong but because it needlessly upsets others within the church. If we truly love Christ and His people, we will seek to be considerate of them and their feelings. Our desire is to help them, not to hurt them, by our actions.

Saying *no* to our rights for the good of others is difficult. Our sinful nature pressures us to do what we want, regardless of how it might affect others. But the gospel calls us to be kind and compassionate. By being sensitive and cautious, we help to ease the problems associated with human togetherness.

*Lord, please help me to be considerate of my
fellow Christians and to avoid doing anything
that might needlessly offend them. Amen.*

TO SERVE: BE ACCESSIBLE TO OTHERS

1 Corinthians 10:23–24

It's not easy for us to put our own interests on the back burner for others. We live in a competitive society, and that has an affect on our personal attitude. Service to others is not only unpopular but also virtually unheard of.

We might acknowledge that being accessible to others is a noble idea, but not for us. We like to leave that job for people who are "more spiritual," such as Francis of Assisi and Mother Teresa. But they're more than altruistic heroes; they're also excellent role models, and, as such, are to be imitated.

People today, like those who lived in ancient Corinth, insisted that they had the freedom to do anything they wanted. But Paul noted that not everything is helpful or beneficial (1 Cor. 10:23). As Christian men, we are called not only to think about our own good but also to consider other believers and what is good for them (v. 24).

It's easy for us Christian men to conclude that we must do something big and bold and splashy to show our consideration for others. Yet it's in the small, simple things of life where our acts of kindness count the most—in the comforting word we say, the open hand we extend, and the smile we offer.

> *Lord, please help me to look beyond myself and*
> *see how I can be a source of consolation to*
> *my brothers and sisters in the faith. Amen.*

DAY FIVE

To Serve: Who Is My Role Model?

1 Corinthians 11:1

Who is your role model? For many men, it's their parents or even famous people, such as athletes, scientists, and artists. For some men, it could be a teacher or a pastor. None of these role models is perfect. They might sometimes break a promise they have made or fail to live up to our expectations.

We learn two key truths about role models from 1 Corinthians 11:1. First, Jesus is our ultimate role model. He was the superlative example of love, humility, and generosity. He alone obeyed God perfectly and sacrificed Himself for the good of others.

Second, Jesus wants us, as His followers, to be role models for others. Think about it. Christ is not visibly present for the unsaved to see and imitate. That's why Jesus wants *us* to demonstrate His kindness and compassion to the lost.

Does this idea seem too overwhelming? Perhaps you feel incapable of being an adequate role model to others, and so you should. The realization of your own inability will move you to depend totally on Jesus in living as a Christian. The more you depend on the Savior, the better example of Christlikeness you will be to others. As others see you living humbly and sacrificially, they will be encouraged to become more like the Messiah.

Dear Lord, I acknowledge that Your Son is the perfect role model for me to follow. Please help me to be such an example of Christlikeness that others will want to follow Him, too. Amen.

DAY SIX

TO SERVE: MAKE ALLOWANCE FOR THE FAULTS OF OTHERS
Colossians 3:13

Unless one happens to be a loner, men tend to stick together (for example, by meeting in clubs and other fraternal organizations). Men like to be with other men who share their interests. Such companionship produces unanimity and camaraderie.

But what happens when a member of a male social group thinks differently about something or does something that the others dislike? Typically, the group will get together and discuss the matter. Often, the leaders convince everyone to oust the offender from their fraternity.

God has called Christian men to think differently. Jesus told us not to have a hypocritical, judgmental attitude that tears others down to build ourselves up (Matt. 7:1). And Paul said that when one of our spiritual brothers is overcome by some sin, we should gently and humbly help that person back onto the right path (Gal. 6:1).

Let's face it, none of us is perfect. In light of this fact, we should relate to one another in a spirit of mercy and forgiveness, not law and order. We can make allowance for each other's faults and forgive those who offend us, for God in Christ forgave us (Col. 3:13). We obey the law of Christ when we share each other's troubles and problems (Gal. 6:2).

Are you put off by the idea of making an allowance for the faults of others? Are you hesitant to forgive those who have wronged you? Just remember that he who is forgiven little shows only a little love, but he who is forgiven much will show much love (Luke 7:47).

Now, which person would you rather be?

*Lord, You have forgiven me much. Please help me
to show my appreciation by making allowance
for the faults of others. Amen.*

TO SERVE:
USING WEALTH TO BENEFIT OTHERS

2 Corinthians 8:9

Men love money! They enjoy earning it, investing it, and watching it grow. They are engrossed by the notion of planning for the future and ensuring that they will have a comfortable retirement. After all, they reason, they don't want to be a burden to anyone when they grow old.

It's not wrong to plan for the future, but it is wrong to make money the object of our affection and devotion. It's far better for Christian men to invest our time, energies, and material resources in the work of God.

Jesus is our supreme example in this regard. As the Lord of the universe, He is infinitely rich and powerful. Yet He set aside His royal wealth and became poor for our sake so that by His poverty we might become eternally rich (2 Cor. 8:9).

In light of what Jesus has done for you at Calvary, shouldn't you be willing to invest more of your earthly wealth in His people? Remember that material riches are not the essence of life (Luke 12:15). The reality of your love for Christ is demonstrated by your willingness to love your fellow believers (1 John 4:11). If you have enough money to live well but refuse to help a spiritual brother or sister in need, how real is your love for God (3:17)?

*Lord, please enable me to devote more of
my material resources to meet the needs of my
fellow Christians. Amen.*

ED SCOTT

A Man and His Church: Prayer

ONE THING YOU CAN'T DO IN PRAYER

Matthew 6:5−8

Did you try to impress your boss today? It wouldn't really be unusual if you did. We all would like to have that much-deserved promotion. What about your wife or girlfriend? We all want the woman in our life to be proud of us. What about your neighbor? We all want our yards to be the neatest on the block!

Working to impress others is almost a daily task. But impressing others shouldn't be our motivation for praying. We can speak to God in prayer and we can listen to God in prayer, but we can't impress God in prayer.

In Matthew 6:5–8, Jesus spoke about people who were trying to impress God and others with their long, complex prayers. He told His disciples to pray instead in solitude and simplicity. Prayer is designed to be an expression of our humility and need. Prayer is best done when we are surrendered and obedient to God.

Jesus noted that God already knows our needs. This observation should not surprise us. After all, the Lord is all-knowing, all-caring, and all-powerful. So we won't be able to impress Him with our accomplishments. The wonder, of course, is that God will hear us anyway, and that knowledge is liberating. In prayer, we depend on His love, not on our deeds!

Father, please help me to see Your greatness and to acknowledge it as I pray. Amen.

DAY TWO

PREDICTABLE PRAYER?

Matthew 6:9–13

Men are "list" people. We tend to be orderly and logical. Do you remember working on your car before the advent of the computerized ignition? If it didn't start, it wasn't getting either gas or "fire." We would just work down the list of system parts until we found the problem.

That "list" habit will serve us well in prayer, just as it does in automobile repairs. Jesus showed us in His model prayer that praying never has to be the same kind of words over and over (see Matt. 6:9–13). Prayer should be a rich and diverse experience.

Jesus started with praise, saying, "Hallowed be Your name." Next, He spoke about the importance of seeking and surrendering ourselves to God: "Your will be done." Then He focused on personal requests: "Give us this day our daily bread." He also talked about confessing our sins: "Forgive us our debts." Furthermore, He mentioned our relationships with others: "as we forgive our debtors." Finally, He talked about guarding the integrity of our lives: "Deliver us from evil."

From this passage we discover that we should not get into the habit of praying only one kind of prayer. You might already be keeping a "prayer list"—namely, a roster of items to pray for—but it would not be bad if you also kept a list of ways to pray. I think that would be a good way for us to live up to our reputation as "list" guys!

Lord, please help me to think of ways to keep my prayer life creative and fresh. Amen.

DAY THREE

GOD WILL HELP YOU TO PRAY

Romans 8:26–27

It may not happen often, but it definitely happens. You find yourself up against a brick wall in life. There doesn't seem to be any way out, and your heart is broken. You don't have to be told that it is hard to voice a prayer in such situations.

But it is still important to be with God in those times of distress, even if you don't know what to say. We still need to feel His comfort, encouragement, and guidance from prayer. We were never meant to function as Christians without such intimacy with the Lord. And so God will never let us go without it!

In Romans 8:26–27, Paul said that the Spirit will "make intercession" for us. He will guide and lead us in prayer when we are bewildered and confused. His guidance might come out in actual words spoken in prayer, or it might just come out in a renewed sense of peace. But no matter how it happens, it is the intervention of God. He is there helping us when we do not know what to do or say.

Father, thank You for all the help You give me
while I'm praying to You. Amen.

DAY FOUR

GOD HEARD EVERY WORD
Revelation 5:8

One morning in the ninth grade, I committed one of those great male errors. I spent five minutes before class telling everyone that I hoped our teacher wouldn't show up. Little did I know that she was sitting right behind me and grading papers! She heard every word I said.

We often wish that we could take back our hastily spoken words. But in prayer, it's just the opposite! We wonder sometimes whether our words ever got out and whether God has heard them. Sometimes we just don't "feel" that we've accomplished anything in prayer.

But the Bible is clear: God hears every word we say in prayer. Even when we don't "feel" that we have made contact, God has heard us! That truth is communicated in a dramatic and wonderful way in Revelation 5:8.

In John's vision of heaven, he saw the throne room of God. And when the Lamb (Christ) entered the sacred chamber, the elders all bowed down. John reported that the elders were all holding gold bowls filled with incense, which the apostle says were the prayers of the saints.

It is a wonderfully poetic way of encouraging us. We discover that our prayers have arrived in heaven safely, have been heard by God, and are even being held and guarded by His holy servants. We can trust God to know all about what we need and what we want.

Father, thank You that You always hear me when
I pray to You. Amen.

DAY FIVE

ENJOYING THE FRUIT
OF A GODLY HABIT
1 Chronicles 16:11

While Christians often have difficult decisions to make about how they live their lives, there are some aspects of the Christian life that are distinctly clear. One such aspect is our need to spend time with God in prayer, and it is taught clearly and lucidly in the Bible.

Such godly men as David and Paul testified concerning the peace and fulfillment they found in a continuing habit of prayer. In 1 Chronicles 16:11, David told us to seek the Lord and His strength and to do it forevermore. A similar truth is recorded in 1 Thessalonians 5:17: "Pray without ceasing."

Most of us, however, don't have that kind of prayer habit. The national average for prayer is still under five minutes a day! And I don't think this average will increase until Christian men make some definite decisions. We won't enjoy the fruit of prayer until we make real plans to pray regularly.

You can start by setting aside a definite time and place to pray. Write a personal prayer list. Choose a book of the Bible to read through, and make it the guide for your prayer time. If necessary, turn off the telephone and the television for a few minutes, and let this be God's time. The habit will grow, and it will bring you joy!

Father, please help me not to go through the day
without praying to You. Amen.

THE BIG MISTAKE IN PRAYER

Ecclesiastes 5:1–2

Sometimes the big mistake in prayer is talking too much and too soon. After thinking a long while about his life, Solomon said in Ecclesiastes 5:1–2 that we just don't think enough when we pray. We don't think about what we are doing, we don't think about who we are, and we don't think about who God is.

Too often we pray out of routine and not out of intention and purpose. And far too often we just don't listen to God. In verse 1, Solomon exhorted us to be "more ready to hear" than to speak. And in verse 2, he admonished us to be careful not to rush into prayer, immediately barraging God with a multitude of requests. Solomon's advice was to stop and get a grasp of what is happening in prayer: a man on earth is speaking to God in heaven.

If that thought can seize us, it will revolutionize our prayer time. This is what Solomon desired, for verse 2 advises, "let your words be few." Don't worry, the words will come, and there will always be time for your requests. But start slowly, seize the moment, and consider what is happening. You might discover that God has something to say to *you* as well!

Father, please never let me take my prayer time for granted. Help me to enjoy my communion with You. Amen.

USING PRAYER TO OVERCOME TEMPTATION

Matthew 26:41

Christian men continually face temptation. Our world seems to thrive on appeals to our desire for material goods, worldly pleasures, and self-gratification. Yet, continued praying strengthens Christian men spiritually, morally, and ethically. With prayer, overcoming our temptation is certainly possible.

Jesus made this truth plain to Peter in the garden the night of the Savior's arrest and trial (Matt. 26:41). Jesus was facing perhaps the hardest night of His life. He was facing the cross, and He knew it! The Bible says that Jesus fell back on His continual habit of prayer to make it through that night. He realized that prayer would be a source of strength for Him (vv. 42–44).

And at one point, Jesus told Peter to learn from what he had seen. Not only on that one night but also for the rest of his life, Peter would have to keep praying, especially if he wanted to fight temptation. Jesus then uttered those oft-quoted words, "the spirit is indeed willing, but the flesh is weak" (v. 41).

We have remembered those words fairly well, probably because they seem to give us an excuse for not performing well. We should have remembered the preceding words—"Watch and pray, that you do not enter into temptation"—for they give us the way to win over sin.

Father, as I now pray, please help me to overcome the temptation that I'm now facing. Amen.

ROSS WEST

A Man and His Work: Purpose

DAY ONE

TO BE SUCCESSFUL: LET GO AND HOLD ON!

Psalm 33:10–11

What's involved in successful living, whether at work, at home, or elsewhere? Psalm 33:10–11 provides two keys to the answer.

First, successful living calls for us to let go of plans that look stable but that are really precarious and going nowhere. For example, sometimes we may be tempted at work to take the easy, maybe even unethical, way. A recent survey of truth-telling at work indicates that a shockingly high percentage of people admit to lying regularly in the workplace.

Maybe such unethical behavior brings positive results for a while. And maybe the work culture even expects it, no matter what the policy manual might say. But what price does such behavior exact of your integrity and of your influence on other people who are important to you and may even look up to you? And what is the cost to your relationship with God?

God has so structured the world that His way lasts whereas the world's way doesn't, no matter how attractive the latter might appear. Behavior that departs from God's way, even at work, reaps dire consequences.

Second, successful living calls for us to embrace those plans that are in keeping with God's goal for our life. Although unethical behavior might pay in the short run, it damages us spiritually in the long run. Also, while ethical behavior might be costly in the short run, it pays rich spiritual dividends for us in the long run. Successful living, as God's Word defines it, lasts forever. That's the way God has structured life in His world.

Lord, please help me to see what's temporal in value and let go of it. And help me to see what's eternal in value and embrace it. Amen.

HOW MUCH IS ENOUGH?

Matthew 6:31–33

So what's the number? That is, how much do you think you need to feel you've got it made? A thousand dollars? Ten thousand? A hundred thousand? A million? Or do you want just to get out of debt? You might say that you'd be willing to try any of these options!

But really, how much is enough? Whatever number you come up with, your real answer is likely to be the following: "Just a little more than what I have right now."

The hefty raise we receive soon disappears in expenditures for increased wants. Then we long for the next raise. Our wants keep spiraling upward, calling for increased income. There's no end to this spiral when we focus on material things. As we run faster and faster to get more and more, our income seems never quite to catch up with our wants. No wonder we worry so much!

Thankfully, Jesus showed us a better way (Matt. 6:31–33). He ordered us to stop worrying, for anxiety just doesn't make sense when we have a heavenly Father who already knows what we need and promises to give it to us. So do we need to work for what God plans to give? Of course! Although God provides food for the birds, He has so designed life that even these creatures still have to scratch for the food they eat!

Working for pay is important. Remember, however, that God, His kingdom, and His righteousness are far more important than money. We should never do anything for pay that will dislodge God's priorities from their place of prominence. He promises to provide for our needs but not for our greeds!

Lord, thank You for providing for all my needs. Amen.

So Where's Your Kingdom?

John 18:36

One of the most striking qualities of Jesus is that He never forgot where His kingdom was based. It was "not of this world" (John 18:36). Did He mean that it was somewhere else geographically and not related to earth? Not at all. Rather, Jesus meant to distinguish His kingdom from worldly systems of thinking and living that are unrelated to God and His purposes. Jesus centered His life on God and on carrying out His will. Jesus would not even let the basic human need for safety come between Him and that commitment. Furthermore, He would always use God's methods, not the world's, to fulfill the Father's plan.

When many Christians go to work, they see themselves as moving out of the "private" sphere of life and into the "public" sphere of life. They tend to relate their faith mainly to their private life—their personal lives, their lives at home, and their lives at church. They find it difficult to see how their faith relates to their work. They leave Jesus' kingdom behind and live in another realm while they're at work. The consequences are tragic. Living thus, Christians fail to be salt and light (Matt. 5:13–16).

You don't have to leave Jesus' kingdom behind when you go to work. In fact, you can keep living in Jesus' kingdom *while* you work. How? Try doing the following: work faithfully so that you produce worthwhile results for your employer; relate with grace and care to the people with whom you work; act with integrity, no matter the cost; engage in actions and attitudes that help your co-workers see Jesus and His kingdom operating in you; and avoid ways of thinking and behaving that obscure the presence of Christ and His rule in you.

Lord, please help me to live in Your kingdom
regardless of where I am, what I'm doing,
or what I'm thinking. Amen.

LIVE A HOLY LIFE (EVEN AT WORK)

2 Timothy 1:9

Do you want to be known as someone who's holy? Few people do. For one thing, we've seen holiness come across as "holier than thou." We don't want that, and rightly so. We're especially not interested in being holy at work. After all, many workplaces don't seem exactly holy.

But 2 Timothy 1:9 (KJV) says that we are "called . . . with an holy calling," meaning that we are called to live a holy life. Note that the verse doesn't add "except at work." All of Scripture is consistent regarding our call to holy living. For example, in Leviticus 20:7 God declared, "be holy." He added the reason in verse 26: "for I the Lord am holy" (A similar emphasis can be found in 1 Peter 1:15–16). The detailed laws of Leviticus spelled out the various ways in which the Israelites were to be holy. These laws dealt with the nitty-gritty of daily life, even the life of daily work.

A minister was leading a group in discussing ethics in business. During the discussion, one person said that he'd been thinking about how his faith ought to influence his life at work and what might happen if he actually put his faith into practice there (e.g., in the decisions he made and in the way he related to people). He concluded that he wasn't sure he could afford that much Christianity.

But since we serve a holy God who expects us to be holy even at work, can we afford *not* to have that much Christianity?

Lord, please help me to honor and serve You as
a holy God in every place I go today, including
my work. Amen.

GOT AN "ATTITUDE"?

1 Peter 4:1—2

Do you know anyone at work who's "got an attitude"? This phrase has become shorthand for saying that the person has a *bad* attitude. He's hard to get along with, or he's always complaining, or he's untrustworthy.

People don't "get an attitude" by accident. They're not suddenly struck by it and thus have no control over it. Neither can anyone say, "I admit that I have a bad attitude, but it's because of this problem." The fact is, similar bad things have happened to other people, and they haven't reacted negatively. They may even have responded positively. They know not only how to make lemonade out of lemons but also how to take a bumper crop of lemons and prosper from them.

In life, you get to choose the attitude you have, whether it's pessimistic or optimistic. You also get to choose your attitude toward temptation—whether you choose to let it overcome you easily or, with the Lord's help, to overcome *it*. There are no excuses for yielding to the sinful nature.

First Peter 4:1–2 calls us to choose the "will," "purpose," or "attitude" of God. In other words, you can choose what you'll make of the bad things that happen to you or the temptations that strike you. You can even make that choice at work today. In fact, you *will* choose. Why not decide to "get an attitude"—namely, the best attitude, the attitude of Christ.

Lord, please help me to have the proper attitude at work today. Amen.

DAY SIX

PROCLAIMING CHRIST AT WORK
Colossians 1:28–29

Can Christ be proclaimed at your workplace? The answer to that question depends on you. That, in fact, is where all proclamation of Christ must begin—with you, not with other people. Of course, many Christians consider the workplace off-limits to expressions of faith. They wince at the thought of proclaiming Christ there.

A few other well-meaning Christians do see the workplace as a great opportunity to proclaim Christ. But their efforts often appear to their fellow workers as either "trying to cram religion down their throats" or hypocritical acting. Such attempts to witness ignite a self-defeating cycle. Fellow employees' negative reactions to such behavior confirms to other Christians that the workplace is no place to share their faith. So no one does so.

But you don't have to err in either of these ways. Here are a few suggestions to help you proclaim Christ in your place of work:

- Work in ways that show you're a competent employee. A poor employee doesn't have much of an opportunity to be a good witness.
- Always act ethically. If you don't, please don't tell anyone you're a Christian, and certainly don't try to get them to be like you.
- Relate with care, concern, and fairness to all customers and fellow employees. Be especially attentive to this matter if you're in management.
- Be respectful of the right of fellow employees to their own beliefs. Respect begins with listening.
- As opportunities for conversation arise, talk with ease about what your faith means to you. Don't let proclaiming Christ degenerate into "arguing about religion." Let your fellow workers know how your faith helps you.

Lord, please guide me today to proclaim You effectively in my place of work. Amen.

DAY SEVEN

ALIGNED WITH GOD'S PURPOSE
Philippians 2:13

Where are we going? Businesses that are successful in making improvements in their work processes and results ask this question and seek answers to it. Unless this question is answered, there's not much use in going any further. However, when a business understands its destination or purpose, it's ready to start going somewhere.

The next step is for all aspects of the business to align themselves with the organization's overall purpose. All parts and levels of the business are included, from each employee to whatever material resources are used. The possibility of business success is greater when all of these elements are aligned to help the organization accomplish its purpose.

Why mention this point in a devotional book such as this? Because there's a parallel here to your Christian life and to your participation in God's work. It all begins with having a purpose. The basic question is this: Whose purpose are you following, your's or God's? If you're following God's purpose, that's good. But are all of the resources at your disposal aligned with the purpose of accomplishing what is pleasing to God?

The good news is that when we align our lives and purposes behind God and His purpose, we are not alone. We find that He is working in us and through us to accomplish His will.

Good management practice calls for providing the resources employees need to accomplish the tasks the business has assigned to them. Similarly, God provides the resources that we need to accomplish His purpose. Here's more good news. When we devote ourselves to accomplish God's purpose, He also assures us that His purpose will prevail. It's absolutely certain. Now that's a great investment!

Lord, please lead me to follow and accomplish
Your purpose today. Amen.

MARK JOHNSON

A Man and His Work: Value

DAY ONE

WORK TO GIVE

ACTS 20:35

Jesus' exhortation that "It is more blessed to give than to receive" (Acts 20:35) is seen in some interesting contexts. Hollywood producers will place that phrase on the lips of a sleazy evangelist as he fleeces the flock to line his own pockets. A pastor with integrity will repeat that phrase when reminding his members to practice responsible stewardship. And the chairman of the building campaign will repeat, "It is more blessed to give than to receive."

Paul repeated Jesus' statement in a farewell address to the Ephesian elders. That notwithstanding, Christ's words are just as applicable to our daily work as it is to the ministry in a local church. What is the goal of our work? Is it merely to pad our bank account? While it is important to save, invest, and be good stewards, our concern for good stewardship ought to be tempered by the realization that God ultimately is the One on whom we rely for our needs.

If we have confidence that God will take care of us, we begin to view our possessions differently. The rationale for our work changes. We begin to see our work as part of our partnership with God in fulfilling His purposes in our life.

We should work hard so that we can have something to give to others. The adage is true: "We make a living by what we get; we make a life by what we give." The guarantee of a bitter, empty, and angry life is to hold as tightly as you can every penny that comes your way. But the key to the abundant life is to be a giver. As St. Francis prayed, "It is in giving that we receive."

*Lord, please help me to become more sensitive
to opportunities for giving that I might
otherwise miss. Amen.*

DAY TWO

FINDING SATISFACTION

Ecclesiastes 3:1, 11, 13

Solomon was certainly not the Robert Schuller of his day! You know the book is going real sobering when the writer's first line cries, "Everything is meaningless!" (Eccl. 1:1). But it's true; apart from God, life is pointless.

Solomon realized that God is sovereign and beyond our comprehension. He alone controls the past, the present, and the future. And He is the One who directs our lives. Solomon also observed that God has established a certain rhythm to life. There is a time and a place for everything (3:1), and God has planted within us an awareness of eternal realities (v. 11). We learn that our work is meaningful when it's done for God's glory. Satisfaction and joy come when the Lord remains the center of our life. In fact, the ability to enjoy our work is a gift from God (v. 13).

Do you like your job? Do you have fulfilling and challenging work, or are you just putting in hours until retirement? Do you go to work confident in the sense that your work matters—that you're filling a unique niche—or are you just earning a paycheck?

In 1:3, Solomon asked, "What does a man gain from all his labor?" The answer is that our work matters when it is seen from God's perspective. The curse of the Fall is not work in itself; rather, it is the wearisome toil associated with our labor that seems like a curse. Yet even in the midst of toil, God can give you satisfaction and joy in your work.

What am I talking about? God can help you to see that your work matters. You are a part of His grand master design to bring glory to Himself. As Paul said in 1 Corinthians 15:58, "You know that your labor in the Lord is not in vain."

*Lord, please help me to derive satisfaction and joy
from my work and thereby bring glory to You.
Amen.*

IF I WERE A RICH MAN
Ecclesiastes 5:13–17

Sean Gilbert of the Washington Redskins was designated the team's "franchise player." Under the terms of the NFL Player Agreement, the team was obligated to offer him the average salary of the five highest players at his position, which was approximately $2.8 million a year. The team offered $3.6 million a year. Gilbert and his agent held out for $5 million a year, saying that God told them this was the figure the player should receive. I wish God wanted me to make $5 million dollars a year!

Like Tevye in *Fiddler on the Roof*, I'm tempted to ask, "Would it spoil some vast eternal plan, if I were a wealthy man?" That's why I'm taken back by Ecclesiastes 5:13–17, which says that we cannot take our riches with us when we die. This truth is hard to swallow! How many times have you awakened in the night and thought about how you'd pay your bills? Solomon knew from experience that having a lot of money is not all that it's cracked up to be.

Contrast the life of Solomon and the palace intrigue of the rich and famous with the lives of people who roll up their sleeves and work hard for a living. There's something redemptive about a good sweat.

When was the last time you had a good day of hard physical labor? When was the last time you worked late at the office and came home tired but with the satisfaction of a day's work well done? God created you with a job to do. As Ecclesiastes 9:10 advises, "Whatever your hand finds to do, do it with all your might."

Lord, thank You for the work that You have
given me to do. Amen.

A GIVER OR A TAKER?
Ephesians 4:28

Every "self-made" man will tell you that the secret of success is hard work. We respect people who work hard and have disdain for those who are lazy. I've known some folks whose only hard work seems to consist in figuring out how to "beat the system."

Ephesians 4:28 urges us to take care of our own needs legitimately and to help those who are less fortunate. This exhortation comes in the context of instruction on how we are to live as children of light. Work is set in contrast to stealing. Do you need to be reminded that giving less than your best in your work is a form of stealing? Perhaps you don't need a lot of convincing that it's wrong to steal and that it's right to work.

Work in and of itself can be satisfying and fulfilling. But what is the goal of work? Is it merely the accumulation of possessions? Is it so that our kids can wear expensive, name-brand clothes?

Paul taught that we should begin using our hands for honest work, and then we should give generously to those in need. It's like the difference between the Dead Sea and the Sea of Galilee. The first is appropriately named, for its salinity is seven times that of the ocean. Nothing lives there. In contrast, the Sea of Galilee is teeming with life. It is one of the most lush and vibrant regions of Israel.

What's the difference? Water flows through the Sea of Galilee but never leaves the Dead Sea. In other words, the Sea of Galilee is a giver and the Dead Sea is a taker. Which are you?

Lord, please help me to use the money I earn
to help those in need. Amen.

DAY FIVE

THE RHYTHM OF LIFE
Genesis 2:3

As I consider the nature of work, I realize that God has created life to have a regular rhythm and cycle of activity. He created the world and everything in it in six days, and then rested on the seventh. In other words, He ceased from His creative activity (Gen. 1:1–2:3).

As a man made in the image of God, you were created to work. But labor, as important as it is, is not to be the sole focus of your life. There is also a time to rest. You have a certain number of days in which to labor. But what if your work's not done in that period of time? Perhaps you're trying to do too much. It's physically healthful and spiritually renewing to regularly step away from your busy activity and take a break. Allow yourself the refreshment that comes from worship, relaxation, and time with friends and family.

Jesus knew when to give Himself completely to His work and

when to rest (see John 4:6). I know Christian workers who have the gall to think that the kingdom of God would collapse if they ever took a day off. They say, "I'd rather burn out than rust out."

Excuse me! Are those the only two alternatives? What's wrong with recognizing the rhythm God has put into life so that you can maintain maximum effectiveness for Him over the long haul? Hey, it's okay to rest! You have God's permission. In fact, He commands it!

*Lord, please help me not only to work hard but
also to relax at the appropriate times. Amen.*

DAY SIX

HOW WILL YOU FINISH?

Matthew 21:28–31

It's amazing how different brothers can be. They have the same parents and basically the same environment, yet they are as different as night and day. One brother can be high-strung and uptight whereas the other is laid back. One can have a heart that is tender and sensitive to the Lord whereas the other is completely apathetic about living for Christ. One brother may quickly say "Yes!" to serving God but "run out of gas." Meanwhile, the other brother will resist coming to Christ, but once he's made a commitment to doing God's will, there's no stopping him.

That's what Jesus is talking about in Matthew 21:28–31. The father asked his two sons to go work on the farm. I can imagine the first one saying, "Father, that's a splendid suggestion! Where would you like for me to begin?" And I can imagine the second son saying, "Not so fast, old man! My friends and I are going fishing. See ya later!" Yet as the day wore on, who's working? It seems that the first son failed to live up to his good intentions. But the second son reconsidered and decided to obey his father.

Jesus teaches several lessons here. First, it's not just how you start that matters but also how you finish. Second, Jesus told the parable to let those who were smug in their religiosity know that the people they despised would enter the kingdom ahead of them. Third, the kingdom of God belongs to those who "walk the walk" rather than to those who just "talk the talk." You say you love Jesus. How will you finish the race of life for Him?

*Lord, please help me to serve You faithfully
from this day forward. Amen.*

A CALL TO DILIGENCE

Proverbs 24:30–34

A man had a beautiful garden. It was obvious to all who saw it that gardening was his passion. One observer, when he saw the plot, marveled at God's awesome handiwork evident in it. The owner replied, "Yeah, but you should have seen it when God had it all to Himself."

We are arrogant to think that we can improve on what God has made. The humble, reverent believer will see himself as a steward of God's creation. The Lord has given us many wonderful raw materials to use. We worship and honor Him by taking what we have to make objects that are beautiful and beneficial to others.

I take pride in trying to beautify the tract of land that Tennessee says belongs to me. I have dreams of azaleas and shade trees placed in the lush carpet of green surrounding my tastefully decorated home. How beautiful our neighborhoods would be if everyone truly did their best in adorning their yards. It's a question of stewardship.

Maybe a pretty yard isn't your dream. Whether you want to plant flowers or cultivate a thick carpet of green grass, there is some area where you have passion and influence. Work diligently to cultivate that passion to God's greater glory.

The operative word here is *diligence*. The sluggard decried in Proverbs 24:30–34 is the one who ceases to work hard. Tomorrow becomes next week, next month, and next year. Ultimately such a person looks back at an idle life with nothing but regret for wasted opportunities.

What passion has God entrusted to you? Why not take the first step in making it a reality?

*Lord, please enable me to pursue the work You
have given me with passion and diligence. Amen.*

JOE JOHNSON

A Man and His Work: Unemployment

GOD CARES FOR THE UNEMPLOYED

Malachi 3:5

The Old Testament prophets denounced employers who sinned against their employees by unjustly firing them and cheating them out of their proper wages. For example, in Malachi 3:5, God declared that He would judge and "testify against sorcerers, adulterers, and perjurers" and "those who defraud laborers of their wages."

At this moment, the United States is seemingly prosperous. The stock market has reached record levels. One political slogan of the recent past was "It's the economy, stupid." But there is a danger of being lulled into false economic security. In spite of recent "prosperity," multiplied thousands of workers are still being laid off, sometimes under the guise of corporate "downsizing." Perhaps you have suffered because of this trend.

Once a man could settle down into a position for the length of his career. If he worked hard and honestly, he could expect to remain with that firm until retirement at age 65, and then depend on a pension and Social Security to live comfortably. That scenario is rapidly changing. People are making dire predictions about the depletion of the Social Security Trust Fund within the first two decades of the next century.

You may not know it, but God is sensitive to your plight. Amid all of the economic confusion—including corporate downsizing, bank closings, and jobs being exported to other countries—God still cares for you. Continue to give your best, plan, and even dream, but, most of all, prayerfully depend on God through Christ. And don't forget Philippians 4:19: "And my God will meet all your needs according to his glorious riches in Christ Jesus."

Lord, I am confident that You will meet all of my needs. Thank You for this reassuring promise from Your Word. Amen.

WHOLEHEARTEDLY TRUST

Proverbs 3:5–8

The "ancient mariner" in Coleridge's famous poem *The Rime of the Ancient Mariner* admitted that he ended up "a sadder and wiser man." The writer of Proverbs 3:5–8 had a similar experience. Although he seemed to "have it made," he prayed for wisdom. But he wasn't always wise, especially in having 700 wives and 300 concubines!

Nothing grants inward peace and serenity like relying on God's goodness. If you are currently employed, praise God for your job and ask Him to help you make the best of your situation. If you are unemployed, lean on Him to grant you wisdom in finding a job.

After working for a company for fifteen years, a dear friend of mine was laid off. He sent out 350 résumés (no joke). I suggested, "Have you ever considered that God wants you on the staff of a church instead of in a secular job?" Sure enough, he is now joyfully serving as an administrator with a church.

I have often heard guys in the work force comment, "Until I began to trust God, I considered myself 'big stuff.' Then tough times taught me hard but valuable lessons." I can relate to those men, for I have often trusted in my own faculties only to fall flat on my face.

Lord, please help me to trust in You, not half-heartedly, but wholeheartedly. Amen.

WOE TO THE DISHONEST BUSINESSMAN!

Jeremiah 22:13

In one sense the prophets of the Old Testament were tort lawyers for the mistreated. If they were preaching today, they might ask, "Have you ever been cheated out of rightful benefits?" "Have folks you trusted refused to honor their agreements, whether oral or written?" "Has anybody ever failed to pay you properly or not at all?"

These same heralds of justice might also ask those of us who are managers, "Have you ever been less than honest with an employee?" I hope not. (As an aside, I've always felt uncomfortable around people who argue against tithing and, of course, don't do it. I feel that if they'll rob God, maybe in a pinch they'll even cheat me.)

Early in my ministry, I realized that some of my parishioners kept their workers in virtual slavery. Their poor laborers had to keep borrowing money or goods from the boss until they were almost indentured servants and could not break free.

The prophets indicated that God frowns on a person who mistreats another person for greedy gain. A few businessmen have confessed to me, "It's the bottom line that counts the most." They believed that profits were more important than people.

Bravo for the businessman in the northeastern United States whose factory burned down. It was a financial disaster for him, but he called together his employees and reassured them, "Don't worry. I'll continue to pay you as long as I can. We'll rebuild, and you'll still be working for me if you want to." His employees wept.

Lord, please help me to exemplify my Savior
in all of my business dealings. Amen.

DAY FOUR

Unusual Employment
Matthew 20:1–14

Matthew 20:1–14 is one of the strangest in the New Testament. The boss agreed to pay a penny a day. Sounds minuscule, doesn't it? Anyhow, that was the agreement. But it doesn't stop there, since the employer hired five crews at different times of the day, some at six in the morning, others at nine, still others at noon, more at three in the afternoon, and the last guys at five—one hour before the workday ended.

What on earth, or heaven, could Jesus be teaching? First, if you agree on a certain pay scale and hours, stick to them without complaining. Experts claim that unemployment is low in the United States. Maybe that doesn't reflect your situation, and you are unemployed just now. But if you do have a job, do it as "unto the Lord." Do the best you can without comparing yourself to your fellow workers. That's why it's advisable not to know what the other guy makes.

The overriding spiritual lesson is: The final reward of our service for Christ does not depend on how long we worked for Him, but on the fact that we served Him and stuck to it—whether we worked for Him ten years or fifty.

For employers, there is a lesson. Pay what is fair and right. Good management and productive labor are reciprocal. Honest, fruitful work must be rewarded with proper pay, working conditions, and benefits. Our Lord declared, "My Father is working still, and I am working" (John 5:17 RSV). As Christians we must be good workers not only to give ourselves dignity and a means of support but also because of Jesus' example.

Thanks for hiring me, Lord, to work in Your kingdom. May I please You in all I do. Amen

DAY FIVE

Do Right

James 5:4

Recently, a Christian woman in the Nashville music industry commented, "It's come to the place where I'd as soon work with an unbeliever as a Christian. Many of them don't practice what they preach in business." Sadly, some professing believers have reneged on their agreements and promises to me, too.

Maybe that is par for the course in the so-called "secular" world, where the practice is "dog eat dog," but this should never be true of Christians! James lambasted those who mistreated and cheated the poor (James 5:4).

Most citizens in the United States think that capitalism is the best economic system, yet it can be abusive to workers. In fact, labor unions were founded to protect workers from inequities and injustices. But let's face it. Labor and management are often equally to blame when an impasse occurs in their negotiations.

If you are a Christian employer, you should be honest and equitable with your employees. After all, without them you would have a tough time producing a product or providing a service. Despite all of the talk about substituting computers and robots for people, we will always need humans.

You have every right to expect diligent work and dedication from your personnel. But, conversely, what can they expect from you? May James 5:4 never be true of you.

Lord, please help me to encourage and
appreciate my personnel. Amen.

WAITING FOR WORK
Matthew 20:6−7

Have you ever gone by an unemployment office and watched the men and women there? In Matthew 20:6–7, Jesus was actually talking about working for Him in the kingdom, but His parable also applies to our job situations. If we're looking for work we must expect the best job possible and pray for it, always understanding that it may take time for our prayer to be answered. When I graduated from high school, I was offered a well-paying job. Sadly, it required working on Sunday, so I turned it down and accepted a newspaper job paying less than half as much. Undreamed-of avenues were opened up for me as a result. That summer job forty-seven years ago profoundly molded my ministry.

Jesus had a rationale for His account of the waiting workers. Sometimes we have to "wait upon the Lord" for wise decisions. "Wait on the Lord: be of good courage, and he shall strengthen thine heart: wait, I say, on the LORD." (Ps. 27:14 KJV). Our human natures, unfortunately, show themselves in our impatience. We are like the demonstrator who shouted, "I demand my rights." When asked what those rights were, he replied, "I dunno, but I want 'em right now!"

At eighteen I prayed that one day I would become an editor with our denomination's publishing company. Two decades of education and Christian ministries followed. Then I received an unexpected call to become an editor with the very firm I had prayed about. I served there almost twenty-three years until my retirement! Doxology!

God, I trust You to open up opportunities for me
according to Your own timetable. I only ask for
Your will to be done. Amen.

REBELLIOUS WORKERS

Matthew 21:33—40

Rebellion from authority is the theme of this parable of a vineyard where the employees revolt against the land owner. Jesus used it to describe the people who rejected His lordship.

If God expects respect as owner, He will demand an accounting of our obedience toward Him and toward those in authority on earth. In another of Jesus' parables, a master confronts his servant: "How is it that I hear this of thee? Give an account of thy stewardship; for thou mayest be no longer steward"(Luke 16:2b, KJV; see Rom. 14:12). "Stewardship" here means management of what the owner has given. All honest work is obedient stewardship, even "flippin' burgers" to the glory of God.

In the parable of the vineyard, the violent employees kill the son of the owner. But even if our workplaces do not reach that level of rebellion toward the vice-president, those who cheat and mistreat others will face a "payback." That accounting must be in God's time. Even the most deplorable conditions do not justify personal vengeance. God's stewards persevere until God opens another opportunity; they leave justice to Him.

They also follow the correct channels with their gripes, then pray that God will change and bless those who are abusive. This is good stewardship in God's workplace.

Commit yourself to glorify God with responsible work in His kingdom.

Lord, please help me to be a diligent steward
at work. Amen.

D O N   M .   A Y C O C K

A Man and His Work: Fellow Workers

DO YOUR FAIR SHARE

Leviticus 19:13

I lost some money recently. No, it did not drop out of my pocket. I gave it to a thief! I hired the owner of a small company to do some work on my house. He required me to pay a third of the cost up front, as many companies do. I checked this fellow out carefully, calling references and examining his licenses and other papers. He seemed to be a good guy. But when he got the check, he practically disappeared. I finally had to take him to court to recover my money. But I was too late; the IRS got him first. Try standing in line behind *them* to get something from a bankruptcy!

So much of our lives depend on trusting others. An honest person will do the right thing no matter what. A crook will cheat you no matter how many references you might find on him.

This point is no less true in our relationships with our fellow employees. Some of them will pull their share and do what is expected of them. Others will go beyond the minimum and give an extra effort. But there is another group. All of us know them. They believe that they are somehow exempt from work. They think that they are getting paid to hold down a chair, regardless of whether they do anything. People like that make our jobs doubly difficult. We have to pull not only our weight but also theirs.

Leviticus 19:13 reminds us not to "oppress" our neighbor or rob him. You don't have to use a gun or fraud to rob someone; you can do it by being lazy and uncaring on the job. At our place of employment, we depend on each other, so let's give what is due.

Lord, please help me to give my best on the job
and to treat my fellow workers honestly. Amen.

PROTECT YOUR COLLEAGUES

Proverbs 11:12–13

Office gossip. Innuendoes. Stretching the facts. Tales spread about coworkers. All these actions are employment homicide. We can kill people with our words, maybe not literally, but we can damage their futures.

Jim heard that Bob, his supervisor, had been hospitalized for cancer. Jim began telling everyone that Bob would soon be too ill to continue his job. Jim was pushing hard to get Bob's job. It did not matter to him that Bob made a complete recovery and continued in his job. To the ruthless, lies and half-truths are good weapons.

I had a recent conversation with an attorney who practiced in a small town for more than sixty years. I asked him whether he knew a story on everyone in town. He laughed and said, "I know many stories on everyone in town. I know things that could ruin people and send them to jail! But I would never reveal any of it. It will go to the grave with me." That is the way to handle delicate and sensitive information on others. Why hurt them?

Proverbs 11:12–13 tells us not to be a tale-bearer revealing secrets. This command is not permission to conceal crimes or serious breaches of ethics. Those, of course, should be reported. The Scripture, however, is telling us to protect our colleagues by refusing to spread gossip about them. If a harmful rumor is flying about a coworker, we can let that rumor stop with us instead of passing it along.

Every office or workplace has a person who always seems to have the lowdown on everyone else and is willing to tell it to all, even if it is not true! Don't let that person be *you*. Help your fellow workers. Protect them if you can. Never slice them to shreds with your tongue.

*Lord, please help me to be a trustworthy colleague
of others by keeping confidences. Amen.*

WATCH YOUR ATTITUDE

Proverbs 22:24–25

I once worked for a crusty old man in the oil fields of Louisiana. He was as rough as a corncob. His temper was legendary. He would just as soon curse a man as speak to him. He would fire men in fits of rage. Once when labor organizers tried to start a union by intimidating workers, this man shot and killed one of them! The act was ruled "self-defense." He knew about drilling oil wells, but he was not much of a human being.

I wonder where this person had learned to act as he did. Did his father act like that? Were all of his friends like that when he was growing up? Had no one ever taught him that there was a better way to live? I don't know. But I did what I could to stay on his good side, if possible, and to stay out of his way when he was angry. I certainly didn't spend my free time with him!

The attitudes of people around us are catching. We can be infected by emotions every bit as much as by viruses, especially if we are not careful. That is what Proverbs 22:24–25 tells us. Don't associate with a man whose only emotional expression is anger. Why? Because we will "learn his ways," and they will become a "snare" for us.

Sometimes work conditions force us to associate with people we do not like. They may be mean-spirited or petty or any number of other things. We may need to work with them, but we don't have to pick up their attitudes and actions. Many people will form a prayer or Bible study group during breaks at work to help them stay morally straight and to keep them from taking on attitudes of people like my old boss.

How about you? Do you need to do something extra to keep straight? If so, take the plunge and get it done. Now is a good time to start!

> *Lord, when I am around others who live in ungodly ways, please help me not to catch their hostile attitudes. Amen.*

DAY FOUR

GIVE IT YOUR BEST SHOT
Ecclesiastes 9:10

There is an interesting legend about creation. It is said that when the world began, four angels approached God and asked Him a question. The first angel said, "How are You creating the world?" The second angel queried, "Why are You creating the world?" The third inquired, "May I have the world when You finish?" And the fourth angel asked, "Can I help?"

Here we find four different questions and four unique perspectives. Maybe the first angel was a scientist interested in the "how" of creation. Perhaps the second was a philosopher interested in "why." The third might have been a business angel interested in corporate takeovers. But what about the fourth angel? He was like a man who takes seriously Ecclesiastes 9:10. Such an individual puts himself into the job and wants to give it his all.

Most people work with a variety of colleagues. Some are lazy and could never be counted on for extra help. Others are focused on doing their job, but only *their* job. Still others always do their best and are willing to give a hand to help others.

The last part of this verse indicates that the time for planning and working is *now*. Whatever you do to earn your living, be good at it. Stretch to learn new things. Try different approaches. Always be ready to help a colleague, if necessary. Whatever you do, "do it with all your might."

Jesus was once a carpenter. I imagine the products He built were both sturdy and eye pleasing. He must have given each job His best effort. I have a friend who is also a carpenter. He treats each project as a special challenge to achieve perfection. Most of the time, he comes very close. He gives his best every day. What about you?

Lord, please help me to do my best at whatever
task You would have me do. Amen.

DAY FIVE

To Each His Own
Matthew 20:1–16

There are two things in which people in a work situation are keenly interested—the clock and the pay scale. To some men, the clock is like a key opening up a prison door. When it's quitting time, they drop everything and zip out as fast as possible. I saw a bumper sticker that says, "If you don't believe in the resurrection of the dead, you should be here at quitting time!"

But the pay scale is probably more important. Many people want to ensure that everyone is treated exactly the same. Why should one person make more or less than others in the same position? Sometimes factors such as skill, seniority, and education make a pay scale go up or down. On the whole, however, we think that no one should make more than we do for the same job.

That's why Jesus' parable in Matthew 20:1–16 is so realistic. The laborers of His time were paid at the end of each day for twelve hours of work. Each worker took his pay home to buy food for the family. But in Jesus' parable, the laborers who worked fewer hours received the *same* pay as the first group the owner had hired. When the original band of laborers found out what those workers had been paid, they "grumbled against the landowner." Today, they would probably go on strike.

Jesus told the parable to illustrate God's generosity toward everyone coming into His kingdom. Those who arrive late are as blessed as those who enter early. But the parable also illustrates a principle in work life. Everyone is different. Some will rise to levels of leadership and greater responsibility. Others will reach a certain plateau and stay there.

We should know ourselves well enough to realize where we will be. And we should support our colleagues when they get promotions and pay raises over us.

Lord, please help me to support my colleagues by being a team player. Amen.

You Can Have Friends at Work, Too

Ephesians 4:25

I had many friends when I was growing up, but one friend was special. His name is Milton. He and I were almost inseparable. We lived a half mile apart in a rural area of Louisiana. Woods, swamps, a bayou, and pastures were all around us, and we knew every square inch of them.

Together, Milton and I hunted, fished, went to school, played basketball at school and softball at home, and threw cow "muffins" at each other. We swung from vines out over Bayou Des Canes and gave our Tarzan yells, especially as we let go of the vines and hit the water. We climbed small pines, grabbed the tops of these saplings, and jumped out so that the trees bent, giving us an "elevator" ride down. Sometimes the tops snapped off, and our ride down was faster than we had wanted!

Milton and I picked mayhaws in the swamps and rode around

in homemade boats during floods. He had a huge abandoned saw-dust pile behind his house, and we spent many hours tunneling through the sawdust with old stockings over our heads to keep the debris out of our eyes and noses. We were true friends, "members of one another" in the fullest sense that Paul talks about in Ephesians 4:25, and we would do anything with and for each other.

Milton and I do not see each other very often now. We have gone our separate ways, as most adults do, although I still hold him in high esteem. Our childhood friendship helps me even now to realize the importance of close ties with other men. We men are not meant to be loners. Competition often seems to drive a wedge between us, but that wedge can be thrown out. Seek male friends at work with whom you can experience an Ephesians 4 relationship.

Lord, thank You for the male friends You have given me at work. Please help me to show them how much I appreciate them. Amen.

DAY SEVEN

Don't Pigeon-hole Your Fellow Workers
Matthew 7:1

All of us have a tendency to make up our minds about other people quickly, perhaps too quickly. We fall into the trap of looking at only the superficial, and we disregard the warning of Matthew 7:1. A friend recently sent me the following fictitious report from a pastoral search committee. It details their work and their final decision. See what you think.

Pastoral Search Committee Report

In our search for a suitable pastor, the following scratch sheet was developed for your perusal. The list contains the names of the candidates and comments on each.

- Noah: He has 120 years of preaching experience, but no converts.
- Moses: He stutters, and the former congregation says he loses his temper over trivial things.

- Abraham: He took off to Egypt during hard times. We heard that he got into trouble with the authorities and then tried to lie his way out.
- David: He is an unacceptable moral character. He might have been considered for minister of music had he not "fallen."
- John: He says he is a Baptist but lacks tact and dresses like a hippie. He would not feel comfortable at a church potluck supper.
- Peter: He has a bad temper and was heard to deny Christ publicly.
- Paul: We found him to lack tact. He is too harsh, his appearance is contemptible, and he preaches far too long.
- Timothy: He has potential but is much too young for the position.
- Jesus: He tends to offend church members, especially Bible scholars, with his preaching. He is also too controversial. He even offended the search committee with His pointed questions.
- Judas: He seemed to be very practical, cooperative, good with money, concerned for the poor, and professionally dressed. We all agreed that he is just the man we are looking for to fill the vacancy as our Senior Pastor.

Lord, please forgive me for labeling people harshly and judging them prematurely. Give me compassion for my fellow workers. Amen.

DOUG HAUGEN

A Man and His Work: Employees

KNOW WHOM TO TRUST

Isaiah 55:2

I thought he was a phony. Yes, he was a Christian, but he was unemployed, and he seemed just a bit too happy. I was visiting him because I had heard about how he and the other people in his congregation were living the gospel.

I spent several days with this man. I waited for him to crack. He had been a stockbroker. Okay, he might have been "financially comfortable," but even if he was, I wondered whether he was like most men I have known and how much of his self-image was based not on who he was in Christ but on what he did "for a living."

I heard about this man's faith. I shared in the intense fellowship he had with other Christians in his congregation. I witnessed his service to others. Finally, I got it. In giving himself completely to God, he had also completely opened himself to the fellowship of his congregation.

This man was not among the seventy percent of us who are anxious because we have less "job security" than we had a few years ago. This man, and those with whom he was in fellowship, had found security in God's promises to them through the fellowship that they had with one another. They found delight, not in circumstances, but in God's promises (Isa. 55:2).

Dear God, please give me the courage to live in real fellowship with other Christians and to find delight in Your promises. Amen.

Pass Along the Encouragement

Luke 15

My cousin was the epitome of encouragement. It was his voice that the Spirit used to help me "come to myself." He thought God was telling me to attend a Bible college with him. I am glad he was listening, for I was not.

It is a long story, but I was nineteen and had no idea what I, or God, wanted to do with my life. After two years of urging, encouraging, and pleading on my cousin's part, I went along with him—partly to get him off my back but mostly because I had no idea of what else I should be doing.

I soon found myself in a small group of people who were taking Scripture seriously and trying to live what they were being taught. At that time, I committed my life to Christ, knowing that He had been committed to me all along.

I was not staring down the barrel of a gun when I responded to Christ's call, and I did not have a needle stuck in my arm. I was not eating with the pigs. Friends who have that kind of testimony tell me that I am fortunate, and I agree.

The point is that all of us need the forgiving arms that the Father extended to his wayward son in the parable Jesus told (Luke 15). If it were not for that moment in my life when I realized the truth, I would not be married to my wonderful wife of twenty years, have the great kids I have, be in the vocation I am (men's ministry), or, most importantly, be where I am in my walk with Jesus.

Somewhere in your life is a person who needs your encouragement. Who knows how God might use you to convince them to trust in Christ for salvation?

O God, please help me to be an encouragement to others and perhaps lead some of them to Christ. Amen.

SALES PITCH
Matthew 24:4–5

I went with my friend to a pep rally for salesmen. It was a day filled with motivational speakers. Excitement grew as each one charged the crowd to think positively and to go out and sell. Thousands of people cheered as one speaker after another exclaimed that we had the innate ability to be successful—in other words, to make a vast number of sales and great sums of money.

Finally, radio commentator and salesman Paul Harvey took the podium. "I am a salesman!" he exclaimed. The crowd applauded wildly. "And I will be a salesman until the day I die!" The crowd responded with a thunderous roar. "In fact, when I die, and God asks me, 'Why should I let you into my heaven? . . .'"

My heart fell. I did not want to hear him say that would be his greatest sales job ever. Our salvation is not about selling ourselves to the Creator, who formed us in our mother's womb. Much professional literature and seminars tell us that personal success is measured in dollars, and they attempt to appeal to our pride in teaching that the ingredients for success lie within us.

Paul Harvey continued, "No reason. I'll just say, 'I accepted the Gift you gave me!'" The arena crowd fell stone silent. In that moment Harvey distinguished a pure motivator (Matt. 24:4–5) from a speaker of truth.

Motivational speakers and literature can be helpful. God does want us to take a constructive and positive approach to marketing our products. But He measures success in terms of our relationship to His Son. We can take joy in who we are, what we do, and the people we know because of what God has done through the Gift that Paul Harvey spoke about—Jesus Christ.

Lord, please help me to have an upbeat attitude about life because of what You have done for me in Christ. Amen.

SERVE OTHERS AS YOU SERVE GOD

1 Thessalonians 3:12−13

Lloyd is ninety-three years old. He retired—sort of—about two years ago from the home improvement business he started in the 1940s. His son now runs the company and still frequently consults him. I visit Lloyd in his office at home. He usually sits next to his computer. (He gave me his e-mail address the last time I visited with him.)

Lloyd is an inspiration to me. Because he is so grateful for God's goodness, he has practiced stewardship in every area of his life. He has given faithfully and generously of himself and his finances to both the church and the community.

From the beginning, Lloyd provided not only a pension plan for his employees but also shared with them 10 percent of the profit. His greatest pride is not in the wealth he has accumulated but in the satisfaction of those whom his business has served and the people he has employed. Lloyd has done all of this without calling attention to himself. Instead, he gives credit to God. And he has never grown weary of caring for those he believed God placed under his oversight. He is the kind of man Paul prayed that the Thessalonian Christians would become (1 Thess. 3:12–13).

What man in your life has provided an example like that of Lloyd? Why not have a conversation with him today, and let him know how much you have benefited from the way he has run his business and lived his life?

O Lord, please help me to serve others as
I serve You. Amen.

SET THE EXAMPLE

1 Timothy 6:1

This man was my supervisor first, and then he became my friend and mentor. I was a teenager, the same age as his own children. He was a Christian, and his greatest concern was to bring glory to God in all that he did.

This man's piety seemed legalistic, and he had a long list of do's and don'ts. But he was also loving. We worked in the grain fields with men who were crude and earthy. Sometimes they laughed behind his back, amused at his struggle to follow God.

I couldn't buy the legalism, but I admired him as a man of Christian principle who was willing to be different and stand up for what he believed. Despite his foibles and regardless of what anyone may have thought about his piety, no one ever questioned his dedication to his work and the fact that he honored those who were in authority over him.

Our work was to develop crop varieties that would be disease-resistant and yet produce larger yields. In short, our work was to develop wheat to feed the world. But my friend and mentor knew that other side of our work. He knew that to be called to a vocation was more than just a job. In his eyes, those fields were a place of ministry. And bosses, fellow workers, and the world benefited because he was there.

Do you see the work God has given you from the same perspective? And do you see the opportunities God has given you to be a Christ-like example to the people whom you employ or for whom or with whom you work?

Lord, please help me to be a positive influence for You in the workplace. Amen.

DAY SIX

Mere Talk?
Proverbs 14:23

"They don't care how much you know. They want to know how much you care." That was a favorite adage of a friend who was the director of a ministry for homeless people.

A lot people talk about the homeless problem. They talk, in some cases, about their disgust with homeless people. Still others talk about what the government (or the church or someone else) should do for homeless people.

My friend, however, is a man of words *and* action. There was profit from his toil. I'm not talking about his pocketbook but his heart and soul, for he knew that he was engaged in the very task God had created him to do. Those who were homeless and now are self-supporting have benefited from his words put into action. The community has prospered from not only having more productive citizens but also the heart and hands this man's work provided on behalf of the community.

Words that are not put into action are empty, benefit no one, and do great damage (Prov. 14:23). But words that are put into action can be powerful. For example, with God's command, the universe came into existence. And with God's promise, redemption was made available to the lost.

What has resulted from the words you recently spoke? In what ways have they benefited your home, workplace, and community?

Lord, please move me from being a mere talker to someone who puts his words into practice. Amen.

ENTHUSIASTIC SERVICE

Romans 12:11

While on a recent tour of Israel, I took a boat ride on the Sea of Galilee. Although I was enthralled with the fact that my companions and I were at one of the sites where Jesus spent time with His disciples, I was most intrigued by the men who ran the boat.

These fishermen reminded me of how I think the disciples might have looked and how they may have acted. They were burly, scruffy-looking men. They were mighty men, men full of zest and life. With their tanned, muscular bodies and rugged souls, they worked hard and laughed heartily. They looked like men who did not do anything in life halfway.

When I think about the disciples, the feminized images that most religious art gives to us are not the pictures that come to my mind. These were men who did hard physical labor. They were being developed to put their lives on the line for Christ.

You may have heard the adage, as I often did while growing up, "If it's worth doing, it's worth doing well." While there may be much truth in that statement, the Christian takes it deeper. We might say, "If a job is worth doing, let's do it, remembering that our purpose is to serve God." To the Christian, our work is more than just a job; it is a part of our calling. Regardless of what we do, we should be enthusiastic in our service for God (Rom. 12:11).

Lord, please help me to be enthusiastic in my work for You. Amen.

HAROLD HAWKINS

A Man and His Work: Employer

THE CHARACTER OF A CHRISTIAN EMPLOYER
Leviticus 25:39–43

Leviticus 25:39–43 concerns the indentured service of one indebted Israelite to another. The Lord through Moses commanded that the wealthier relative was not to charge interest on whatever he lent. Similarly, the wealthier relative was not to treat the bankrupt family member as a slave or exercise power over him ruthlessly.

In today's workplace, we have different kinds of employers. Some employers have only one focus—the "bottom line." To run the company, these employers ride the employees hard, for they believe that is the only way to make a profit.

Other employers think the profit line is important, but they are just as concerned to be fair, virtuous, and considerate of their employees. Scripture teaches that this is the way to have a successful company. Christian love, understanding, and patience are the qualities that keep the workers in their jobs, not ruthless, demanding attitudes from the management.

Dear Lord, please help me to be an example of Christ's love to those in the workplace. Amen.

DAY TWO

AN UNFORGIVING EMPLOYER
Job 31:13–15

Supervisor John Towns had suspicions that several of the workers were slacking off in their jobs during the day. They would take their breaks and return later than allowed. He spoke to the men about this, but they said there was no reason to be concerned and that it would not happen again. John accepted their explanation and did not report the incident to his plant manager. Later, he discovered that the men with whom he had talked were caught distributing drugs to other plant workers.

During an inquiry conducted by the company lawyers, the president reprimanded John severely for not reporting the men, and John was fired on the spot. John asked the president to forgive his mistake and to have mercy, but the president would not relent. The executive was unable to forgive John for a seemingly small mistake. His heart was so hardened that he refused to consider what it would mean to be fired.

Have you acted like this company president and been unable to forgive someone you employ or with whom you work for a mistake he has made? If so, look at Job 31:13–15. The writer said that if he had been unfair to his servants or had refused to hear their complaints, he would be unable to face God when questioned by Him for his actions. After all, God created both Job and his employees. The implication is that both the employer and the employees were to treat each other fairly and kindly.

In your relationships with your coworkers, learn to understand the reasons for their actions. Then, discern through prayer and God's leading what you should do.

Dear Lord, please help me to show love and mercy to my coworkers who have made mistakes. Amen.

DO YOUR BEST AT WORK
Proverbs 18:9

In the workplace are several types of workers. There is the ambitious worker who is prompt to satisfy his employer at all times and displays a personality that blends well with his associates. He is respected and admired by those who know him. The management is favorably impressed with his performance, and his future with the company seems bright.

The lazy worker has little ambition other than to collect his paycheck regularly. He finds time to do little on the job and will usually look for someone else who shares his feelings. When he finds that individual, they usually become close friends. As the relationship grows, their work deteriorates further. Before long, the management realizes the situation and may fire one or both of the shiftless workers.

Here are three men. One is a success and the other two are failures because of the presence or absence of diligence in their work habits. What is the cure for a lazy and self-pleasing attitude? Proverbs 18:9 suggests that it is taking pride and joy in what we do for a living.

Dear Lord, please help me to do my best at work so that You might be glorified. Amen.

DON'T BE A MISER
1 Timothy 5:17–18

It is God's will that we work. A company looks for men to work so that it can sell its products or services. The benefits for the worker and the employer are mutual: the worker receives wages and the employer obtains a profit for the goods and services he has rendered to the customer.

First Timothy 5:17 says that church leaders who do a good job should not only be given due respect but also adequate pay for their diligent care of the congregation. Verse 18 contains two Scripture quotations, one from Deuteronomy 25:4 and another from Luke 10:7. The point of both passages is that church leaders should not be taken for granted and criticized unfairly. Rather, they should be given adequate financial compensation for the work they do.

These verses include a broader principle applicable to the workplace. Employers should pay their employees regularly and adequately, and the workers who do an especially good job should be rewarded for it. It is discouraging to work and not be paid. In the absence of appropriate financial compensation, people have little incentive to go on living.

If you are employer, take Paul's words to heart. Don't cheat your employees out of the wages they've earned. And don't take your most diligent workers for granted. Instead, reward them financially for their faithful service.

Dear Lord, please help me to do whatever
I can to pay my employees adequately and
appropriately, giving them what they deserve for
the work they perform. Amen.

DAY FIVE

DEPENDING ON GOD
FOR WISDOM AND STRENGTH

Luke 10:7

Jesus sent out seventy-two disciples into the villages to preach, teach, and heal the sick. They were to take no money or extra clothing. Jesus said that because they labored diligently in His name, they should be compensated for their work. Christ did not give a monetary amount but left that decision to the recipients of the disciples' ministry (Luke 10:7).

Wages can be paid only if you do work. Because many people in our society do not want to work, we have a tremendous welfare system that drains our national economy. (Of course, there are people who wish to be employed but are unable to find work, and our government gives them financial assistance.)

Work is a blessing from God to us. We praise Him for His plan to allow us to use our skills and talents to serve our families and communities. Whether you are an employer or an employee, Christ is the reason for all that you do on the job. When conflict arises between labor and management, He will give you wisdom for how to handle any situation. And when a downturn occurs in the economy and your business might have to let some people go, Jesus can give you the strength to weather the storm. You can depend on Him, for He will never fail you.

Dear Lord, this day I look to You for wisdom and
strength to handle the problems I am encountering
in the workplace. Amen

WHY ARE YOU WORKING?

John 10:12–13

The hired hand mentioned in John 10:12–13 was interested only in the money he could get from the job. Because he didn't care about the sheep, he ran at the first sign of danger. The good shepherd wasn't doing his job simply to get a paycheck. Rather, he truly cared about the sheep and wanted to protect them, provide for them, and guide them to safety. In these verses, Jesus is the good shepherd, whereas Israel's religious leaders were the hired hand.

What is your motivation for working? Are you like the hired hand whose with a particular company only because they pay more than the competition? Or are you there because you see your job as an opportunity to serve the Lord and make a positive difference? How great is your commitment to the organization and its workers? Would you stay there even if a higher-paying job came along, or would you switch jobs at the drop of a hat?

These are hard-hitting questions, and it's tough to answer them honestly. But doing so can be therapeutic, helping you to see more clearly what your true attitude is toward the work you do, those for whom you work, and the people with whom you work.

Dear Lord, please help me to cultivate the right attitude about working. Amen.

TREAT YOUR EMPLOYEES RIGHT

Ephesians 6:9

Let's face it, the business world is a cutthroat place! If you don't come in with a lower bid than the next guy, chances are that his firm will get the job. And if you can't deliver the goods by the end of the day, most likely there's someone else in the industry who says he will.

It's no wonder that businessmen are feeling pressured to squeeze every last ounce of energy and profit from their employees. When the "bottom line" is at stake, some owners will resort to threats, blackmail, and broken promises just to get what they want from their laborers. They don't care whether they've mistreated or manipulated the people who work for them.

If you are a Christian businessman, the way you handle your workers should be vastly different. After all, as a child of the King, you should desire to do what is right, not what is wrong. For example, Ephesians 6:9 says that you should treat your employees rightly, meaning that you shouldn't threaten them, for both of you have the same Master in heaven, and He plays no favorites. No one is more important than anyone else. Christ is as displeased when you mistreat your workers as He is when they take advantage of you.

Dear Lord, please help me to be honest and fair in the way I treat those who work for me. Amen.

LEONARD GOSS

A Man and His Work: Ethics

DON'T ATTACK THE RIGHTEOUS!
Proverbs 24:15–16

Many people plot against the righteous and covet their belongings because the wicked are by nature selfish. The only thing of interest to them is their own interests. But Proverbs 24:15–16 warns them that if they try to oppress or scheme against the godly, they will be defeated. The reason? God is against the wicked and for the righteous; thus, to attack the latter is to attack God.

Someone might knock down the righteous seven times (i.e., very often), but the righteous will keep coming back because the godly are resilient. Like the Energizer bunny, they keep going and going. The righteous have a spiritual elasticity similar to that of a young sapling, which springs up and rebounds after it has been bent low to the ground.

Yet, as futile and self-defeating as it is to mistreat God's people, the wicked will do it anyway! Every Christian man frequently will fall into trouble. But we should never be impatient or fretful, and we should never lose our trust in God. We are never really secure against worldly problems, including unfair attacks from those who oppose us on the job. But we can always be secure in knowing that God watches over us and can deliver us from all evil (Matt. 6:13).

Lord, thank You that You're always here to help
me make it through the darkest moments of life.
Amen.

LET GOD BE THE JUDGE

Proverbs 24:17–18

At times, the wicked experience calamity. When it happens, it's easy for us to gloat over their misfortune. But Proverbs 24:17–18 warns against doing so, for our glee over their demise displeases God. When we gloat, we make ourselves the avenger. In other words, we put ourselves in the place of God, Who alone is the true Judge of both the wicked and the righteous.

Romans 11:18–21 says that when our Christianity lacks humility and gratitude and when we show a spirit of contempt and arrogance, we are not acting like citizens of the divine kingdom. Members of God's spiritual family remember that their adoption is by His grace, not by their good works. Humility, not haughtiness, should characterize their attitude and actions.

The warning against vindictiveness when our enemy falls applies especially to Christian men in the workplace. Jesus told us to love our enemies and to pray for those who might persecute us (Matt. 5:44). The duty to love is extended even to competitors and those with whom we work but do not get along. Without the command to love, we would lack the fear of God, which is what humanizes us.

Lord, please help me not to take perverted pleasure in the misfortune of others. Amen.

GIVE A TRUE WITNESS

Proverbs 24:23–26

Proverbs 24:23–26 teaches that a court of law has no room for prejudice or favoritism. No virtue is so great and ethical as true justice. This truth definitely applies to judges, but it also applies to all of us who call ourselves Christian men. We should give a true witness, not only in the courts of justice but also at work. To bear false witness strikes at the root of our conscience and moral obligation to God. The same is true of volunteering false information against another in a spirit of hatred and revenge. People who are full of sinister tricks pervert the plain sense of justice.

When a judge willfully perverts what is right by setting the guilty free (rather than rebuking and punishing them), the just suffer and the public good is undone. It is no wonder that the "peoples will curse him and nations denounce him." Individuals and whole communities will turn against a crooked judge. But an honest judge who gives a just answer is like a true friend. Straight speaking may sometimes be costly, but in the end it is the only kind of utterance that glorifies the Lord.

William Temple once said that "if we choose between making men Christian and making the social order more Christian, we must choose the former. But there is no such antithesis. . . . There is no hope of establishing a more Christian social order except through the labor and sacrifice of those in whom the Spirit of Christ is active, and the first necessity for progress is more and better Christians taking full responsibility as citizens for the political, social and economic system under which they and their fellows live."

Lord, regardless of where I am or what I'm doing, please help me to give a true witness to others. Amen.

DAY FOUR

SWEETER THAN VENGEANCE
Proverbs 24:28–29

Proverbs 24:28–29 warns against bearing false witness against our neighbor. (To do so is perjury, which is a serious crime in a society that honors justice and truth.) We are not to offer false testimony against another person, whether through misrepresentation as busybodies or maliciously as slanderers. The Christian code calls for a much higher morality.

For us to render evil for evil may seem natural and even just. Certainly, human nature *wants* to avenge wrongs, but we shouldn't do it for at least three reasons:

1. the sense of revenge springs from our sinful nature, and there is nothing noble in it;
2. God does not authorize us to execute a sentence of judgment on our fellow human beings; and
3. our duty is to forgive those who wrong us and to avoid retaliation and vengefulness.

We are not to use the courts for settling personal scores. And we should never set ourselves up as judge and jury. What, then, is the answer to our desire for justice? Leave vengeance in God's hands. Let Him Who is our Savior and Judge repay the wicked for what they do. Even he to whom actual injustice is done should commit his case to God. Above all, take God as your example. He treats sinners who seek His forgiveness, not with the justice they deserve but with grace. Grace is much sweeter than vengeance.

Father, please help me to rise above
vindictiveness and retaliation by showing
a spirit of love and forgiveness to those
who have wronged me. Amen.

DAY FIVE

WHAT DOES GOD REQUIRE?

AMOS 5:21–24

Are you more concerned with religion than with God? That was the case with Israel during the time of Amos. God became disgusted with the religious ceremonies Israel organized in His honor. The people were certainly arduous in never neglecting "feasts" and "assemblies" and in practicing all of the "offerings." But God flatly rejected this religious activity (Amos 5:21–24). It seems that God's people were inundating Him, not with rivers of righteousness, which would have delighted God, but with rivers of religiosity and false worship, which were a foul odor to Him.

How would Amos evaluate your worship of God? Is it displeasing and unacceptable to Him? Is it a hypocritical formal activity that should be condemned? God turns aside from the mere noise of your songs and offerings when they are not based on obedient conduct. It is as though He stops up His ears, closes His eyes, and shuts His nostrils to your hypocrisy. What, then, does God require of you? He wants justice, righteousness, and complete faithfulness.

We should not think that God rejects all types of worship as evil or unnecessary. For example, He never rejects worship that is inward and moral. But God rejects "alibi religion," which has no place for justice in the lives of worshipers. It's only when we become justice-intoxicated Christian men—at church, at work, and in all other areas of life—that God will receive our worship as genuine and acceptable.

Lord, please help me to be a justice-intoxicated
person whose worship is genuine and acceptable
to You. Amen.

THE SEVEN DEADLY SINS

Proverbs 6:16–19

The medieval church had seven deadly sins: pride, anger, envy, impurity, gluttony, slothfulness, and avarice. Proverbs 6:16–19 gives us another version of these sins to consider. Of the seven vices there listed that God hates, five are associated with body parts (eyes, tongue, hands, heart, and feet) and two deal with types of people (liars and troublemakers). All seven vices are equal objects of the Lord's abhorrence, and all of them are taboo for men of God.

The proud look reflects the haughtiness within one's soul and is opposed by God. A lying tongue is hateful to Him, for it contradicts the truth. God will avenge murderous hands for He alone is the Lord of life and death. A heart that devises wicked schemes is full of depravity, thus God condemns it. Feet that rush quickly to evil carry out the wicked schemes already devised in the heart. A false witness is odious to God. The one who stirs up dissension among believers destroys harmony and unity. The man whose eyes, hands, or feet perform such deeds has a perverted soul and therefore invites God's censure, not His commendation.

What then does God commend? Among the virtues He applauds are humility, truthful speech, preservation of life, pure thoughts, eagerness to do good things, an honest witness, and the cultivation of harmony among believers. Are any of these qualities true of your life?

Dear Lord, please help me to make Your loves
my loves and Your hates my hates. Amen.

ABOUT PRAYER AND FORGIVENESS

Matthew 6:13–15

At the end of the Lord's Prayer, we are told to pray thus: "And lead us not into temptation, but deliver us from the evil one." This statement confuses many people. Does God actively "lead" or "bring" Christians into temptation? Not according to James 1:13.

Then what does the word rendered "temptation" (Matt. 6:13) mean? It probably means "trial" or "test." Although God does not tempt us to do evil, He does on occasion allow our commitment to Him to be tested. More than anyone, Jesus understood what it meant to be tested. In the Garden of Gethsemane, He said to Peter, James, and John, "Pray that you will not fall into temptation" (Matt. 26:41). He was not telling His disciples to pray that they wouldn't be tested, but rather that they wouldn't give in to temptation.

If God allowed His Son to go through testing and trials, we should expect that in God's timing it might also happen to us. Our constant prayer should be that we will not yield to enticements to sin. It is the proud prayer of the self-righteous man that invites God to test his character. What he asks for he just might get! We should not ask God to test our faithfulness but rather to deliver us from our temptation. Even in the midst of tests or trials, however, we should remember that God will never allow enticements to drive us to be unfaithful to Him.

What about Matthew 6:14–15? How are our willingness to forgive others who have wronged us and God's forgiveness of us interrelated? Jesus meant that men and women of God must have a forgiving spirit if they are to receive the benefit of His forgiveness. We are to forgive others when they sin against us, for as we forgive others, so God forgives us. This statement does not mean that He is unwilling to forgive sinners. Rather, when we refuse to forgive others, our hearts lack the capacity to receive God's forgiveness through faith in Christ.

Lord, please help me to forgive others just as You have forgiven me freely—and unconditionally—in Christ. Amen.

DENNIS HILLMAN

A Man and His Work: Integrity

WHAT YOU DON'T SEE MATTERS MOST
Matthew 7:24-27

Along a tree-lined country road in rural Michigan stands one man's pride and joy: a weekend getaway cabin. This particular cabin sits at the end of a private lake where the bass jump out of the water and the passerby feels the almost irresistible urge to jump in. The cabin sits atop a slight rise in the ground, surrounded on three sides by large boulders. The man who spent countless weekend and evening hours building his dream house was justifiably proud of it—until the dream became a nightmare.

In spite of the fact that the cottage is an architectural gem and that the owner bought the best materials, it is sinking. It is slowly settling into the marshy soil, the weight of the structure compacting the soft ground beneath the footers. Short of expensive excavation of the foundations or moving the whole structure to a new sight, it will continue to sink. And despite its above-ground appearance, it is unsalable and may be eventually unlivable.

The owner of that home probably wouldn't be comforted to know that his problem is nothing new. Jesus probably drew upon actual construction flops of His own day in Matthew 7:24–27 when He contrasted the house built on rock and the house built on sand. And while Jesus' parable addresses a more general principle—our lives must be grounded upon His Word—it is also instructive concerning the specific issue of integrity. The parable basically tells us that the strength of what is underneath the visible structure determines the ultimate survival of the structure.

Like a building, the inner person, or self, depends upon an invisible base to support the visible structure. Integrity is that base, the foundation to self-esteem and fulfilling relationships with others. Architects speak of the "structural integrity" of a building.

In human life, our persons can only have structural integrity—
wholeness and soundness—to the degree that they reflect inner
integrity. Without personal integrity, love relationships crumble:
vows of faithfulness are broken and trust is destroyed. Without
integrity, family relationships disintegrate: lies undermine love and
anger consumes respect. Without integrity, friendships splinter,
partnerships dissolve, and reputations are sullied.

Integrity matters, and it makes a difference.

> *Father, what others see of me is the only "me"*
> *they know. What I know of myself may well be*
> *only partly true for I am skilled in self-deception,*
> *like all sinners. Help me to have an inner*
> *wholeness built on the rock of Your Word,*
> *an integrity that underlies my thoughts,*
> *my words, my relationships with others.*
> *I want You to delight in me. Amen.*

DAY TWO

How to Make It to the Majors
Luke 16:10–11

"Minor league"—it's a phrase that is synonymous with second-
rate, unimportant, inconsequential. Yet in professional baseball,
progressing up the ranks of the minor league teams is the obliga-
tory training process for the aspiring major-leaguer. It's in the small-
town, backwater ball clubs that the young player demonstrates his
abilities and hones his skills. To the public at large, the minor leagues
are only a sideshow to the "big show," but in reality they are the
proving grounds of the sport.

Almost every profession or trade has its minor leagues. Who
hasn't heard the story of the respected CEO who started out, not in
the boardroom, but in the mail room? Every famous architect began somewhere as a draftsman, and every renown surgeon pulled
down the grueling hours of the medical residency. Every master
plumber or carpenter began as a lowly apprentice, and every plant
foreman began by pushing a broom or working on the assembly
line. Each step up the ladder of recognition and promotion is crafted
by faithfully executing a task, by sweating the small stuff.

Jesus drew upon this principle of career development, but his
concern wasn't for the future Fortune 500 executives or professional

athletes. His concern was for how one handles "the true riches" (Luke 16:10–11). Money and everything that goes along with it—status, power, and personal freedom—are a part of the spiritual minor leagues. Christ's ultimate game plan is for us to receive responsibilities and rewards far greater than any earthly achievements. Eternal rewards, however, are earned by faithfulness in what God considers the "small" areas of life.

Are the deals we make ethical? Do we "borrow" company equipment or supplies? Are we willing to cut corners to get ahead? Are we always on the lookout for the loophole, for the opportunity to help ourselves, even if it costs our employer or associates? No matter how high we rise in a field or profession, we'll never make it out of the spiritual minor leagues without integrity in handling money and responsibilities.

Lord, I don't want to be in spiritual bush leagues, always regretting that I'm missing what is real, what is deep, and what is eternal. Help me to be faithful, to be Your reliable servant who is worthy of Your trust. Amen.

DAY THREE

A LITTLE SOMETHING OF OUR OWN
Luke 16:11–12

It had imitation pearl handles and two polished blades that glistened under the glass of the display case. It was the prettiest pocketknife my six-year-old eyes had ever seen. The only problem was that I didn't have even a dime, much less the considerable sum of two dollars, for my pearl-handled prize. So I stood there with my face almost touching the glass and wished for some way to walk out of the hardware store with that little beauty in my pocket.

My dad, who had been observing my nose-to-the-glass inspection of the knife case, sized up the situation and proposed a deal: I would dry the dishes each night for two weeks and earn the money to purchase the pocketknife. Every night, without fail, I would report for kitchen duty, and in two weeks, I could walk back into the store with two dollar bills. Deal!

For the next two weeks I stood by my mother in the farmhouse kitchen and dried dishes, handling the dinner plates carefully, being sure to get both sides dry, pushing the towel into the glasses and making them shine, sorting the silverware and stacking the forks and spoons in their plastic holder in the drawer.

Two Saturdays later I walked into the hardware store and dutifully placed my two dollars and a few odd cents on the countertop and watched almost without breathing as the owner put the sleek penknife in my hand. Walking back to the truck with the knife's cool grips clutched firmly in my small fist that was pushed deeply into my jeans pocket, I was the proudest boy in the county, if not the country. Almost forty years later, it still lies ready in my dresser drawer.

What turned that insignificant little pocket knife into a treasure? It was the first possession in my life that was truly *mine*. Not a gift, not a hand-me-down, but something I had worked for and waited on.

In Luke 16:12 Jesus spoke of that which is one's own, that which will belong uniquely and distinctly to each of us as a reward for faithful service to Him. It's a parallel to the phrase used in verse 11 that mentions "true riches." He wants to give us the deepest sense of fulfillment and joy. There is a payoff for faithfulness, a reward for serving with integrity and selflessness. One day we will be able to have a pure pride, a sense of accomplishment free of self-centeredness, because Jesus is going to give us what we worked for and wanted.

What are you working for and what do you ultimately want? What can be only possessed in this life and lost forever, or what can be achieved now and enjoyed forever through faithfully following the Lord?

Lord Jesus, I need great spiritual heroes to challenge and inspire me, but I also need my own success stories, times that I can look back on and feel holy pride in having done Your will. I don't want a pat on the back from others, Lord, but Your approval. That's my deepest desire, for Your sake, Amen.

DAY FOUR

Go Figure

Leviticus 6:1–5

We've all heard the old saw, "Figures never lie, unless liars figure." You don't have to be a liar to get into trouble with figures. Did you hear about the statistician who drowned crossing a river?

Its average depth was only three feet. Averages may not lie, but they don't tell the whole truth!

In Leviticus 6 Moses sets forth some legal standards for dealing with the crimes of embezzlement, extortion, perjury, and theft. The average person today would certainly agree that we need laws against such crimes. But would the average person agree that finding a lost item and telling a little fib to keep it is a "crime"? How about borrowing a power tool from a friend and conveniently forgetting to return it? Or failing to draw attention to the box of laundry soap on the bottom of the grocery cart that the checkout person missed? Maybe the issue is a ream of paper taken from the office and sitting by the printer at home?

What the "average" person would do is hardly the correct standard when it comes to questions of honesty and integrity. God's standard is, "You shall not steal." Period, end of discussion. Stolen property must be returned, and restitution must be made. The Mosaic law mandated a payment of 120 percent of the value of the stolen property, and the guilty party was required to provide a guilt offering: a ram without defect or its equivalent in silver.

For the Christian, the guilt offering for sin was paid by a Lamb without spot or blemish. We can be forgiven, but forgiveness doesn't eliminate the responsibility of restitution if we have taken advantage of another person or a company. Maybe our offense isn't a crime, but it does show a lack of integrity, a failure to respect the rights and property of others.

Let's start by looking in the garage or workshop—is that your brother-in-law's power saw? Put a new blade on it and return it with an apology for keeping it so long. How about the extension ladder behind the garage? Take it back to the neighbor with a coffee cake as an extra thank you. How many company pens, pencils, or other office items clutter the top of your dresser or desk at home? Paper clips? Sure, everyone accumulates a few, but what about the box you borrowed from the supply cabinet?

Coming clean before God may mean cleaning up around the house first. Sure, the average person wouldn't think twice about taking a towel from a hotel room or about how many ink pens are in his desk drawer, but a Christian isn't an average person—he's under new management with a mandate to not accept business as usual. Now, go figure.

My world is filled with ethical shortcuts, Lord.
The world's way of getting things done has no

sharp edges, only rounded moral corners. I want
the sharpness, the exactness of your way, Father,
that cuts through the self-deceit and wrongness of
the world's way. Amen.

WHO WRITES YOUR PRESS REPORTS?

I Chronicles 29:17

Without benefit of radio, television, direct mail, or the Internal Revenue Service, King David completed one of the most profitable fund-raising drives in history: 188 tons of gold, 10,000 gold coins, and 375 tons of silver, all given by the citizens of Israel in response to David's own example of generosity.

If a modern public relations agency had been running the show, they would have made sure that there were plenty of media on hand to cover the event. Press releases would have been printed by the chariotful; pictures of the smiling donors, standing in front of the mountain of coins, would show up on the covers of magazines and tabloids from Damascus to Nineveh. No doubt several stories would play up the theme of David's rags-to-riches rise through military and political life. And a couple of glamour shots of attractive women from the king's harem certainly would perk up interest at the newsstand.

That's not the way it happened, of course. David didn't need a public relations specialist. His fame had already spread widely in the ancient world. He had been in the public's adoration ever since he dealt with a pesky Philistine named Goliath and returned to Jerusalem with the songs and shouts of the city's populace ringing in his ears. He didn't need to toot his own horn; he had plenty of loving subjects to do that, thank you very much. In fact, this could have been another occasion for David to bask in the adulation and near-worship of the people.

But unlike most of the big-wig movers and shakers, hotshot politicians, self-made billionaires, and fame-craving philanthropists, David passed up the opportunity to glorify himself, to toot his own horn. In fact, David disclaimed any personal ownership of his own wealth but acknowledged that everything he had came from God and belonged to God. David's motives in giving were solely to honor and express adoration for the Lord (1 Chron. 29:17).

Interestingly, David identifies in this passage one of the few occasions in the Bible where it is said that God rejoices or takes delight in response to human action. It wasn't the fabulous quantity of gold and silver nor the incomparable pile of precious stones that gladdened the heart of God. Nor was He overwhelmed by the enormous generosity of the people. God rejoiced in response to the integrity of David's actions. Because God knew David's heart, God knew that David's motives and his actions were pure, untainted by ambition or ego.

How generous are we? And more importantly, why do we give? Are our motives pure? Does God take delight in us?

I get puffed up by the applause and admiration of others. Lord, break the bubble of my silly self-conceit. Create in me a heart of integrity, a heart that desires Your glory before my own, that wants others to admire You ahead of me. For Your kingdom's sake, Amen.

DAY SIX

A FEW GOOD MEN
Nehemiah 7:1–2

The stories are too numerous to have much shock value anymore —a government official gets caught up in a sex scandal. Tawdry details of the affair emerge as aides to the politician are forced to testify, but the case drags on and on. With each new detail the public's appetite for more scandal fare seems to grow.

In another case the second-highest official in the government keeps a list of all the appointees and agents who have accepted bribes. When the records are finally uncovered, they provide a detailed record of the web of corruption that maintains the regime's power—a most useful tool for blackmail among the power-hungry government elite.

Neither of the stories are from recent pages of the *New York Times* or even *People* magazine. The first case involved Kushshiharbe, the mayor of Nuzi, a town in northern Iraq, sometime around 1400 B.C., and a young woman by the name of Humerelli. Their story was recorded on clay tablets that were unearthed in 1928. The second comes from approximately 1300 B.C. and involves Ashour Adein, a royal minister of Assyria whose accounts are preserved in clay tablets found in one of the empire's administrative centers during recent excavations.

Apparently, finding a few good men for government work has always been something of a challenge. The allure of power and the ready opportunities for personal gain through extortion, kickbacks, and "cookin' the books" is too much of a temptation for many. It's not surprising, therefore, that Nehemiah chose a man for an important job based on one major qualification—integrity. When it came time to choose someone to man the city gate and keep the citizens secure from secret attack, Nehemiah turned to Hananiah because "he was a faithful man and feared God more than many."

Both qualities go together: the person who fears God will usually be the most faithful person. That is, when we have a deep respect for and are in awe of God's holy character and incomparable glory, we act with integrity. We know that anything less would be unacceptable to Him. Therefore, it is unacceptable to us as well.

If (and when) God needs a big job done, can He count on you?

Lord, I so often want to cop out, to plead majority rule and say that everyone else is doing it, so that You will understand and overlook my selfish bent. In reality, I need my bent straightened. I need to be laid against the straightedge of Your holiness and painfully (if necessary) be made whole in heart and action. Help me be the man You'd choose when someone needs to stand tall. Amen.

DAY SEVEN

HARD CHOICES
Mark 12:13–17

Between a rock and a hard place; out of the frying pan and into the fire; between the devil and the deep blue sea—all these are proverbial expressions for impossible situations with no satisfactory alternatives. For the religious leaders who opposed Jesus, how diabolically delightful it was to have Him in just such a place!

Taxes were the scourge of the ancient world, and no one was more despised than the tax collector. The Roman Empire exacted heavy taxes from its conquered territories—there were land taxes, crop taxes, import taxes, sales taxes, road taxes, entry taxes, salt taxes, census taxes—all collected at rates that amounted to legalized extortion. One commentator observed that the Roman provinces and territories almost "bled to death" paying taxes, so it's little wonder that taxes formed the basis for much of the civil unrest in the conquered territories. Acts 5:37 records one such ill-fated rebellion.

So when Jesus' enemies wanted to trick him into making a public statement that could be used against him, either in the court of popular opinion or in the court of the Roman governor, the issue of taxes seems to be the perfect vehicle for self-incrimination. If Jesus supports taxes, He betrays His fellow countrymen and sides with the Romans. If He opposes taxes, He is opposed to Roman law and therefore is an enemy of the state. It seemed so simple: heads you lose, tails you lose (Mark 12:13–14).

Except Jesus "knew their hypocrisy" (v. 15). The Herodians weren't interested in "the way of God in accordance with the truth," as they professed in their patronizing approach to Jesus. They were political activists, hoping to see the Herodian dynasty back in power in Jerusalem. The Pharisees, for all their pretensions to spiritual devotion, had erected a false system of religion that was all show and no substance. Their false piety and pretentious prayers were favorite targets of Jesus' most frequent condemnations. Did they really want His opinion on taxation? Hardly.

Is this incident an example of the need to be honest in our accounting, of no cheating on our income taxes? Is Jesus directing us to get our 1040s and Schedule Cs straightened out? No. It's primarily about motives and integrity, about trying to accomplish seemingly good ends by devious and discredited means, about impure hearts and compromising methods.

Are you caught in situations where the only way out seems to be a moral shortcut? Where cutting corners is the quickest means to an honorable end? It won't work. It didn't almost two thousand years ago. Jesus saw right through it then.

He still does.

Dear Lord Jesus, I need Your clarity of thought and your purity of heart. I like to scheme in order to win my battles at work. Sometimes I manipulate even those closest to me to get my own way. Forgive me, and give me singleness of purpose. My "yes" to You needs to be "yes," rather than "Let me get back to you on that." Amen.

RICK BRAND

A Man and His Community: Citizenship

DAY ONE

BEING FAITHFUL CITIZENS

1 Peter 2:13—14

A consistent emphasis in the New Testament deals with the place of the Christian in society. We are to cooperate with the ruling authorities. And we are to obey the leaders of this world in their exercise of their civil responsibility (1 Peter 2:13–14).

When Jesus was being interrogated by Pilate, the Savior offered the defense that His Kingdom was not of this world (John 18:36). He did not come as competition or a threat to the political realities of this world. Likewise, His church does not set itself in a revolutionary or rebellious posture toward the civil authorities of this world.

God's people have remained faithful citizens in a host of forms of government, including oligarchies, monarchies, dictatorships, and republics. Of course, believers should never compromise their consciences (see Acts 5:29). But, in most circumstances, it is possible and desirable for Christians to obey the laws of their government. This fact ensures that when they are persecuted, it will be for their Christian testimony, not for their having violated any moral or civil code.

O gracious God, please enable me to be a good citizen of both Your kingdom and the country in which I live. Amen.

BEING CONSTRUCTIVE, NOT DESTRUCTIVE

Acts 23:5

As Paul stood before the Sanhedrin, he declared that he had served the Lord with a clean conscience (Acts 23:1). When Ananias commanded an attendant to strike Paul on the mouth, the apostle stated that God would judge the high priest for giving such an illegal order (vv. 2–3). And when Paul was questioned about the appropriateness of his statement, he claimed that he did not know he had spoken against the high priest (vv. 4–5).

The apostle mentioned Exodus 22:28, which prohibits speaking evil of a ruler. This commandment seems to be broken quite frequently these days. For example, we are not shy about saying uncomplimentary remarks about those in charge of our communities. Sadly, Christian public speakers seem to be in the forefront of those who are uttering unwholesome statements about elected and appointed officials.

Rather than be cynical and suspicious of those in authority, we should pray for them (1 Tim. 2:1). For example, we can ask the Lord to be merciful to them, and we can express thanks for the job they are doing (v. 2). Also, we can pray that God will use the rulers over us to maintain law and order so that we can live in peace and quietness as well as godliness and dignity (v. 3). Perhaps most importantly, we can pray for their salvation (v. 4).

Dear God, please help me to be constructive, rather than destructive, in my demeanor toward those in authority over me. Amen.

READY FOR ANY HONEST WORK

Titus 3:1

When we come to faith in Christ, we are set free from the control of sin. Martin Luther celebrated this freedom by saying, "Love God and sin boldly." Unfortunately, some people misinterpret this to mean that they can live as they please and do whatever they want.

However, this attitude represents a profound misunderstanding of the gospel. God did not free us from sin so that we could live in sin. Rather, we are free in Christ to love and serve God.

Part of our commitment to God includes submitting to the government and its officers (Titus 3:1). For example, we should seek to be good citizens and always to be ready to do good. Doing so does not mean that we are compromising our allegiance to Christ. On the contrary, by acting as good citizens, we prove that we are truly followers of the One who established all human governments.

Admittedly, we must struggle to live this way consistently. After all, the sinful nature wants to rise up in rebellion against all forms of authority. Through the presence and power of the Spirit, we can resist the temptation to live in sin. In fact, He is ever with us to do what God desires.

Lord, please help me to glorify You by heeding
the civil and moral codes of the land. Amen.

DAY FOUR

SUBJECT TO AUTHORITY

ROMANS 13:1

During the last few years, as the effort in the United States to reduce the welfare rolls has gone forward, programs have been developed between churches and businesses that seek to help needy people adjust to the workplace. One component in many of these programs is to teach the importance of submitting to authority. For example, participants learn that everyone has a boss.

Often it comes as a real surprise to some people that authority is something that God has instituted (Rom. 13:1). Just as He has ordained and established marriage for the welfare and happiness of humanity; so He has created and instituted the links and lines of authority and responsibility, in the absence of which anarchy would result.

Ultimately, human governments are God's gifts to us. Thus, our willingness to obey our rulers is an indication of our willingness to share in the goodness of God's perfect will. It also signifies that we are in submission to God. If we refuse to acknowledge our earthly authority, how will we ever be able to learn to acknowledge the ultimate and supreme authority of God over our lives?

*Father, please give me the strength to bend to
the authority of my local, state, and federal
representatives. Amen.*

THE RIPPLES OF GOODNESS

Proverbs 11:11

Every year different magazines try to tell us the best places to live. The editors look at the crime rate, examine the schools, and measure the percentage of unemployment. They also compare the hospitals and death rates.

These nonreligious surveys confirm what the people of God have known for a long time: there is a connection between the blessing upon the community and the conduct and obedience of its residents. Good and devout people make communities that prosper because their virtue blesses the whole citizenry. By the same token, a community is cursed when deceit reigns among its citizens. A lack of integrity in speech will tear apart the very fabric and bonds of the city or town.

So what are you doing to send ripples of goodness through your community (Prov. 11:11)? Are you known as an upright citizen who blesses your city or as some who tears it apart? With God's help, you can become just such a blessing to your community.

*Heavenly Father, please enable me to be a source
of goodness and blessing in my community. Amen.*

WHOSE MONEY?

Matthew 22:21

Nobody likes taxes. After all, America was virtually founded on a tax rebellion. To listen to talk radio is to know that resentment over taxes seems to be growing. The idea seems to have become clearly established that "It is *your* money, and you should be able to keep as much of it as possible!"

Have you looked at the money in your wallet or pocket? If its a paper bill, printed on it are the words "Federal Reserve Note" of the United States of America. That means it is *not* your money. Rather, it belongs to the government. They made it, and they are responsible for giving it value.

Jesus taught that there is nothing wrong with giving to the government the things that rightly belong to it (Matt. 22:21). Because we are citizens of the nation in which we live, we are required to pay money for the benefits and services that the government provides. And because we are citizens of the kingdom of heaven, God wants us to be faithful in giving the ruling authorities the honor and taxes due to them.

Think of it this way. The air we breathe is on loan to us. The sunsets are ours only to enjoy but not to keep. And we neither bring anything into this world nor take anything out of it. Even the money we use is on loan to us. This realization should set us free from not only coveting money but also withholding that which rightly belongs to the government.

Lord, please help me to have the right attitude
about the money my government makes available
for me to use. Amen.

DAY SEVEN

A Debt of Honor

I Peter 2:17

Do you remember what people typically said during the last political campaign? Many of them verbally attacked and cursed the candidates who were running for office. Have you ever paid attention to what the fans usually say at sporting events? The language is what I call "trash talk." Have you ever listened to what your coworkers say about the people who run the company? They often sneer at and ridicule the officers.

First Peter 2:17 directs us to show respect to everyone, which means that we are to speak in a respectful and affirming way about others. The Lord wants us to give all people the gift of dignity that is theirs because they are created in His image. This point remains true even though people do not always deserve to be given respect. In the play *Man from La Mancha,* the honor and respect with which

Don Quixote treats Dulcenia challenges her to become an honorable woman.

Honor all people so that they might be encouraged to live up to that honor. Also, be sure to love the brotherhood, thus encouraging them to respond in kind. Above all, revere God, for He is your Lord, and respect the authorities, who serve in His name. Doing so will greatly please your Maker and Master.

Dear God, please help me to give people the respect and affirmation that they should receive as those who have been made in Your image.
Amen.

A Man and His Community: Neighbors

ONE ANCESTOR

Acts 17:26

One of my preoccupations when traveling is to watch people. They come in all sizes and shapes, wear all kinds of garbs, and speak all kinds of languages. During a recent breakfast in a Denver motel, I visited with a young family from Germany. They were most friendly and talked about hiking in the Rocky Mountains and the wild canyons of Utah.

Hundreds of languages are spoken in the United States, by not only tourists but also legal immigrants and long-time citizens. Is one language really better than another? After all, God has created all humanity. And more and more new churches serve immigrants speaking different dialects and having distinct customs from China, Indonesia, Vietnam, Ethiopia, and Latin America (to name a few places).

Acts 17:26 is part of the narrative describing Paul's preaching to the sophisticated Greeks at Athens. He appealed to these cynical debaters with the profound truths of Scripture, beginning with God's creation of the world and ending with Jesus' resurrection from the dead. Paul's witness to the Gentiles living in the eastern part of the Roman Empire ultimately led to the conversion of barbarians all over Europe. The apostle's words challenge us to witness to people regardless of their background and heritage.

Lord, please give me a heart for people from all different cultures, races, customs, and languages. Amen.

THE GREATEST COMMANDMENTS

Mark 12:30-31

My parents were fleeing Bolshevik terror in the 1920s when they were detained for months on the Turkish border. Their meager supplies of food and money were finally used up. Then money arrived from a church agency in North America to buy bread. Later, caring Christian families in the United States loaned money to pay for their passage to safety.

In the last week of Jesus' life on earth, He was preoccupied with His upcoming death on the cross. Nevertheless, He found time to answer a sincere question about the greatest commandment. The first commandment, he said, was to love God with all one's heart, soul, mind, and strength (Mark 12:30). But then He moved on to the second commandment, which is to love one's neighbor as oneself (v. 31).

True Sunday worship moves on to influence the way we care for those around us, which means showing unconditional and self-sacrificing love. The early church shared generously with fellow believers. Christians raised money to help the poor in other lands, beginning with Paul's fund drive to aid the poor in Jerusalem. The monks in the Middle Ages continued to help the poor. Today we should help a neighbor in need. The needy throughout the world are aided by agencies such as World Vision and the Mennonite Central Committee.

Lord, please help me to discover what I can do
to show Your love in tangible ways to those
in need around the world. Amen.

ETIQUETTE FOR ENEMIES

Romans 12:20

During the horrific Civil War in the United States, brother fought against brother over slavery and states rights. Seth Loflin opposed this mutual killing, for he believed in the biblical teaching of showing love for one's enemies. When he was drafted, he refused to shoulder a gun. He was imprisoned and tortured in an attempt to get him to murder. When he still refused, he was sentenced to death.

On the appointed day of execution, men gathered to witness the event. The prisoner was led out, but first he asked to pray. His simple prayer was, "Father, forgive them, for they know not what they do." When the command came to "Fire," the riflemen could not pull the trigger. A wave of approval came from the gathered soldiers, and Loflin was led away.[1]

Romans 12 deals with the transformed life that results from faith in Christ. No longer do believers follow the ways of society. Instead, their lives are molded by the risen Lord. Out of thankfulness to God they humbly serve others. How wide is this circle? Family? Local congregation? Denomination? Nation? Not only friends but also enemies need our love. As verse 20 says, we should be willing to feed them when they are hungry and give them something to drink when they are thirsty.

> *Gracious God, please enable me to be*
> *compassionate even to my enemies. Amen.*

DAY FOUR

FOR THE COMMON GOOD
Romans 13:10

During World War II, some of my relatives lived through exile, hunger, and slave labor camps in the Soviet Union, not only because of the stringency of wartime but also because of religious and race discrimination. Yet they continued to pray and praise God together whenever they could. While others may have fought over the last crust of bread and the last coat, these believers shared with and cared for each other. The common bonds of Christian love led them to survive.

Contrast this attitude with that prevalent in North American society, where people tend to regard the Bill of Rights as their "ten commandments." The result has been such things as aggressive driving, the enormous wage spread between management and labor, and the publication of pornography.

But a recent study showed that lower rates of violence exist in urban neighborhoods that have a strong sense of community and values. These are places where most adults discipline their children for missing school or scrawling graffiti.[2] This influence overrides such problems as poverty, unemployment, single-parent house-holds, and racial discrimination. What would motivate such cohesion and care? Certainly the gospel outcome of love for neighbor plays a major part.

Romans 13:10 teaches that our love for our neighbor reflects our love for God. Giving up rights to serve others is our thanks to Him for His undeserved grace!

Lord, please open my eyes and ears to the neighbor I can serve today. Amen.

DAY FIVE

ESTABLISHING REAL HARMONY

ROMANS 14:13

Some of the most gratifying experiences of my life have been working through genuine differences of opinion with others in the church. Once I was privileged to stand by at the reunion of two congregations that had once separated. Although the intervening events were painful, the resolution of these two congregations' differences led to a much stronger witness to their community.

Unfortunately, I have observed congregations splitting over terminology, styles of worship, and evangelism strategies. Pious reasons are given to mask power plays. Romans 14:13 challenges us to rise above such differences to establish a genuine harmony under the lordship of Christ.

Paul called for respect between Christians despite their differences of opinion about food, drink, and the keeping of holy days. Some of these differences came about because new believers, "the weak," still clung to pre-Christian taboos instead of enjoying the freedom of the gospel. The "strong" were those who knew that Christ had freed them from the old customs and emphases.

Mature Christians should respect the sensibilities of new-comers. And all believers should remember that God will one day evaluate their actions. In light of these truths, we should avoid doing anything that might cause a brother in the faith to stumble.

Lord, please help me to exercise my freedom in Christ wisely so that the brethren are encouraged, rather than discouraged, in their faith. Amen.

BUILDING UP OUR NEIGHBOR

Romans 15:1—2

Recently, I visited a mission church aimed at poor immigrants to Dallas. A gifted, bilingual couple were devoting their older years to serving others with both a spiritual and a social ministry. The good news was unashamedly proclaimed. Members were built up through Bible study, English classes, employment, and solutions to immigration problems. The love within the congregation was most apparent.

Similarly, our Lord did not please Himself but accommodated Himself to the ways of His time and the people. He knew that the temple and synagogue worship of His people would one day pass away, yet He observed the feasts and the Sabbath gatherings wherever He was. In this way, He reached out to His people with the good news.

Romans 15:1–2 likewise urges us to be considerate of our less mature brethren for their spiritual growth and edification. Note that the weak described here are those with religious scruples about foods, keeping of holidays, and mode of worship.

Today's Christian customs grow out of not only the Scriptures but also the culture of our forebears, fallible human wisdom, and the fallen nature of the human race. Sadly, this fact leads to dissension and divisions. God grant us grace to accept each other and to build one another up, rather than tear each other down.

Gracious Lord, please help me to join You in
Your building program for others. Amen.

HANDICAP AWARENESS

1 Corinthians 8:13

About 15 years ago, my wife broke her leg the day before she was to read Scripture before a large Christian gathering. After first aid was administered, we were told that she had to ride a wheelchair for the coming week. I became her loving and willing servant to push her to her public duties and private needs. Needless to say, we both got a major lesson in care for the handicapped. We have never been the same since.

What does this have to do with 1 Corinthians 8:13? Paul stated that the Corinthian church had people with weaknesses who were in danger of stumbling. Most of the meat sold in the public market was left over from pagan rites. New converts from paganism were in danger of returning to the offering of meat to idols and thus slipping away from the faith. Strong, mature Christians knew that idols were a figment of the imagination, so they had no qualms about buying and eating such meat. Some new converts, however, believed that such meat was contaminated with evil forces and therefore abstained from it.

How should these opinions live together in one church? Again, love for the other person outweighs one's rights and privileges. The strong dare not offend the sensibilities of the weak. What sensibilities of new Christians do you need to respect?

O Lord, please help me to respect and love the brethren as You do. Amen.

Notes

1. Adapted from *He Had No Revolver* by F. L. Coutts (London: The Bannister Press, n.d.).
2. *The Wichita Eagle,* August 17, 1997.

DAVID McCRACKEN

A Man and His Community: Service

RIGHTEOUSNESS BRINGS PEACE

Romans 5:1

I have always been somewhat overwhelmed by words such as *righteousness* and *holy*. It seemed to me that my sin was overwhelming and that I could never live without fear of being "found out." So aspiring to be righteous was beyond my comprehension until the day I sat in Sunday school and listened to Fred Sunday describe his search of the Scriptures to find divine approval for divorce. He related that he had searched the Bible from cover to cover and could come up with only one conclusion: All divorce is sin. He also said that his search had convinced him that all sin is *forgivable!*

That was the day I finally understood that Christ came to forgive my sin and that in His holiness I could live a righteous life. It's not because of my personal piety or perfection, but because His love allows me to live in His righteousness and therefore without fear of condemnation (Rom. 5:1; 8:1).

As those who accept and follow Christ, we can live without fear, not only the fear of being found out but also the fear of what life or others may bring to us. You see, nothing can separate us from the love of God in Christ Jesus; therefore, we have nothing to fear (Rom. 8:38–39). So I can live throughout this day with the calm assurance that God will be with me in all circumstances and that I can trust His holy presence to strengthen and guide my actions toward His righteousness.

O God, please help me to live in Your
righteousness, unafraid and knowing that You are
beside me in all of my circumstances. Amen.

An Exalted Nation

Proverbs 14:34

Sometimes it is easy to be overwhelmed by the thought of how small and unimportant one person is when contemplating national events. How can my desire to live a holy life before God make any measurable difference in whether my country is a land exalted by righteousness or a sinful reproach to the Creator. Despite my tendency to want to pass off as inconsequential the actions of one person, I must face the reality that my actions today *do* have an effect on the lives of each person with whom I come in contact. If I act with integrity and honesty, I will be part of the force for good in my land (Prov. 14:34).

I can affect for good this land I call home. I am responsible for the actions of my life, and my voice can be used to promote justice. I can join with other Christians in working to improve the lot of the least and the poorest of our brothers and sisters. I can be a friend and advocate for the children of my community, especially those who have the least voice in forming the policies and programs that directly affect their lives. I can pray for the leaders of my nation and community. And I can live this day as one of God's righteous sons because of my faith in Christ.

O God, please help me to find ways to serve
Your cause of justice and righteousness in
this land I love. Amen.

At Home in the Lord

Jeremiah 29:4–7

For the first forty-five years of my life, I spent nearly every Thanksgiving and Christmas at my grandmother's house. During those years, my life went through many changes. I lived many different places, each of which was okay, but my real home was the big old house where Grandmother lived. Then, when I was forty-six, she died. The house was sold and demolished. Today, no evidence remains that it ever existed. I can never go "home" again.

Only now can I relate to the message of Jeremiah to "seek the welfare of the city where I have sent you" (Jer. 29:7). I can determine to be at home in the Lord no matter where I live. Many refugees have left home never to return or see the place of their childhood. Each of us suffers losses and finds that in many ways we are away from home. It is easy to find ourselves in a "foreign" place even in the midst of our work or family.

Finding ways to be at home within the love of God requires intentional time in study and prayer daily. God is the unchanging factor in a world that changes daily. Jeremiah instructed us to go on with our lives in the middle of change, even when we find ourselves in a strange place.

It is easy in a time of estrangement to want to say that this is not my home, that these are not my people, and that I do not belong here. But the assurance that God goes before us and surrounds us with love can help us to feel at home in whatever circumstances we find ourselves. To be at home in the Lord is a blessing that the world cannot give or take away, no matter what the circumstances of our life.

Dear God, please help me always to find my home in You. Amen.

SALTY PEACE
Mark 9:50

Mark 9:50 calls us to have ethical "flavor" in our lives. In other words, we are to be a positive moral influence on the world as well as to live at peace with one another. It is a difficult task to be an individual with definite ideas and strong feelings about life, to live a life of ethical and moral piety, and at the same time to live at peace. Often the divisions and disagreements within the church have been anything but peaceful.

Peaceful behavior is not necessarily milquetoast submission to avoid conflict. At the same time, the divisions within the body of Christ surely must grieve the heart of God. It is never easy to live as "salty" Christians and at the same time avoid the quarrelsome behavior that can come from confronting the differences of opinion as we endeavor to apply the Scriptures as a guide to our daily life.

A minister's wife who offered much guidance to my early life used to say, "We can disagree without being disagreeable!" Today, let us strive to speak the truth in love (Eph. 4:15). Love is never quarrelsome but rather always a force for peace in the world. Any truth we discern must be offered in true humility, for it is a gift from our gracious God.

Lord, please help me to be moral "salt" in a needy world and Your ambassador for peace in the midst of strife. Amen.

LIVE IN PEACE WITH YOUR ENEMIES
Romans 12:17–18

Romans 12:17–18 is hard to practice. This world is not a place where men who try to live in peace with their enemies are rewarded. We want to believe that good comes to those who live rightly and that those who do evil will fail. The Old Testament's call for an eye for an eye seems much more equitable than the New Testament injunction to feed your enemies and offer them hospitality (v. 20). Trusting God is at the heart of Paul's message. To leave all vengeance to the Creator (v. 19) is to trust that God is working for good in all situations, even those that seem so unfair to us.

It is natural for human beings to want justice and therefore to struggle with repaying evil for evil. The old saying "I don't get mad, I get even!" reflects our natural tendency to try to balance the scales when we are mistreated. To live at peace certainly requires us to think about what is noble at all times and in all places.

To leave God's business to Him is to let Him be God instead of acting as if we were God. We are always faced with the temptation to try to be God instead of worshiping and serving the true God. May this word from Romans speak to us daily as we live.

Lord, thank You for this reminder that I am called not to live in judgment but in peace. Amen.

PEACE AND JOY IN THE HOLY SPIRIT

Romans 14:17–19

Romans 14:17–19 reminds us that the kingdom of God is not measured by the world's standards. Food, clothing, and shelter, since they are often the measure of one's monetary wealth, are not the measure of the presence of the kingdom of God in one's life. His rule is always measured by justice and righteousness. Also, where the kingdom of God truly reigns, there is joy. The man who walks with the Lord leads a life of joyous behavior (Neh. 8:10).

An old preacher used to remind me that persons would not likely want to be part of a group of sour-faced Christians. Today, we are reminded that serving Christ is pleasing to God. What a joyful affirmation of our life in Christ to know that our joy, not our possessions, reflect our relationship with the Lord! Joy is a gift from God to those who love Him. This gift cannot be earned or purchased but is freely given by the Father. Our lives, then, must be filled by the pursuit of peace and the building up of one another in love.

Precious Lord, please empower me this day to
live in the joy of the Spirit. Amen.

PEACE WITH ALL

Hebrews 12:12–14

Hebrews 12:12–14 challenges us to use our God-given strength to make a smooth path for those whose lives are more difficult than ours so that they may not stumble. That path must be smoothed by our holy actions, which aim for peace. We cannot be at peace with one another unless we are at peace with God. Peter Marshall reminded the Senate of the United States, "The strength of this nation does not lie in armies or navies, but in the integrity of her people; that peace is born out of righteousness and nothing else."

We must live our lives, not for selfish gain, but for others. Our actions do make a difference in the world. We must model holy actions that will help keep those who follow us from falling. The passage says nothing about "being right" but about righteousness.

It is easy to believe that being correct in our opinions is the same as being right with the Lord.

It comes down to living a prayer life that consistently asks of God, "What would You have me do in this situation?" Or, as some would say, "What would Jesus do?" We cannot live holy lives outside of the power of the Spirit. Therefore, seek to live this day in peace with all people.

O God, help me this day to be a minister of mercy and an ambassador of kindness for You to others. Amen.

CURTIS MILLER

A Man and His Time: Priorities

THE FIRST PRIORITY OF TIME
Matthew 22:36– 38

Men are "people of the clock." It matters little whether we are talking about the clock on the mantle, the clock on our wrist, the biological clock, or our spiritual clocks. We like order; we like schedules; and we like to know when it is time to work, time to play, time to be at home, time to be with our child, grandchild, or those we enjoy the most in life. We also like a clear understanding of what are the most important activities of each day, so that we can spend our best energies and the best of ourselves on those tasks or relationships that are most important.

Matthew 22:36–38 is the familiar account of the Pharisees testing Jesus with the question, "Which is the greatest commandment?" or "What is the first priority for men of faith?" They obviously were expecting Him to speak against one of the hundreds of laws that governed life in Israel. Then they could attack Jesus for ignoring the other commandments of God.

However, Christ saw the treachery of His opponents. He said that the first priority for the man of faith is to use one's time to show unconditional love for others. The Savior quoted Deuteronomy 6:5: "You shall love the Lord your God with all your heart, and with all your soul, and with all your mind."

The first step for any man of faith begins with loving God. Here we find not only empowerment for life but also purpose, direction, and the grace necessary to prepare us to live daily as men of God. For many men, identity comes from their work, but Jesus says that such is not true identity. That comes only when we love God, and then, in that love, find who we are, whose we are, and what we are to be about.

Loving God, then, is the first commandment, the first priority for our time. The spiritual clock begins ticking when we give ourselves to God, and from that point the rest of our time begins to move forward. Loving Him wholeheartedly is the beginning of life and the foundation upon which everything else is built.

Gracious God, please let my love for You be the first priority of my time. Amen.

DAY TWO

KEEPING THE COMMANDMENTS
John 14:15

Several years ago, a cartoon in *The New Yorker* depicted an American couple dashing up the steps of the Louvre in Paris shouting, "Where's the Mona Lisa? We're double-parked!" So often we men approach faith in this same hurry. We know that it is important, but we just don't have time to spend on it, so we make our dash at faith as if we are double-parked.

As a young boy, I learned that if I could not devote myself to a task or a project, I had to be honest, say "I cannot do it," and leave it undone. The choice for many men is to give no attention or only a little attention to anything that lies outside of what they consider to be the immediate needs for survival or success as defined by their culture.

But what happens when our first priority becomes loving God? Is a little love better than no love? Does our hurry through life make us approach God saying, "This is all I can give for now, so You'll have to be happy with it, and I'll get back to You later." Is this acceptable to God?

In John 14:15, Jesus stated that seeing ourselves as workers, members of civic organizations, husbands, fathers, and even church members is secondary to loving God and keeping His commandments. When our priorities are set in this order, we are empowered to do all other things. But without first loving God and keeping His commandments, we are left with only our own limited powers and energies, which will keep us in a hurry and throw our lives in turmoil.

Great God of life, please keep me focused on loving You and keeping Your commandments. Amen.

THE SECOND PRIORITY

Matthew 22:39

As an avid golfer, I learned quickly that if I loved the game, I wanted to play well, and that to play well I had to know and follow certain rules: keep your left arm straight; take the club away from the ball slowly; keep your eye on the ball, but never move your head, except as your shoulders turn it after impact; keep your lower body "quiet;" etc. Because I loved golf, I wanted to learn as much as possible and incorporate what I had learned as a natural part of how I played. I must add that I still have much to learn, but I have not quit even though I don't do everything perfectly.

Although the life of faith is not a game, some of the same disciplines of golf still apply. In Matthew 22:39, Jesus said, "The second commandment is like it, 'you shall love your neighbor as yourself.'" This is one of the foremost rules for faith.

If we love God, we will be true men of faith. Our love for God dictates that we also show love to others, which leads us to be faithful and supportive husbands. We will likewise be responsible fathers. Furthermore, we will help others become the best people they can become. Moreover, we will accept as our primary vocation being the servants of God. In all, we will love and take care of others as we would take care of ourselves.

At times, keeping the commandments of Jesus might be enjoyable, maybe even fun. But on other occasions, it will be difficult, for it means loving those who are hard to love, laboring in unfamiliar surroundings, and, on occasion, taking great risks. We are trusting that Christ will stand beside us in performing God's labors of love.

Whether we live in the cities or the farmlands or in apartments or homes, and whether we wear suits and ties or jeans and T-shirts, God has called us to love Christ and to keep His commandments. The challenge is not to waste our time and to be about loving God and loving our neighbors.

Glorious Lord, please help me to be bold in my service and gentle in my relationships so that I might reflect Your presence here and now. Amen.

ETERNAL REST FOR THE SOUL
Hebrews 4:9

Men have been accused of never being able to stop working. When we get lost on a trip, we won't ask for directions but rather will attempt to work our way back to the correct route. When a problem arises, we strive to resolve it. When we have an argument, a disagreement, or some other form of conflict, we seek to make peace and restore harmony. Sometimes we work so much that we exhaust both our physical and our spiritual energies. Yet we fail to know when it is time to disengage from a matter.

The solution is to find our eternal rest in Christ (Heb. 4:9). Jesus invites *all* people to come to Him in faith and find such rest (Matt. 11:28–30). It is the invitation to trust and to find relief from the demands of life. He quietly encourages us to be inseparably joined with God—the God through whom all things are possible—and then learn from Him what it means to be a man of faith.

Paul Tillich once wrote that Jesus was the perfect man because He presented to the world a perfectly clear window on God. Jesus' love was God's love. His wisdom was God's wisdom. Christ's justice was God's justice. His total life was the working of God. So it can be for us. We need to let God work through us, and in doing so we will find eternal rest for our soul.

Ever-caring God, please remove my busyness and help me to find eternal rest in Your Son. Amen.

WHO IS YOUR GOD?
Ecclesiastes 5:12

I once heard a pastor comment that people today are as much idolaters as were the people of the Old Testament period. What makes it worse today is that they do not know that they are guilty of idolatry. Here's the crucial question: Before what altar do you worship? Is it money? Is it position? Is it sex, alcohol, drugs, materialism, success, or anything else than God? If it is, you are bowing before a pagan deity.

Ecclesiastes 5:12 is instructive. Solomon certainly was not talking merely about those who have money and those who do not, for that is too narrow and too small an interpretation of this verse. The laborers are the servants of God, namely, those who use their gifts in loving Him and in loving their neighbors. They can sleep at night in the assurance that they have worked for God and improved the quality of life for others. In contrast, the rich are those who use their gifts to indulge themselves.

The righteous have made God's love real. They have satisfied the hungers of neighbors who hurt and struggle and, in doing so, found peace and rest for themselves. The wicked "rich," on the other hand, have found only indigestion and heartburn in their excess. They live in fear of the thief, the beggar, or anyone who would challenge their position. They worship and are controlled by what they have.

What about you? What is on your altar? Are you controlled by God or the idols of the world?

Dear Lord, please give me the wisdom and grace to worship and serve only You. Amen.

DAY SIX

WITH WINGS LIKE EAGLES
Isaiah 40:29–31

God has a purpose for Christian men! This statement comes as no surprise to those of us who have made loving God and our neighbors our foremost priority and who know that all the time of life belongs to Him. Such loving requires a listening ear, a giving spirit, and a desire for the best in life for others, even as we offer our best to God. Men of God are His servants. They are also ambassadors for Christ. They are reflections or channels of God's love for all people.

To be men of God means to live life to the fullest, but it also means hard work. Isaiah 40:29–31 reflects an awareness of this truth. Following are some principles from this passage that are worth considering.

First, God does not expect you to do by yourself what only He can do by working through you. The Lord gives the energy, power, and tools you need to do your God-given tasks. Second, even the young and energetic will become exhausted if they try to serve

God in their own strength rather than in His power. Third, through all the difficulties of life, God renews the energy of the faithful. He grants men and women of faith new strength so that they can fulfill their call to service.

God loves you! That is the good news of faith. And God can use imperfect people like us to do great things for Him. In those moments when we fail, become weary, or feel discouraged, God will give us the strength to continue to the end.

Great and powerful God, please give me the
strength I need to do Your work. Amen.

TIME TO CHOOSE
Matthew 6:24

Many men today are finding it necessary to work more than one job. The economic demands placed on a family are great, and the larger the family, the greater the demands.

Otis Jones is a pastor, his wife works outside the home, and together they run a small wholesale distributorship. Frank Morgan is a physician, but he also owns several apartment houses that he manages and where he serves as the primary maintenance person. Frank Adams is a social worker, his wife teaches, and he is part-owner and manager of the local movie theater and a recycling center.

These men are bright, ambitious, and successful, but to give their families some "extras," they work several jobs. These men are also finding that some days they are so tired that neither job goes well. They are finding less time and less of themselves to give to their families. They are also finding less joy in life for themselves, even as they are providing more for their families. "More" is quickly becoming "less" for them.

Jesus had seen this happen in the lives of men who tried to serve two masters. Soon they would love one and hate the other or be devoted to one and despise the other because they felt emotionally and physically torn. Jesus clearly stated that it was impossible to serve two masters, especially when one is God and the other is money. Either both will be cheated out of the best the person can offer, or he will "shut down" from the stress and pressure of what he is trying to do.

Matthew 6:24 is still true. At some point, you must choose to be either a man of God or a man of the world. You must choose between the gifts of God and the trinkets of the world, the eternal and the temporal. The choice is yours. What will you decide?

Merciful God, please help me to understand that true success comes in following and serving Your Son. Amen.

HAROLD BRYSON

A Man and His Time: Decisions

CONFRONTED BY A CHOICE

1 Kings 18:21

Long ago, a prophet of the Lord confronted Israel with a choice. King Ahab of Israel had married a woman named Jezebel. She came from a foreign land and worshiped pagan deities. Many Israelites became attracted to the idols that Jezebel venerated, especially the idol to Baal, the supreme fertility god of the Canaanites.

Elijah thought that a confrontation with this idolatry was in order. He assembled the prophets of Baal and the people of Israel on Mount Carmel. Elijah told the spectators that they could not continue serving both Yahweh and Baal. It was time to decide. If Baal was God, follow him, but if the Lord was God, follow Him (1 Kings 18:21). Elijah then challenged the prophets of Baal to ask their god to answer by fire; but nothing happened, for Baal was a powerless and lifeless idol. But when Elijah called for fire from the Lord, it flashed down from heaven.

How does this account relate to you as a Christian man in today's world? Well, we may not serve Baal, but we do have our idols. The world, like Jezebel, brings its gods and goddesses to our attention. We can be attracted to materialism, success, popularity, sinful sexual indulgences, and dozens of other vices. God has given us His Word so that we can make a choice. We are confronted with choosing either the false gods or the true God.

Is this choice a one-time matter? No, idols get into our life continually. Each day we need to choose to serve the Lord and not to give our allegiance to idols. We cannot follow the Lord's way and the world's way at the same time. At the beginning of each day, look for any idol in your life, ask God to remove it, and then devote yourself exclusively to Him.

*Father, please help me to abandon all forms of
idolatry in my life. Amen.*

UNDER CONTINUAL CONSTRUCTION
Philippians 2:13

In 1976, I moved to New Orleans, Louisiana. My work required
that I travel weekly by airplane in and out of the city. On my first
visit to the airport, I discovered construction taking place. Over
the course of the next twenty years, I continued to notice continual
construction. Runways were resurfaced. Concourses were rebuilt.
The terminal building received a face-lift. Parking lots were con-
structed. A parking garage was built. At no time over the last two
decades have I once seen a sign that said, "Completed: No More
Construction!" One of the facts of life about busy airports is that
improvements and changes are always being made.

Do you see the analogy to the Christian life? No man of God has
"arrived" spiritually. He is always "under construction." The work
started the moment you trusted Christ. The Lord immediately moved
into your life and began to change the way you think and act. This
transformation does not come instantly. Rather, it develops over a
long period of time. And it also does not happen by your human
effort alone. Instead, it occurs daily as you allow God to work in you
(Phil 2:12–13).

Do not become frustrated when you look at other Christian
men and notice that they are farther along in their walk with the
Lord. Growing in the grace of Christ is a personal matter between
you and the Savior. Just yield to His control and let Him do His
"reconstruction" work in you!

*Dear Father, please make me more Christ-like today
through Your work of grace in my life. Amen.*

RESISTING TEMPTATION
Matthew 4:4

Have you ever thought about how many decisions are involved
with a simple meal? We frequently ask, "What do I have in the

house to eat? Should I eat a heavy or a light meal? Does this food have a lot of calories? Do I want to eat now or later?"

Jesus had to make a choice about eating. He had gone without food for forty days and forty nights. In other words, He fasted. The Devil tempted Jesus by directing Him to command the stones lying on the ground to become bread. Although Jesus could have done so, He knew that such an act would be using God's power selfishly. Jesus refused to yield to the Devil's enticement. Instead, He declared that people need more than bread for their life. They must feed on the Word of God (Matt. 4:4).

In addition to our daily choices about meals, we have to decide whether we will gratify our sinful desires or glorify God. If we opt for the first choice, we might get some short-term satisfaction, but we will reap long-term disappointment.

At the moment when the enticement to sin feels strongest, giving in to it might seem logical, but it isn't. Remember, Jesus gives you the power to overcome temptation and thus glorify God.

Sovereign Lord, please give me the wisdom and strength to say no to temptation today. Amen.

DAY FOUR

BEING LED BY THE SPIRIT
Matthew 4:1

Every day of our lives the Devil tries to lead us away from God. Such satanic attempts are called temptations. The Devil is a master at creating enticements to sin. He appears at moments of weakness to lure us away from God's will.

How can we win the battle against Satan and his temptations? One expression in Matthew 4:1 helps us to see how we can be victorious: Jesus was led by the Spirit. Although Satan is powerful and influential in getting us to sin, Jesus is more powerful and effective in helping us say *no* to temptations. Jesus, the Son of God, was led by the Spirit. He listened to the Spirit's direction rather than to the Devil's temptations. By relying on the Spirit's power and direction, Christ refused to yield to Satan's enticements.

The Devil uses a variety of snares and tricks to get us to sin. Each such strategy is designed to get us to think more about ourselves and less about God. To imagine that we are immune to temptations is incorrect. Equally erroneous is thinking that we cannot resist Satan's enticements.

The key to victory is to be led by the Spirit. At the moment the Devil attacks, we should rely on the power of God to enable us to resist the pull of our selfish desires. We can also remember how Jesus defeated Satan when the Devil attacked Him. Victory over temptation is never automatic. It comes each time we decide to allow the Spirit to lead us.

> *Heavenly Father, thank You for Your Spirit,*
> *whom You have given so that I might win the*
> *daily battle against the attacks of Satan. Amen.*

DAY FIVE

DECIDING TO PLEASE GOD, NOT PEOPLE
Matthew 4:7

The attempt to please people begins early in our lives. For example, young boys want to get a hit in Little League to please their fathers. In school, students sometimes work hard, not to enhance their education, but simply to please their teachers. Employees often work hard just to appease their boss. And owners might have only one focus—to please their customers.

In Matthew 4:5–7, Jesus faced the decision to be merely a people pleaser. The Devil led the Savior to the highest point of the temple in Jerusalem. Satan proposed that the Son of God leap off the pinnacle to see whether God, in fulfillment of Psalm 91:11–12, would rescue Him from danger. Clearly, the Devil misquoted and misapplied the passage. In fact, he tried to portray God as some sort of cosmic magician who is ready to perform at a person's request. The Devil was also trying to convince Jesus to gain the applause of the people unworthily.

But Christ rebuffed Satan's proposal by quoting Deuteronomy 6:16. Jesus said that it was wrong to presume on God's goodness and grace. If the Savior had done what the Devil suggested, it would be an indication of doubt, not faith in God. Jesus, however, decided to please God by doing what the Father wanted and in the Father's way.

Satan wants you to be merely a people pleaser. You should resist this temptation by remembering that you worship and serve the Lord. The finest compliment God could give would be to say to you, "This is my faithful servant in whom I am well pleased." How do you please God? You do so by trusting and obeying Him.

Heavenly Father, please help me to think
primarily of pleasing You. Amen.

DAY SIX

DO YOU WANT
CONVENIENCE OR COMMITMENT?
Matthew 4:10–11

Is the best way always the easiest way? Sometimes it is, but often it is not. For example, when Israel left Egypt and began journeying toward Canaan, God did not have His people take the easiest route. Instead, the Lord had the nation take a longer, harder way. Why? Because God, in His infinite wisdom, used the Israelites' wilderness experiences to humble and test them.

Satan tried to get Jesus to choose the easiest way to win the world rather than the best way. The Devil took Jesus to the peak of a high mountain and showed Him the nations of the world and all their glory. Satan then pledged that he would give everything in view to the Son of God in exchange for His worship. The Devil said in effect, "Jesus, why not lower Your moral standards, use my quick and easy methods, and You can have the world!"

Thankfully, Jesus chose the best way. He refused to compromise with evil and chose instead to worship the Father. In rejecting the easiest way—the way of convenience—Jesus chose the path of service, suffering, and sacrifice.

Each day we face the choice of convenience or commitment. From Matthew 4:10–11 we learn that the easiest way is not always the best way. God's way is for us to deny ourselves and follow Christ. That might not be the easiest way, but it is certainly the best way for us to live as children of God.

Dear Lord, please help me to choose Your way,
which is always the best way. Amen.

THE BENEFITS OF COMMITMENT

Proverbs 16:3

Webster's New Collegiate Dictionary defines commitment as "a promise or pledge to do something," "the act of doing or performing something." To achieve excellence in work, marriage, or any other endeavor requires commitment. For example, athletes improve their performance because of their commitment to practice. Employees enhance their skills because of their dedication to improve their work. And marriages grow stronger when both partners are committed to making the relationship work.

Proverbs contains many practical instructions that relate to our work, our home life, and our leisure. For example, Solomon instructed us to commit our work to the Lord and then our plans will succeed (16:3). This proverb implies that God is interested in our performing our daily tasks in the best possible way.

How do we commit our work to the Lord? First, we should give our best each day in the workplace. Second, we should be respectful of the people with whom we work. Third, we should make every effort to improve in our job skills.

We must maintain the right perspective about the work we do. We should trust God as if everything we do depended on Him and work as if everything depended on us. In what hot project are you currently involved at work? Have you committed it to the Lord?

Father, please help me to commit my work to You.
Amen.

DONALD ROCK

A Man and His Time: Time Management

GOT A TIME PROBLEM?

Ecclesiastes 3:1

Is there really a time for everything, as Ecclesiastes 3:1 says? When I look at my weekly and monthly calendar of activities, I occasionally wonder. There are so many places to be, meetings to attend, jobs to do, and people to see that there just doesn't seem to be enough time to do everything!

How, then, is it possible for me to accomplish every task that I need to do? I admit that at the beginning of each month my calendar looks doable. Many days and evenings are open to do some of my favorite things. But somehow by the end of that first week those empty spaces have filled up with all sorts of unexpected but urgent activities.

Have you noticed anything conspicuously missing from the two preceding paragraphs? Have I mentioned God anywhere? My problem is that I often don't include Him in my planning. I look at what *I* have to do, not at what God wants me to do in His power and for His glory. When God is the master of my plans, I know that there will be time for me to get things done in their "season."

Dear God, please help me to give control of my plans and my time to You. Amen.

THAT WAS DUMB!
Ephesians 5:15–16

"That was a dumb mistake. I should have known better!" Yes, I say that to myself many times when I discover how foolish I was in doing something the wrong way. I've assembled such things as tricycles, wagons, bicycles, and furniture. It's easy for me to see myself as an "expert" in such tasks. But then I find myself all thumbs in putting together something that's really simple to assemble. It's humbling to realize that if I had only read the directions first, I would have saved myself a lot of time and aggravation.

What's even dumber for us Christian men is to live foolishly. Ephesians 5:15–16 cautions us to be careful how we think and act. Instead of wasting our lives, we should make the most of every opportunity, especially in doing good.

I admit that it's hard to keep my moral standards high and to act wisely when evil is all around. But when I consider the alternatives, I soon realize that God's way is the *only* way to live. As this passage of Scripture teaches, we should use our time to do good whenever we can.

Lord, please help me to avoid wasting my time
on frivolous activities and to do good whenever
I can. Amen.

WHOSE PLANS ARE RIGHT?
Proverbs 19:21

God's plans for me aren't over yet (Prov. 19:21). I look back on my life and see all the things I've done and can only imagine what God has planned for me in the future.

In high school I wanted to be in the engineering field, but I graduated from college in Food Service. From there, I went into retailing, which gave me the opportunity to become more active in my church. I then became a Sunday school teacher and got involved in lay ministry. I was given opportunities to lead congregations in worship while they were seeking a pastor. From that experience,

God led me to seminary and to the church I now serve as an ordained minister.

The question is not whether God has a plan for you. He does! Rather, it's whether you are open to doing His will. His will might not be ordained ministry, but it could involve fixing things, chairing a committee, visiting the sick and shut-ins, or preparing meals for a soup kitchen. Why not take a few moments to listen with your heart for what God has planned for you. Don't be surprised if He directs you in ways you never imagined!

Dear God, please guide me in Your path,
especially as I go about my daily work. Amen.

DAY FOUR

WHO ARE OUTSIDERS?

Colossians 4:5

What did Paul mean when he referred to "outsiders"? The apostle meant unbelievers, that is, those who were not part of the body of Christ (Col. 4:5). Paul urged his readers to be wise in their contacts with non-Christians. In fact, he advised that believers make the most of whatever opportunities they had to share the gospel with the unsaved.

How many unbelievers do you know? Perhaps they might be neighbors or family members. You might have some unsaved acquaintances at work, at the athletic club, or at the grocery store. Regardless of who these individuals might be, all of them need to hear the gospel, and God might want to use you to share it with them.

Perhaps you think that you don't have the time to waste on evangelizing the lost. But is witnessing to unsaved acquaintances really a waste of time? What could be more important than sharing the truth about Christ? What could be a better investment of one's time? So what opportunities might you have to tell the good news to an "outsider" you know?

Lord, please help me to make the most of every
opportunity that You give to share the gospel with
the lost. Amen.

WHOSE TIME IS IT?

2 Peter 3:8–9

When I served in the military, and was going through boot camp, the drill sergeant used a favorite phrase to hurry us to the next training site. He would yell, "You're on your own time!"

I often wondered whose time he thought it really was. It certainly wasn't his or mine, for ultimately all time belongs to God. After all, He created day and night. And even though the Lord is not bound by time, He still remains sovereign over it.

It's easy for me to become impatient with God, especially when He seems to be slow in answering my prayers. Yet 2 Peter 3:8–9 reveals that God is never slow in carrying out His perfect plan. Rather, His timetable for doing things is vastly different from mine.

For example, why has Jesus taken so long to return for His church? Scripture says that He is being patient for our sake. Because God does not want anyone to perish, He is giving them more time to repent of their sins. So, the next time you find yourself wondering why God is not doing something as fast as you'd like, just remember that His perfect patience gives the lost more opportunities to get saved.

Lord, thank You for this reminder from Your Word that when it comes to spiritual matters, I should operate on Your timetable, not my own. Amen.

MAKING THE MOST OF TIME

Psalm 90:12

Young children generally have a poor concept of time. For them, ten minutes can seem like a long wait. And two weeks is impossible to fathom. It's hard for them to figure out why adults seem so controlled by the clock and why certain activities must be performed on certain days.

As we grow older, we discover that childlike concepts of time can lead to a wasting of precious hours, days, weeks, months, and (sad to say) even years. Therefore, we should take Psalm 90:12 to heart. The older we get, the more we realize that life is short and that we should be wise in the use of what little time we have left on earth.

The point is not to worry about time already wasted. Rather, we should evaluate where we are in life and consider what God would have us do in the remaining days He gives us. Once we have an idea about this, we should then think about what small step we can take today toward achieving that purpose. If we follow this plan, we will not only begin making the most of our time but also grow wiser in the proper use of it.

Gracious God, please help me to grow wiser in the proper use of my time. Amen.

VERY MERRY UN-BIRTHDAY TO ME

Ecclesiastes 12:1

News flash! I'm one day older now than I was yesterday. Perhaps you're thinking, "Big deal!" It *is* a big deal to *me*, especially when I total all the days of my life. I remember when my birthdays couldn't come around fast enough. I also remember telling relatives proudly that I was not six years old, but six and a half. For some reason, that made me feel older. Back then I didn't have all the responsibilities I have today. Now I must earn a living, make payments, and so on.

When I'm not wrapped up in my own concerns, I remember how God came to my rescue on many occasions. When I was younger I didn't have the time to give to God. But He didn't forget me. He looked after me and led me back to the right path.

Ecclesiastes 12:1 reminds me to use whatever time I have left on earth to honor God. After all, He has given me life, loving parents, a loving wife, and loving children. Most of all, the Lord has given me a loving Savior, who suffered and died on the cross so that I may have eternal life. Yes, it is time for me to remember my Creator while I'm still able to do so!

Lord, please help me to use whatever strength I have left to honor You. Amen.

A Man and His Time: Leisure

WHERE'S THE SAFETY VALVE?

Exodus 20:8–11

When I was a young man, I worked as a roughneck on an oil-drilling rig in Louisiana. The job was brutal and dangerous. One day we hit a pocket of high-pressure gas and had a blowout. Crude oil blew up through the drill pipe and sprayed all over the rig and the workers. A blowout is dangerous, for a spark can set the oil and gas on fire.

We kept a safety valve handy for just such emergencies. The valve is about two feet long and can withstand 25,000 pounds of pressure. The trick was to position it over the open drill pipe about waist high, screw it into the pipe while oil was spewing out, and then close it off. When the blowout happened, we all began asking, "Where's the safety valve?" We couldn't find it! Everyone ran around on the raised floor of the rig looking for it. Finally someone located it, and we got it on and closed. The blowout was over.

Exodus 20:8–11 tells us about another kind of "safety valve." It's called rest. I call leisure time a "safety valve" because it can keep us from blowing our tops! These verses encourage us to work six days and then take a day off from our labor. A day off is an opportunity for relaxation and recreation. Think of it as time for "re-creation."

Every man needs to be able to slow down, shift gears, and re-charge mentally and physically. The fourth commandment of the Decalogue is not just good theology. It's also good psychology and physiology. We are tempted to brag about how hard we work, but as the proverb says, "All work and no play makes Jack a dull boy."

Lord, please help me to slow down and take time to rest and relax. Amen.

DAY TWO

THE HABIT OF REST

Psalm 55:6

You can hear the weariness in David's soul as he wrote, "O that I had wings like a dove! I would fly away and be at rest" (Psalm 55:6). You probably have had times like that, too. You envision yourself on a deserted island surrounded by nothing but sun and water. Or you see yourself putting on the back nine for weeks at a time. Or you are hunched over your band saw working on your latest project.

Leisure is not just a lazy man's escape. It is a time to refresh the mind and the body. All of us need it. The guy who brags about putting in sixty or seventy hours a week is fooling himself and isn't doing himself any good. We all need time to put ourselves back together after the concerns of our jobs and families seem to pull us apart.

Maybe you have never thought about it this way, but one of the best things you can do for yourself and your family is to make a habit of getting proper rest and nutrition. Day by day, year by year, learn to use leisure as your spiritual "filling station." Then maybe you won't have such a need to run off to a deserted island.

Lord, please give me rest in my leisure time. Amen.

DAY THREE

REST IN GOD

Psalm 116:7

If you are like most Christian men, you don't go to church to rest. Far from it. From the minute you walk through the door until you leave, you may have many duties—teacher, usher, deacon or elder, door closer, and floor sweeper. Even worship may not be restful because the pastor calls on the congregation to get involved in some project or serve in some capacity. By the time you leave, you feel as though you have put in a long, hard day of work.

A friend was a deacon in his church, served on several committees, and directed major plays. He became so busy that he hated to go to church because so many people pulled at him for something when he walked in. He had to give up some of his duties simply to be still and learn to worship again.

The author of Psalm 116:7 praised God for His bounty. Knowing the Lord personally enabled him to say, "Return to your rest, O my soul." Genuine rest and leisure comes to us when we accept our place in God's family and know that He loves us. We don't have to prove anything, and we don't need to act as if we must earn God's approval.

The Lord has dealt bountifully toward you, hasn't He? You have more than you need. According to much of the world's standards, you are practically rich. Thank God for your life, even with all of it trials. Learn to rest in Him. Accept the fact that He loves you and is with you. Don't feel guilty when you engage in some leisure activity (or inactivity). The rhythm of life requires it.

*O Lord, please help me to learn to rest in You
and to accept Your bounty toward me. Amen*

DAY FOUR

GO FISHING
John 21:3

After the crucifixion of Jesus, Peter was at a loss. What should he do? He went back to the one task he knew well—fishing. For him and the other disciples, fishing wasn't a leisure activity—it was their job. But undoubtedly it also gave him time to collect himself and figure out what to do next.

I have been an angler since my youth in Louisiana. For me, fishing is more than hauling in a day's catch. It is a metaphor for life. It is leisure that helps me recreate myself and my thoughts. Whenever I am at a loss as to what to do, I go fishing.

I have also enjoyed teaching my sons to fish. I admit my impatience with them at times, but we generally have fun. Recently, we went fifty miles out into the Gulf of Mexico from Galveston, Texas, to deep-sea fish. My father-in-law also went with us. My son Ryan got seasick and spent much of the day hanging over the rails. But he caught his limit of Red Snapper just as the rest of us did. In all, we had a great time of family fun.

I also enjoy taking my Gibson Tennessean guitar and trying to figure out those wonderful tunes played by Chet Atkins. That, too, has been a life-long interest.

You might not enjoy fishing or guitar playing. Your leisure-time activity might be fixing up that old '57 Chevy in your garage, or bagging your limit of ducks, or following a ball around the golf course. Every man needs a hobby, something to help him unwind, catch his breath, and remember that life is a rhythm of work and play. To lose yourself in some leisure activity is to find yourself for work and other important duties. Learn to play. Go fishing.

Lord, thank You for the activities that help me to unwind and regain my perspective on life. Amen.

A TIME TO LAUGH

Ecclesiastes 3:4

Sometimes we simply need to laugh (Eccl. 3:4). No explanations or apologies are necessary. A friend recently sent me a list of bumper stickers. Here are some of my favorites. Read them, laugh at them, and pass them on!

- All generalizations are false.
- Cover me. I'm changing lanes.
- Forget about World Peace. . . . Visualize using your turn signal.
- We have enough youth. How about a fountain of Smart?
- He who laughs last thinks slowest.
- *Lottery:* A tax on people who are bad at math.
- I love cats. . . . They taste just like chicken.
- Out of my mind. Back in five minutes.
- The more people I meet, the more I like my dog.
- Laugh alone and the world thinks you're an idiot.
- Rehab is for quitters.
- I get enough exercise just pushing my luck.
- Sometimes I wake up grumpy. At other times I let him sleep.
- I didn't fight my way to the top of the food chain to be a vegetarian.
- I took an IQ test and the results were negative.
- OK, who stopped payment on my reality check?
- Few women admit their age. Fewer men act it.
- IRS: We've got what it takes to take what you've got.
- Time is the best teacher. Unfortunately it kills all its students.

- Very funny Scotty. Now beam down my clothes.
- Consciousness: that annoying time between naps.
- i souport publik edekashun.
- Be nice to your kids. They'll choose your nursing home.
- There are three kinds of people: those who can count and those who can't.

Lord, thank You for the gentle leisure of a belly laugh! Amen.

DAY SIX

GOD'S PLACE OF REST
Isaiah 28:12

Ty Cobb was a legendary baseball player. He had a lifetime batting average of .335. He stole 892 bases, made 4,191 hits, scored 2,245 runs, and batted .367 from 1905 until 1928. Cobb had so much going for him. But a sportswriter recently summed him up thus:

> His talents for collecting base hits was equaled only by a perverted genius for alienating people. So to hear Cobb described by his peers as the game's greatest player is a most telling tribute, because most of the encomiasts despised him, usually with evidence in hand, because Ty at one time or another had spiked them, turned them down, slugged them, bedeviled them, insulted them, or otherwise unsettled their digestive tracts.

Two of Cobb's sons, Ty Jr. and Herschel, died before their father. As age caught up with him and forced him to retire as an active player, he became a manager, but he never matched the success he had enjoyed before. At the age of 71, Cobb tried to move back to his old home near Cornelia, Georgia. He wanted to settle down, but he couldn't. He crisscrossed the country several more times searching for peace and happiness, but he never found it. Cobb apparently could not accept life with its family tragedies.

Many men dream of making a living at sports. But we should consider that success is not in having a dream job. It is in learning to love what we do now. Ty Cobb seems to have had it made, but he could not seem to adjust to the ups and downs of life.

Leisure is a gift of God to help us pull aside from the normal burdens of life. Let's not turn our leisure into more work and stress. Relax. Enjoy. Accept from God what He offers (Isa. 28:12).

Lord, please help me to use my leisure time for unstressful activities that I love doing. Amen.

ULTIMATE RETIREMENT
Revelation 14:13

I read about a lady who began investing in the stock market in 1944 and kept doing so until her death at age 101 in 1995. She built a portfolio worth $22 million! But she lived a loveless, shallow life. Someone who knew her said "a big day for her was walking down to Merrill Lynch to visit her stock certificates." She seems to have lived a wasted life because close relationships with others and love for God were lacking.

I want to spend my life doing something more than chasing sheets of paper, whether dollars or stock certificates. I also want to accept God's promise of being with Him forever. Don't you? I sometimes tell people, "I'm a pastor. The pay is not so hot, but we have a great retirement plan!"

Ultimately, we will all sit down to a large banquet of consequences. The table will be set with our deeds and garnished with our attitudes. Revelation 14:13 reminds us that those who have trusted in Christ need not fear death or judgment. We have the promise of the ultimate retirement system—we will be with God for eternity! Those who know Christ will "rest from their labors for their deeds follow with them."

Leisure is not wasting time. It is resting in the present and preparing for eternity. Someday our life on the earth will end. Faith tells us never to fear death. It is the gateway into the presence of God. That is the ultimate retirement plan, a time when we "rest from our labors."

Lord, I look forward to the day when I can be with You forever. Amen.

TERRY ETTER

A Man and His Emotions: Anger

WHEN GRIEF SHOULD LEAD TO ANGER

Mark 3:1–5

The anger Jesus expressed in Mark 3:1–5 is linked with the word translated "grieved." Jesus was deeply disturbed by the hard hearts of the religious leaders. He was also saddened by the fact that they thought the way to gain God's favor was through conformity to the law. This deception created an emphasis on legalism, which bred arrogance, a sin that God despises.

Read this passage again slowly. What do you notice there? Do you see anything that would lead you to grieve over the plight of others?

Anger in response to a God-discerned understanding of injustice or tied to grief over the human condition is not a destructive emotion. When one becomes angry at what divorce, crime, abortion, abuse, and drugs are doing to our culture and people, he develops a compassion and perspective to do something beyond passive acknowledgment. God wants us to be grieved about those things that deeply disturb Him. In some ways, we are a culture that is not angry enough!

*Father, please create within me a deeper
awareness of what grieves You so that I might
bring passion to my understanding, action to my
rhetoric, and courage to counter my passivity.
Amen.*

211

ANGER AND RELATIONAL CHAOS
James 1:19

One of the challenges of our Christian journey is to have consistency between our talk and our walk. As James 1:19 declares, I am to be slow to anger and slow to speak. But am I, in reality, able to do that? The answer is both "yes" and "no." Although I have been redeemed through the blood of Jesus, I nevertheless groan with the tension of living between the realities of the present and future worlds (see Rom. 8:22–23).

In my spiritual walk, the most challenging application of James 1:19 is in my relationship with my wife and teenage daughters. How often I've wished that I hadn't said what I said or brought condemnation into a situation requiring grace.

Perspective is lost when one experiences uncertainty, powerlessness, and fear. Anger is often the destructive and damaging expression of my own insecurity and immaturity in a matter or a relationship. Only as I am in deliberate daily communion with the living Christ can I keep perspective and overcome my insecurities about roles and relationships.

*Lord, please forgive me for the relational
wounds I have inflicted, usually upon the ones
I love the most. Amen.*

ANGER'S MIRROR IMAGE—MYSELF
Proverbs 14:29

I was driving to my favorite thinking and writing place to begin working on this devotional when I came upon a slow driver who was "camped" in the left-hand passing lane. Because I was on my way to write about a spiritual discipline, I was sensitive enough to keep my impatience with the slow driver in check. Suddenly, a large car filled with four young men whipped around us both, and the driver gave the slow driver in front of me the universal salute to express his disdain.

After passing, the young driver had to break hard and slow down immediately to negotiate a turn into a gas station. His impatience and speeding was pointless. I immediately had two reactions. The first reaction was anger. The second reaction was to think that I needed to be the one to reprimand those guys about their poor judgment and rude behavior.

Do you have the same problem as I do? I'm angry over how easily angered people get. Actually, I am appalled and deeply concerned by the low flash point of emotions and the lack of civility many people display toward others. The irony is that I was ready to go after those guys myself. Although they were wrong, the fact is that I often exhibit the same lack of civility in my own behavior. I've just learned to be a bit more sophisticated (Prov. 14:19).

Lord, help me to replace my anger and sense of indignation with compassion and intercession for the person or persons causing my response. Amen.

DAY FOUR

ANGER EQUALS VULNERABILITY
Matthew 5:22

When I used to fly fighter planes in the Air Force, we practiced a four-ship formation called "fluid four." Each element could easily watch out for the others. Everything we did reinforced the concept of interdependence and mutual protection. We would literally give up our lives for our colleagues.

Matthew 5:22 says that being angry at a brother makes us guilty. What is the effect of anger toward a brother? At least one effect is that we act toward him as if we don't care what happens to him. We withdraw our attention, affection, and protection.

In many instances, we men relate to our Christian brothers as if we *are* angry with them, even though we would never describe ourselves as angry. The result is the same. We withdraw our interest and our coverage, and they become vulnerable. Instead of "elements" providing 360 degrees of coverage, we become more like single-ship formations passing each other at random angles. This is why the growing men's small groups and accountability groups are so important.

Lord, please help me to become part of a small group and to be more of a loving and caring brother to others. Amen.

ANGER—A FORM OF ARROGANCE

Proverbs 16:32

In my own life, anger has primarily manifested itself as a reflection of two conditions—fear and unmet expectations. It is a feeling of loss of power and control. As I have reflected on the role of anger in my life, I've discovered that anger can be and often is a form of arrogance.

Over the past thirty years, I have traveled and done many things. Many of the positions I've held and the things I've done have unwittingly contributed to a sense of power, entitlement, and self-importance. When circumstances didn't go my way, I felt not only frustration but also anger. God has been dealing with me, sometimes gently and sometimes not, about these feelings.

Have you ever considered that the source of your anger is really arrogance? You can express anger in so many ways, but ultimately anger says that you are better than someone else. Does it mean that there aren't appropriate times to express anger? No, at times Jesus Himself expressed anger. But when our anger demeans others and creates chaos, we need to repent of it (Prov. 16:32).

Lord, please help me to submit my anger
to Your redeeming love. Amen.

ANGER'S PRODUCT—CHAOS

Proverbs 15:18

I was a teenager in the late 1950s to the mid-1960s. In that era, my father was the undisputed authority. Deference and compliance are terms that come to mind when I think of him. Imagine my shock when I became a father in the 1990s and my example of fathering didn't seem to work. Terms such as *deference* and *compliance* are more descriptive of Golden Retrievers than teenagers. In my frustration, I became a hot-tempered man. My anger toward what I perceived to be my children's lack of respect and rebellion created complete chaos in our family (Prov. 15:18).

That season in our family is past and by God's mercy we are intact, but I look back on that period with great contrition, regret, and humility. Once again, I experienced how, when my need for control gets undermined, I default to anger.

The valuable lesson I learned is that although I love my children very much, God loves them even more. And as they grow into young adults, I cannot manage all of their choices and behaviors. My posture now is to back off, speak truth in love, affirm them, and love them as unconditionally as I am able by God's grace.

Guess what? The contention is gone, and my girls are turning out great! Even better, they are growing to communicate and express affection toward their dad. But, more importantly, they are drawing closer to their heavenly Father.

*Lord, please make me slow to anger and quick
to ask forgiveness when I lose my temper.
And let the predisposition of my heart be to
affirm and praise my family. Amen.*

Anger As a Cultural Strategy
Ecclesiastes 7:9

Many people have developed the idea that to produce results one has to exhibit outrage. It's the "squeaky-wheel-that-gets-the-grease" syndrome. Anger has become a strategy. All you have to do is drive around or go to an auto service counter or customer service center to see the strategy in use.

Throughout Scripture are countless illustrations that God's ways are not our ways. As Christian men, we are continually confronted with the need to be positive influences of our culture rather than negative examples of it. We cannot allow anger to become part of our strategy to get things done, for God says that anger resides in the bosom of fools (Eccl. 7:9).

Increasingly, we live in a world where exasperation and unmet expectations are becoming the norm. Servers in restaurants aren't quick enough, poor-quality merchandise falls apart, electricity goes out, and aging parents or sick kids cause cancellation of plans. These situations lead to exasperation. We have developed a predisposition toward anger. We need to repent of it and find our peace and contentment through gaining a godly perspective toward all things.

*Lord, please help me to understand that a
gentle tongue can turn away wrath. Amen.*

ED SCOTT

A Man and His Emotions: Loneliness

LIKE THE PLAGUE!

Psalm 38:11

Have you ever heard the expression "They avoid me like the plague"? It must have its roots in Psalm 38:11! David said, "my friends stand aloof from my sore." The word rendered "sore" was used by the Hebrews to describe leprosy. David was saying that his friends avoid him as if he had leprosy!

But in this case, a good reason existed for this separation between David and his friends. David confessed that he had separated himself from God through the sin in his life. He talked of "sin," "iniquities," and "foolishness." He had moved his life in the wrong direction, and it had affected not only his relationship with God but also his relationships with godly friends. Perhaps they should have been able to do a better job of encouraging him to make things right, but David admitted that *he* was the main problem!

Although we might experience lonely times in our lives, we need to ensure that they are not the loneliness of sin. Transgression interrupts our fellowship with both God and our Christian friends. And that is simply too high a price to pay for the temporary pleasures of sin. We always need our communion with God, and we always need the support of our Christian friends. We can't afford to move away from that kind of joy!

Heavenly Father, please help me to recognize any sinful attitude or pattern in my life, and show me what You want changed. Amen.

THE MOST MISERABLE MAN

Luke 16:20–21

There may never have been a person more miserable than Lazarus. He was crippled, reduced to begging, and physically tortured by a condition that left him "full of sores." Every day he begged at the gate of a rich man for only the crumbs from his table, but Lazarus did not get even those. And as if things weren't bad enough, the Bible says that the dogs came and licked his sores. Lazarus apparently was not even able to beat off the stray dogs in the street (Luke 16:20–21).

This is an incredible description of a lonely and forsaken man, and it is a description that we may never fully understand. But we certainly should respond to it! We can ensure that this kind of loneliness never happens to anybody we know. For example, we can get involved in meeting the needs of the poor, the homeless, and the struggling.

In the process, something unexpected might happen. While we are meeting the needs of the lonely, the problem of our own loneliness will be met without our even knowing it. We will simply recognize one day that our lives have been made full because we were willing to give in the name of Jesus!

Lord, please show me how I can begin meeting the needs of others and thereby watch my life become spiritually enriched. Amen.

DOWN TIME

John 5:1–9

The account of the lame man at the pool of Bethesda (John 5:1–9) gives us an opportunity to think about the loneliness of downtime. Do you know what I mean by that? Men are accustomed to being on the job and around coworkers. We seem to thrive on that. But when we are sick, we are isolated and cut off from the busyness that we enjoy. Men are generally "doing" creatures, and downtime frustrates us.

But down time can be a learning experience. It has become a common testimony that Christian men laid up in bed with seemingly nothing to do recognize the opportunity they have to fellowship with God. Men who have been too busy for personal devotions imagine God asking them, "*Now* do you have time for Me?"

The next time you are sick, or the next time you are off work because of the weather (or for whatever other reason), you may be able to reenergize your devotional life with God. But why wait for downtime? You could start doing that today. Simply plan the time, pick the place, and start giving God a piece of your day!

Dear God, please help me to nail down a piece of my day for You. Amen.

THREE LONELY BIRDS
Psalm 102:6–7

You know you are in trouble when you think about birds and it makes you feel alone! The psalmist said there were days when he felt like "a pelican in the wilderness, an owl in the desert, and a sparrow alone on a housetop" (Ps. 102:6–7). He was feeling that way because he was surrounded by trouble.

But one truth gave the psalmist encouragement. He realized that God was greater than whatever problems he had. In verse 8, he spoke about enemies rising up against him, but in verse 13 he was able to speak about God rising up triumphantly. In verse 9, he spoke about eating ashes for bread, but in verse 14 he was able to say that the servants of God love even the dust on the streets of heaven. Near the end of the psalm, in verse 26, the writer said that the enemies of God would perish, "but You will endure."

Knowing that God will always be sovereign was the confidence that the psalmist needed to get through these disasters. It was the only truth in his life greater than his loneliness and frustration. With that confidence, he knew that God would somehow bring him through every problem. Can you believe that for yourself?

Lord, thank You for the way in which You continually help me through times of loneliness and frustration. Amen.

A COSTLY STAND
2 Timothy 4:16

Taking a stand for God is costly. When Paul preached the gospel without hesitation, it landed him in court—not for a lawsuit but in a trial for his life! And as if that wasn't bad enough, Paul reported that he was completely alone at his first hearing (2 Tim. 4:16). No friend would even come and stand with him!

We may never see that kind of persecution or feel that kind of loneliness. But it's possible that we will get a taste of it. Our reputations could be slandered because of our faith; promotions could be lost; and neighbors might turn their backs on us.

What will our reaction be if those things happen? Paul prayed that God would not be angry with those who deserted him. Even in hard and lonely times, will we be able to rise to that level of trust in God?

It's not just our own souls that are at stake in our response (although that would be enough reason to trust God); the souls around us are also at stake. As long as we are alive, the world will watch us. So even when we are in trouble, even for our faith in Christ, we need to be godly in our actions.

Lord, regardless of what might happen to me,
please help me to continue to trust in You and
remain godly in my actions. Amen.

HE'S BEEN THERE
Mark 14:48–50

You hardly go a day anymore without hearing someone say, "Been there, done that!" Such a comment in conversation is more of a complaint about not having anything new to do, but in the case of Mark 14:48–50, it is a refreshing reminder.

The Son of God did not deserve to be left alone, especially since He had done so much for others. He did not deserve to be apprehended like a thief when He had spoken plainly in the temple. It was unfair. But it still happened.

The soldiers came and the disciples fled. In a way, we can understand the soldiers being misguided, but the fleeing of the disciples hurts. Their leaving is an everlasting monument to the weakness of humanity.

So whenever we find ourselves alone, especially through the neglect and weakness of others, we know one truth—Jesus has been there. He does, in fact, know just how we feel. And so one of the most important things we can do as we pray is to be honest with Him about our loneliness. Jesus has been down this road before. If we ask Him, He will walk down it again with us.

Dear Lord, please walk with me as I journey down a lonely path. Amen.

DAY SEVEN

NEVER ALONE
John 16:32

A Christian man may feel lonely, but he is never really alone. Jesus made that clear on the last night of His life as He spoke with His disciples (John 16:32). And His statement is especially remarkable, because He knew everything that was coming! He knew the disciples would not be strong enough to stand with Him. And He knew that He would be alone in His trial before the authorities.

But despite the loneliness, Jesus said that He could keep on going. The reason was simple. He was not really alone, for God the Father was with Him! What Jesus did in this case was to see the unseen. Of course, that is not often regarded as a practical skill, and men may struggle with that idea. We are so practical! But it is a habit that we need to cultivate, for the unseen (the spiritual) is the most real part of life.

Don't neglect or disregard the spiritual dimension of your life. God can supply you with a level of strength, courage, and confidence that is infinitely beyond the little you can summon yourself.

Lord, please supply the guidance and the strength that I need in my time of difficulty. Amen.

AL SAUNDERS

A Man and His Emotions: Despair

BEING A FOOTBALL
Job 17:11–16

Have you ever felt as if life's a football game and you're the football? I'm sure you have! In fact, probably more than once. When you feel this way, it's a sure sign that you have lost your perspective on things. Perhaps, as was the case with Job, some cherished dreams and plans that you had have crumbled at your feet.

Here was Job, a wealthy man with a spotless reputation, a wonderful family, and a large flourishing livestock business. He was highly respected and admired. Suddenly, in a matter of hours, everything he had was wiped out in a series of catastrophes. On top of this, Job lost his health. Then his wife, probably as a response to seeing him suffer so much, encouraged him to curse God and die.

Job's best friends tried to load him with guilt and badger him to confess what he supposedly had done wrong to bring this tragedy on himself. Their philosophy seemed to be that his misfortune was due to some secret sins in his life. In the midst of all this, Job began to lose his perspective, and despair quickly set in (Job 17:11–16).

When this situation happens to you, it's an indication that you are no longer walking by faith but rather by sight. When you start feeling as if life's a football game and you're the football, realize that you have lost your spiritual perspective and ask God to restore it by helping you to refocus on Him and His blessings.

Dear Lord, please help me to see my life from
Your perspective. Amen.

LESSONS FROM PAIN

Jonah 4:8

Jonah's pain was a result of his bad decisions and attitudes (Jonah 4:8). Inevitably, when we consistently insist on exerting our will over God's will, we get ourselves into difficulty. We need to understand, however, that God did not intend Jonah's difficulty to punish him for his disobedience. Rather, it was God's way of getting his attention so that He could steer Jonah onto the right track again.

When life seems to be going wrong, and you find yourself in a state of despair and enjoying a good pity party, it's time to call a halt to your actions and ask God to give you insight into what's happening. James 1:2–5 says that when trials settle in on us, we should ask God for wisdom in how to handle the ordeal.

Ask God to show you the cause of your pain. Is it deserved or undeserved? What can you learn from it? What do you need to do to grow through this experience? What changes do you need to make in your attitude or lifestyle?

Dear Lord, please help me to view every
experience in my life as an opportunity to grow
into the man You want me to become. Amen.

FORSAKEN?

Hebrews 13:5

It was June of 1993. I had just resigned from the staff of a large church where I had been director of the family ministry and counseling center, director of Christian education, and director of music and worship. The reason for my resignation was burnout and related health problems.

I decided to take a two month sabbatical before hopefully continuing in ministry. Morning after morning I sat on my porch with my cup of coffee and my Bible. Initially, I felt despair. I felt that God had forsaken me. I had been in the ministry thirty years. Was this the payback for all those years of faithful ministry? Was I through?

No, God hadn't forsaken me! I had just taken on more than He expected and run through too many doctor's red warning lights. God allowed me to crash in a heap to refashion, refocus, and redirect me in ministry.

Remember, God has promised never to fail or forsake you (Heb. 13:5). Do you think God has failed you? Are you feeling forsaken by Him? Perhaps it's time to step back a bit and let Him give you His perspective on your life and activities.

Lord, thank You that You have promised never to fail and forsake me. Please help me never to lose sight of this fact. Amen.

DAY FOUR

DISAPPOINTED
Luke 24:17

Have you ever felt let down, abandoned, or confused because you really believed something or someone was the answer but it never turned out the way you imagined it would? Such was the case for the two men on the road to Emmaus.

The depth of the despair that the two disciples felt was written all over their faces. It usually is! Note the words, "their faces downcast" (Luke 24:17). As they shuffled along, they had been rehearsing the events of the past few days surrounding the crucifixion of Jesus. They were so downcast that when Jesus joined them, they never even recognized Him.

If you find yourself confused about the way certain situations seem to be unfolding in your life, you need to redirect your attention to Jesus. You see things only from the perspective of the present, but He sees the big picture. So place your trust in Him!

Dear Lord, please help me to place my trust completely in You and allow You to work things according to Your divine plan and purpose for my life. Amen.

DAY FIVE

WHERE WILL YOU GO?
Ephesians 2:11–12

"If God allows this to happen, then that's it; I'm leaving church and God!"

During the past thirty-five years in ministry, I've heard such statements many times. My immediate response is, "Where are you going to go?"

We forget too quickly from where the Lord has brought us. Usually such an expression comes when our comfort zone has been invaded. God never promised that the Christian life would be a bed of roses. He never promised that we wouldn't have hardships or challenges along the way. However, He did promise that He would not allow us to be tested beyond that which we were able to endure, but would, along with the trial, provide a way of escape (1 Cor. 10:13). *He* is that way of escape.

In Ephesians 2:11–12, Paul reminded his readers from where they had come and where they were now in Christ. Formerly they were separated from Christ, excluded from divine citizenship, exempt from God's covenants and promises, without hope, and without God. Now through faith in Christ, even though there were hardships and persecutions, they had Jesus as their Lord, they were citizens of heaven, they were included in the divine covenants and promises, and they had hope in God.

Take a moment right now and reflect on where God has brought you. Then thank Him for His love and faithfulness!

Dear Lord, please help me to remember where
I have come from and all of the heavenly riches I
now have in You. Amen.

DAY SIX

LIFE'S LOSSES
1 Thessalonians 4:13

Losing a loved one through death is one of the realities of life that can cause us to despair. Whether the death was sudden and unexpected or the culmination of a long period of illness, we are never totally prepared for it.

The death of a loved one, as any major crisis, usually takes eighteen months to two years for us to work through. Although believers do not sorrow as those who have no hope (1 Thess. 4:13), we still do sorrow when our loved ones pass away. This grieving is normal and acceptable. In the midst of our grief, however, it's comforting to know that we will one day be reunited with all of God's people.

Some people struggle with thoughts about the unfairness of life, especially if the loved one who died was young. Other people may become angry with God for taking that loved one away from them. Unless these feelings are dealt with honestly, depression can result. Recognize that all these feelings are normal, acknowledge them, and then seek help to deal with them in a practical and scriptural way. Find someone with whom you can talk freely about your pain, and go to God with it as often as necessary.

Dear Lord, I bring my pain of loss to You right now, knowing that You understand what I'm experiencing. In this time of sorrow, please console me with Your presence and love. Amen.

DAY SEVEN

DEATH WISH
Job 10:1

Sometimes the pain of life gets so great that we may even despair of life itself. In such situations, even Christians may have a death wish.

The Bible records a number of instances in which people of God expressed a death wish. Job 10:1 is an example. In 1 Kings 19:4, we also see the great prophet Elijah expressing a death wish. The stress and pressures got so great that he slipped into a state of despair and begged God to end his life.

God's treatment plan for Elijah is still being used today. Notice what He did for the prophet. He relieved him temporarily of his responsibilities, rested him, fed him, counseled him spiritually and psychologically, and then restored him to ministry.

This plan of God is not only good when you have reached the end of the proverbial rope but also for preventative maintenance.

If you are feeling right now like either Job or Elijah, maybe it's time to step aside for some rest, relaxation, and counseling. That counseling may or may not need to be with a professional. You might just need to share your feelings with your wife, pastor, or some other trusted friend. Of course, be sure to take your feelings to God, just as Job and Elijah did.

Dear Lord, please help me in my time of despair. Amen.

C.W. FOGLEMAN

A Man and His Emotions: Joy

REFRESHING WATER
Isaiah 12:1–6

The farm on which I grew up in central Louisiana had no electricity until I was practically grown. When we needed water, someone had to draw it from the well that had been drilled in the yard. That task often was mine, but when I was thirsty, it was a treat to draw the cool, clear water from the well to quench my thirst.

Isaiah 12:1–6 praises Yahweh for His salvation, forgiveness, and comforting presence in the midst of His people. Verse 3 is special to me because it speaks of the endless joy the believer may experience "out of the wells of salvation." Unlike water wells, the source of our salvation doesn't become polluted and dangerous, it can never be made unacceptable by bad taste, and it never runs dry.

Just as our physical bodies require water for survival, our spirits require "water out of the wells of salvation" for both life now and assurance of eternal life. No man can rightfully claim that he holds exclusive "water rights" to the life-giving water of salvation, for Jesus is available to any and all who will trust in Him as Savior. You have reason to rejoice, for this wonderful gift doesn't diminish, even when it is shared among a vast throng of people!

Lord, thank You for the availability and the abundance of Your refreshing salvation in Christ. Amen.

DO YOU AGREE?

AMOS 3:3

Several of my grandchildren were playing a game on the living room floor when they became louder and louder in their arguments. I asked what seemed to be the problem. Several of them pointed to one of the older girls and said, "She keeps changing the rules!" When I suggested that they take a few minutes to read the rules and work out how they would play the game, they did so. The noise level dropped significantly, and the children began to laugh as they played.

In a time of rapid change, such as we are experiencing today, we should not be surprise that difficulties occur in the interaction of persons in all sorts of groups, including the family and the church. It is more difficult, but no less important, than it has ever been for people to give attention to achieving a common understanding of the norms and expectations that are brought into interpersonal behavior (see Amos 3:3). When we adults agree on the norms (rules) for interaction in any situation, we are likely to achieve greater success and find increased satisfaction in our tasks.

A common love for Jesus and His church will be an effective means of building "ties that bind." It is a foretaste of the "joy and gladness" (mentioned Isaiah 35:10) of not only the return of Jews from Babylonian captivity but also Christian families, friends, and churches, especially as we await the return of our Lord.

Lord, please help me to do whatever I can to be as agreeable to others as possible. Amen.

TRUE JOY

Nehemiah 8:1, 8–10.

When we see the winners of a hard-fought game celebrate with exuberance, we understand and are happy for them. This, in a small way, demonstrates what happened when ancient Judah was successful in overcoming opposition from without and corruption from within. Nehemiah had led exiles back to Jerusalem from Babylon, where their parents had been carried captive about four decades earlier.

The Jews established their defenses and then attended to ensuring that the corruption that had brought about the defeat of their parents' generation was not repeated. Then, in the public reading of the law of Moses, the leaders reestablished the worship and commitment that was the basis for their existence (Nehemiah 8). They encouraged the people to enjoy the renewal that came as a result of their repentance and rededication to the God of their ancestors.

The Bible says that there is joy in heaven when a sinner turns to Christ in faith (Luke 15:7). Being right with God is reason enough to "shout" with joy.

Lord, thank You for enabling me to get right with You through faith in Your Son. Amen.

DAY FOUR

THIS IS THE DAY

Psalm 30:5

One of the most rewarding abilities one can develop is the ability to let go of negative feelings, to learn not to nurse grudges or to give in to lasting grief. Psalm 30:5 extols each of these virtues.

My father-in-law, who lived to be 103, loved to quote Psalm 118:24: "This is the day which the Lord has made; we will rejoice and be glad in it." (But he consistently said, "This is *a* day.") He did not believe in starting a day with a load of negatives from the day before.

God will forgive our sins when we ask Him to do so, and He will respond favorably to our prayers when we pray for others who need His forgiveness in Christ. The Lord will help us treasure the good and lasting blessings that come from our relationships with others and, simultaneously, enable us to realize that we are not responsible for the failures and shortcomings of others.

Let your repentance of sin be real and, in humility, accept God's forgiveness in Christ. Also, let grief do its work quickly, but then thank God for treasured relationships that have blessed you and helped to prepare you for heaven's treasures. Furthermore, thank God for His acceptance of you and for giving you the ability to start each day with the realization that it is another opportunity to serve the Lord and rejoice in His goodness.

Lord, please help me to live today as if it were the last day of my life. Amen.

SING WITH JOY

Psalm 16:11

Some years ago, a comedian used in his routine the idea of "saying a song." Maybe he was on to something good! Consider this stanza of "I Love Your Kingdom, Lord":

> *Beyond my highest joy*
> *I prize her heavenly ways,*
> *Her sweet communion, solemn vows,*
> *Her hymns of love and praise.*

Many gospel hymns and songs were inspired by the profound spiritual experiences of their authors. Such experiences make known to us God's paths for our lives (Ps. 16:11). Try "saying a song," and you may share vicariously in the moving experience of the writer.

Corporate worship in your church may also call your attention to this facet of kingdom work. Who knows, maybe you will add some hymns to your "shower repertoire" to the enrichment of your own soul and the surprise of family members who happen to hear you.

"Talking church" may not be comfortable for you, but "saying (reading or singing) a song" allows you to tell the Lord about a need or explore a spiritual experience that will bless your life and, in the end, make you a blessing to others. A poem or a melody may express your prayer of praise to the Lord as well as or even better than any other way you could choose.

Lord, thank You for hearing me and putting a
song in my heart. Amen.

A CHALLENGE TO PRAY

John 16:24

In the last hours that Jesus spent with His close followers, He spoke about the immediate future, when He would leave them and return to heaven. He reassured them that they would be able to carry on His work through the power of the Spirit.

The disciples had difficulty understanding all that Jesus said. But with the coming of the Spirit after Jesus' crucifixion, resurrection, and ascension, they were empowered not only to understand what Christ had taught but also to proclaim the gospel throughout the world.

In John 16:24, Christ encouraged all of His followers to pray in His name, meaning that He would intercede for them as they brought their ministry requests to the Father in prayer. The Savior's authority would undergird their work, give them success in their evangelistic outreach, bring glory to God, and give them great joy.

About what do you pray to God? Do you ask Him, in Jesus' name, to give you an effective ministry? Do you petition the Lord to make your joy full by enabling you to do His will successfully? If not, perhaps today would be a good time to start. Remember, it's never too soon to do so!

Lord, please give me abundant joy by enabling
me to do Your will in ministry. Amen.

DAY SEVEN

FREE INDEED!
John 8:34−36

What does it mean to be a slave to sin? In John 8:34–36, Jesus meant that we are controlled by sin. Regardless of what we might say or do, sin dominates our thoughts and dictates our actions. For all practical purposes, we are powerless to resist its advances.

How can we be freed from this horrendous slave master? Jesus said that He can liberate us from the shackles of sin. Through faith in Him, its power can be broken so that we can become the persons God created us to be. We no longer have to be restrained, mastered, or enslaved by sin.

Now that's good news! And it should bring joy to your heart! Take a few moments to tell God how thankful you are for the freedom that you have in Christ. Also, express how joyful you are that God is helping you to become a virtuous person of faith.

Father, please help me to rejoice in the freedom
You have given me through faith in Christ. Amen.

SCOTT SHAVER

A Man and His Special Problems: Selfish Ambition

DAY ONE

SUCCESS DESTINED TO FAIL

Genesis 11:4

Show God a man whose primary goal is to occupy the place of preeminence among his peers, and God will show you a man who has entered into a binding contract with failure. The words "blind ambition" imply the possibility of forgetting that we exist to glorify God. A commitment to uphold God's purpose of goodwill for all people is the central characteristic of a life that reflects His glory. In God's rule, failure is guaranteed if our desire to get to the top makes us insensitive to the thoughts and needs of others (Gen. 11:4).

An interesting thing happened during the course of the Babel building project. God confused the language of the workers and caused the construction to stop. He saw self-centered motives driving the hearts of ambitious men, so He took away their ability to communicate. Consequently, the kind of relationships needed to finish such a project could not be maintained.

God's blueprint of the heavenly city calls for us to be rightly related to Christ by faith and rightly related to each other. Blind ambition detracts heavily from both of these relationships. Selfish, unchecked desire is something that will cause men to climb over each other in their efforts to achieve a position that God alone must occupy.

Never underestimate the value of others in your efforts to live for God's glory. God cannot be worshiped at the expense of sacrificing human relationships for positions of power.

Father, please help me to structure my life
around right relationships instead of ambitious
struggles for power. Amen.

PLAYING TO THE CROWD

2 Samuel 15:1–4

Loss of integrity is the price a man pays to purchase a name for himself. Such certainly was the case with Absalom (2 Sam. 15:1–4). The chink in his armor was unbridled ambition. His determination to gain the throne of Israel killed him inwardly long before his outward demise at the hands of Joab in the forest of Ephraim. Absalom played to the crowd as a man without guile and thereby proved to God that he was a man without integrity.

The people saw a prince who promised them justice in the absence of a judge. God saw a man who was unwilling to honor his father. The people saw a diligent man who would rise up early to settle civil disputes by the city gate. God saw a ravaged man who would rise up early to create problems for divinely appointed leadership. The idea of Absalom dispensing justice for all was ridiculous to God! How could justice ever be served by a man who lacked the integrity to deal justly with his own father, the king?

Therein lies the problem of playing to the crowd. The perspectives of a throng and a king are rarely the same. Without integrity, it is impossible for a man to see the world through God's eyes. Just as it was with Absalom, so today the spiritual blindness of an overly ambitious man will prompt him to steal rather than win the support of his followers.

Father, please help me to be a man of integrity,
rather than someone who merely plays the crowd.
Amen.

TRUE GREATNESS

Matthew 20:21

Despite nearly two thousand years of hindsight, people still have a hard time understanding that the path of honor for Jesus was a cross. Pagan desires for power and recognition blind people to the fact that true greatness is best represented, not by a throne, but by a willingness to sacrifice for the welfare of others.

Obviously, the welfare of others was not a major concern of James and John in their quest for greatness. How else does one explain their sending their mother to make request to Jesus for something that they were unwilling to make themselves (Matt. 20:21)? Neither did the rest of Jesus's disciples demonstrate the potential for greatness when they deserted Him the night He was arrested by the authorities.

Do you want to be a great man of God? As Jesus' life and teachings demonstrate, you must learn to be the servant of others. By saying *no* to your selfish ambitions and *yes* to the needs of others, you will be on the path to true and lasting greatness in the divine kingdom.

> *Lord, please help me to understand that*
> *true greatness is measured by my willingness to*
> *sacrifice for the welfare of others. Amen.*

DAY FOUR

THE CURSE OF BACKSCRATCHING
John 5:44

"You scratch my back, I'll scratch yours!"

"Tell everybody how wonderful I am, and I'll surely return the favor!"

Have you ever seen such sentiments at work in a congregation? I have. One curse resting upon the modern church is men who would curry the praise of their counterparts rather than promote the purpose of God. They forget that it is better to seek the honor that comes from the One who alone is God (John 5:44).

During the days of Jesus, more than a few religious leaders were fond of calling attention to themselves. This fact is well-documented in the writings of the New Testament. The insatiable appetite of the human ego has always been a problem.

Religion is heading in the wrong direction when it directs more attention to the creature than it does to the Creator. Such religion put Christ on the cross! Why else would Jesus, who was so determined to do the will of God, be so despised and rejected by those who claimed to desire the same thing? If the practice of your religion includes receiving glory and honor from others, get all you can now while it is still possible, for that brand of religion will be useless in the hereafter.

*Father, please help me to seek Your honor,
not my own. Amen.*

RUNNING THE WRONG WAY WITH THE RIGHT CROWD

1 Kings 1:5

Adonijah knew that his half-brother Solomon had been chosen as successor to the Davidic throne. That fact is made obvious by the political maneuverings that accompanied Adonijah's announcement to gain the throne for himself (1 Kings 1:5).

In addition to recruiting a show of outrunners from the royal forces, Adonijah managed to garner the support of Joab and Abiathar, two of David's most trusted allies. The biblical writer had a subtle way of informing us that Adonijah understood the value of image and physical appearance in the game of politics. Verse 6 says that he "was a very handsome man."

In a recent television commercial, tennis player Andre Aggassi echoed the attitude of our culture when he said, "Image is everything!" In other words, the right clothes, the right looks, and the right connections will take you a long way in the eyes of the world. An important point to remember, however, is that the world has always tended to move away from God rather than toward Him.

Even with the right image, Adonijah could move no farther than the boundary lines of God's will. With respect to the Davidic throne, those lines had been drawn around Solomon. When ambition prompted Adonijah to challenge God's boundaries, he ended up sharing a tragic fate similar to that of his brother Absalom.

*Father, please help me to do things Your way
rather than my way. Amen.*

BIG FISH IN LITTLE PONDS

2 Kings 14:9–10

Amaziah was the typical "big fish in a little pond." His decisive victories over the Edomites in the Valley of Salt and at Sela led him to believe that it was time to move on to higher bushes and bigger berries. The Judean king's challenge to Jehoash of Israel was met initially with the fable of the thistle and cedar of Lebanon (2 Kings 14:9–10).

Within that ancient culture, such fables would have been employed to emphasize the weakness of a national power like Judah as compared to the superior strength of a nation like Israel. The response of Jehoash would have also given Amaziah a second chance to consider the ridiculous nature of his aspirations to glory.

Tragically, big fish in little ponds have a hard time understanding how the food chain in a larger body of water is significantly different from that to which they are accustomed. Amaziah learned that lesson the hard way during the battle of Bethshemesh.

Speaking on the subject of self-promotion, Jesus suggested that the wisest course of action would be for a man to wait on God's timing and initiative. Jesus' words to a group of dinner guests who contended for the seats of honor were clarified by the following remark: "Everyone who exalts himself will be humbled; and he who humbles himself will be exalted" (Luke 14:11).

Lord, thank You for the reminder that true
greatness is found in humbly serving others.
Amen.

THE PATTERN OF PREFERENCE FOR OTHERS

Luke 22:24–30

The world may never offer us any more tangible expressions of God's presence than opportunities for service to others. However, by watching the world we cannot learn the pattern of relationships that will prevail in the eternal community of saints called the church. Instead, while living and acting in the world, we should cultivate a strong desire for the divine pattern. Our desire is kindled as we submit to the example and teachings of Christ.

The first disciples were a lot like us. They lived in a society in which those who possessed and exercised power over others were considered great. Jesus told them that this pattern is to be completely and forever reversed. His example of selfless and sacrificial service teaches us that men who strive to get ahead of one another will ultimately finish far behind those who strive to serve one another (Luke 22:24–30).

What things are of concern to you right now? As you look back on these worries ten years from now, will they seem petty and insignificant? Why not take this opportunity to get your eyes off yourself and redirect your attention to the Savior of the world? As you wait for His return, focus on being His humble servant.

Lord, please help me to forget about my petty worries and give more attention to serving others for Your glory. Amen.

RANDY DAVIS

A Man and His Special Problems: Bad Companions

MAKE LIKE A TREE
Psalm 1:1

When I was a little boy, there was a twig of a tree in my grandfather's front yard. That tree and I grew up together. It eventually became tall, straight, and shady. It has seen many grandchildren over the years. We hung our swings in that tree. I have climbed it several times and broke several of its limbs. Like me, my brother climbed to the top and carved his initials in it. Some of us fell from that tree, and I believe that a cousin broke his arm falling out of it. Today its low limbs are gnarled and curled from not just the storms but also us kids as we played and swung from its limbs.

That tree grew tall and strong because it had deep roots. Similarly, our lives need to be strong to endure both the storms of life and the play time of our children. We become strong by being deeply rooted in the Word of God.

The psalmist said that when we are deeply rooted in the law of God, we do not go the way of sinners. The walk of the sinner is inviting. Notice the progression. It begins with the counsel of the wicked. This counsel leads to the path of the sinner, which is a deliberately chosen lifestyle of evil. Finally, the walk leads to the seat of the scoffer, who is the enemy of God and rejects His wisdom (Ps. 1:1).

God has called us to be like a planted tree. We should sink our roots deep into His Word. In Scripture we find all that is necessary for us to remain spiritually healthy. And, in due season, a man firmly planted yields his godly fruit.

Lord, please help me to be deeply rooted in Your Word. Amen.

BUT EVERYONE DOES IT!

Exodus 23:2

"But everyone does it!" is the cry of most little boys. As children, we used this phrase to explain why we should be allowed to do something. Even society has resorted to an "everyone-does-it" mentality to explain and excuse mob action. More than once, defense lawyers have successfully used the excuse of group behavior to defend otherwise illegal action.

Exodus 23:2 says we must not follow a crowd in doing evil. This injunction is based on the truth that we are responsible for our own behavior. Tragically, modern social philosophy seems to find all kinds of excuses for why we are not responsible for the way we behave. We are told that poverty is an excuse for criminal behavior. Hardhearted fathers and unaffectionate mothers are the justification for men to be unloving to their wives and children. More than once an innocent man has gone to jail because justice was perverted by a "follow-the-crowd" mentality. And sometimes a guilty man goes free because the crowd refused to hold him accountable for his evil deeds.

Despite the warped mentality of the world, the truth of God still stands. We are responsible to Him for our behavior. We have no excuses. We are free moral agents. We are made in the image of God with the capacity to discern right from wrong. We cannot stand before the Lord and mutter the excuse, "But, everyone does it!" Biblical manhood calls us to take personal responsibility for our actions, meaning that we can't blame our misdeeds on anyone else.

God, please give me the courage to resist the world's diseased way of thinking. Help me to take responsibility for my behavior. Amen.

AGAINST THE LAW

2 Thessalonians 3:6

The first year of college can be challenging, even in a Christian school! I remember some guys in the men's dorm who had discovered their freedom. The result of liberty plus immaturity led them to a non-Christian lifestyle. Unfortunately, for a time, I was negatively influenced by them.

The Bible reminds us that sinful lifestyles can be very seductive. Thus, it behooves us to discern truth from falsehood. It is fairly easy to spot the errors of the sinner's lifestyle. But what about the behavior of so-called Christians who lead an unruly life (2 Thess. 3:6)?

Here is where caution and wisdom come in. We may be easily confused by a person's behavior that does not conform to biblical standards. He may take the position that since he is saved, he can do whatever he wants. This view is called *antinomianism* ("against the law"). A lawless person claims that since his soul is saved, he can live like the Devil and get away with it.

We should flatly reject this way of thinking and acting. Only the lawless person would suggest that we should continue sinning so that God can show us more and more of His kindness and forgiveness (Rom. 6:1). If we are truly saved, it makes no sense for us to continue to wallow in sin (v. 2).

Watch yourself when you are around those who seem lawless in their attitudes and lifestyle. Rather than spend time with them, choose friends who will enhance your Christian walk.

Lord, please give me the wisdom and courage to
keep aloof from those who are lawless. Amen.

DAY FOUR

APPRENTICESHIP
Proverbs 4:14−17

Few professions allow a newcomer to work without some sort of apprenticeship. Doctors, lawyers, plumbers, and carpenters all require that a man new to the profession work with an experienced journeyman before he is allowed to operate on his own. We do not become experts and authorities without the supervision of others.

The same is true of the Christian life. Proverbs 4:14–17 warns us not to follow the path of the wicked. That sounds like good advice, but how do we avoid this path? Are we born with that kind of wisdom? Clearly not.

God, in His wonderful wisdom, has given us the church. One of the purposes of the body of Christ is to teach us to become spiritually mature men of God (Eph. 4:11–13). The church is a community of believers who equip each other for the Christian life through the teaching of biblical principles.

A wise course of action is to be mentored by a spiritual brother who is experienced in the Christian life. Likewise, it is important to teach those who come after you so that they, too, will learn not to walk in the path of the wicked.

Lord, please lead me to someone who will give me wise counsel about how to live for You. Amen.

DAY FIVE

THE ENVIRONMENT
1 Corinthians 5:11

According to the experts, our personalities are a mixture of our genetic makeup and our environment. Some people say that we inherit our father's temper and our mother's moodiness. This might prompt us to blame our behavior on our parents!

Similarly, we are tempted to blame our behavior on our environment. Some people might claim that they act a certain way because they were raised in a poor family. Others might explain their outbursts of anger by the fact that their father abused them.

But the Bible teaches that we are free moral agents, meaning that our behavior is our responsibility. We really can't blame our genes or our parents or our environment for our bad behavior. We can blame only ourselves (1 Cor. 5:11).

Coming to terms with our moral responsibility takes a level of maturity that many of us would like to avoid. The boy in us wants to blame others for our wrongdoing. We may choose a role model and try to emulate his behavior. But ultimately we can't blame him for our sin.

If our environment plays an important role in our personality, we should take this into account. For example, we should choose friends, acquaintances, and role models who live exemplary lives. Even in church we should be careful about whom we emulate. We need to choose men of God who live consistently Christlike lives to be our role models and friends.

Father, please help me to find godly friends who will encourage me to remain faithful to You. Amen.

A TERRIBLE MISMATCH

2 Corinthians 6:14

Could Paul really mean that we should not associate with unbelievers? Are we, as Christians, supposed to separate from the world so much that we associate with only other believers?

No. Paul had already noted that we cannot avoid the people of the world, nor should we. The key to understanding 2 Corinthians 6:14 is the word rendered "yoked." Paul had in mind a farming scene. Two oxen would be harnessed together to drag a plow. However, if a farmer joined a big ox and a little donkey, the smaller animal would be in trouble. For example, there would be no way for the donkey to pull as much weight as the ox. Together, the two creatures would be a terrible mismatch.

Let's apply this verse to the church. Congregations should not have on their membership rolls people who bring ungodly ways into the fellowship. How long would it take for a congregation to go astray if unbelievers were making major policy decisions? It would soon be a disaster!

The same is true for your personal relationships. Consider your marriage, friendships, and business relations. These are associations where your philosophy of life is either in agreement or in conflict with that of others. It only makes sense that if you are to share the most intimate moments of your life with a mate, that person should be someone who shares your faith in Christ. Otherwise, disaster is certain to follow. As you can see, there is great wisdom in Paul's admonition not to team up with those who are unbelievers.

Lord, please give me supportive relationships
with other Christians. Amen.

THE NATURE OF LIGHT

John 15:19

A fact of physics is that light expels darkness. Creatures that love the darkness will run when they are exposed to light. If cockroaches could talk, I'm sure they would say, "I hate the light!"

When we become followers of Christ, our spiritual darkness is replaced by God's wonderful light. But if you are filled with light, you can expect a reaction from a world, which lives in darkness and detests the light of God's truth and love (John 15:19).

I once worked with a young man who was living with a woman outside of marriage. He was rather proud of his live-in girlfriend and of the fact that her father did not seem to mind their arrangement. I had talked to him about the Lord and I had tried to live the Christian life before him.

One day this fellow told me that I had no right to condemn him for his sexual immorality. I responded by saying, "Tim, I have never said anything to you about living with your girlfriend. I think your conscience is getting the better of you." "Oh," was the only reply he had. It was my presence that had made him uncomfortable. The light of Christ exposed Tim's world of darkness.

You might as well admit that you shouldn't be like the world. You will always be rejected because you reflect the light of Christ. The lost might respect you for your morals. They might even like you to a certain extent. But at some point your faith will conflict with their attitudes and ways. That's how things work when light invades the realm of darkness.

Father, please help me to shine the light of Christ into a world lost in the darkness of sin. Amen.

A Man and His Special Problems: Enticements

DAY ONE

LIVING BY FAITH, NOT BY FEELINGS

Judges 14:3

Samson had taken note of a Philistine woman. He then asked his parents to arrange a marriage to her. He demanded, "Get her for me; for she pleases me well" (Judg. 14:3 RSV).

How often do we men say to ourselves, "She's beautiful. I must have her!" We may or may not be married. Regardless of our marital status, if we are truly men of God, we should first deal with our faith. Samson's faith taught him that an Israelite did not marry pagans. More importantly, Samson knew that he should not choose a wife just because her looks pleased him. Rather, pleasing the Lord was of paramount concern.

Think about yourself for a moment. Your feelings might say, "When I'm around her, I get excited. She turns me on. I want her!" But your conscience says, "This woman is a person to be respected. She has feelings and a mind of her own. God created her in His image. She's not a thing to be used."

When it comes to relationships with the opposite gender, don't let your feelings dictate your actions. Instead, define your behavior by the teachings of the Christian faith. Ask yourself, "Is Jesus my Lord?" If so, He is Lord of your feelings as well as your faith.

O Lord, please help me to respect and value women rather than regard them as objects to be exploited. Amen.

DON'T GIVE IN!

2 Samuel 11:3

David was the king of Israel. His armies, under the command of Joab, had gone to war against the Ammonites. Meanwhile, David remained in Jerusalem (2 Sam. 11:1–2).

Late one afternoon, David got out of bed after napping and took a stroll on the roof of his palace. (In ancient times, roofs were flat and served as a place where one could retreat from the commotion of life.) As the king looked out over the city, he spotted a woman of stunning beauty taking a bath (v. 3). David used his authority as king to have some aides escort her to the palace. After he slept with her, she returned to her home (vv. 4) .

David had every opportunity to do what was right. For example, when he first noticed Bathsheba, he should have turned away from looking at her. Instead, he stared at her for a long time and possibly imagined what it would be like to have sex with her. Rather than repent, he gratified his sinful desire.

Can you identify with David? Do you struggle with lust, as most men do? If so, don't deny it and certainly don't give in to it. Rather, when you find yourself enticed by the beauty or charm of a woman, consider the trail of shame and loss that resulted from David's transgression. Let it be a reminder that you should shun all forms of sexual sin.

Gracious Father, please give me the discernment and self-control I need to say no to sexual sin. Amen.

FINDING A GODLY MATE

1 Kings 2:17

Adonijah was David's son and Solomon's brother. Adonijah asked the king, through Bathesheba, for Abishag as a wife (1 Kings 2:17). What was wrong with Adonijah's request? Simply this. No person made in the image of God is to be treated as a piece of property to be given away. Abishag was to be given the respect that is due every person, regardless of their gender.

How does a man of God find an appropriate mate? The Golden Rule is a good starting point. It says that we should do for others what we would like them to do for us (Matt. 7:12). This principle works well in both courtship and marriage.

A second suggestion is that you adopt the biblical teaching of mutual submission. Ephesians 5:21 says that Christian men and women should submit to one another out of reverence for Christ, meaning that men of God don't try to domineer and exploit women. Thus, if you're single and dating someone, you must treat her as your spiritual equal and as your sister in Christ (see 1 Tim. 5:2; 1 Peter 3:7).

A third suggestion is that you remain sensitive to the teaching of God's Word, the leading of His Spirit, and the counsel of mature, knowledgeable Christians. If you follow these guidelines, there's a greater likelihood that you will find a godly mate.

Lord, please help me treat all women with respect. Also, give me the wisdom and discernment I need to find a godly mate. Amen.

DAY FOUR

Are You Being Seduced?
Proverbs 5:1–6

Seduced is a word that is used more and more in our culture to explain the fall of a good man or woman into sexual sin. Samson was seduced by Delilah. You can read more about this in Judges 16.

Proverbs 5:1–6 urges us, as men of God, to avoid an immoral woman. We learn that although her lips might be as sweet as honey and her mouth as smooth as oil, giving in to her allurements leaves a trail of shame, bitterness, and loss. We discover that she despises the path of godliness. Imagine how many Christian men have become intoxicated by her charms and, like a drunk, have staggered down her crooked trail to ruin.

As men of God, we are responsible for our actions. We can't blame the circumstances of life or the alluring woman we see. God wants us to run to Him for help when we are tempted to fall into sexual sin. There's no other way to fight its evil, seductive power.

Lord, please help me to remember that I am responsible to You for my sexual behavior. Amen.

GIVE YOUR HEART TO GOD

Proverbs 5:7–14

"We are Borg. Resistance is futile. You will be assimilated!"

That's the claim the Borg make on *Star Trek: The Next Generation*. (The Borg are enemies of the Federation.) Do you sometimes think of sexual sin this way—as something that can't be resisted and that will eventually overpower you?

Proverbs 5:7–14 says that you *can* resist sexual sin. Resistance is not futile and will not lead to defeat. What's the key? It's deciding long before temptation strikes that you won't allow yourself to give in to the enticement. For example, figure out how you might avoid sexually tempting situations and also how you might get out of a potential mess. If you don't—if you give in to your forbidden desires—you could end up like the tragic fellow in the text who wept over his indiscretion.

These verses are based on the seventh commandment of the Decalogue: "You shall not commit adultery" (Exod. 20:14). Someone has compared the Ten Commandments to a fence around quicksand. They are there to keep you safe from harmful activities and attitudes. Each decree, when broken, brings pain to you and others.

Why not decide ahead of time to avoid such a tragedy? Give your heart to God, and avoid the public disgrace that sexual sin can cause.

Lord, I give my heart to You. Please help me to resist, rather than gratify, my forbidden desires. Amen.

A FOUNTAIN OF BLESSING

Proverbs 5:15–20

Proverbs 5:15–20 is filled with vivid imagery. For example, the idea of a man drinking water from his own well is a picture of him enjoying the closeness of his wife. Spilling the waters of our springs in public is a graphic way of referring to having sex indiscriminately. The sage urges us to reserve our love for our wife, rather than share it with strangers.

Physical intimacy in marriage is one of God's greatest gifts to us. A Christian man's wife is like a fountain of blessing, a loving doe, and a graceful deer. The Lord says that He wants us to be captivated by our mate's love and to relish her beauty.

But it's a different matter with an immoral women. God cannot bless an illicit relationship. Rather, He condemns all forms of adultery. Despite what the world might say, we, as men of God, must look to our wife—and her alone—for lifelong satisfaction and companionship. Any other outlet for intercourse is forbidden!

Lord, please help me to be faithful to my wife.
And help us to bring joy to each other. Amen.

TAMING THE SEX DRIVE
Matthew 5:27–30

Take a moment to read Matthew 5:27–30. Now consider your own thought life. How does it match what Jesus said? It's sobering to realize that even looking at a woman with lust is a violation of the seventh commandment of the Decalogue (Exod. 20:14).

What does all this mean, anyway? Christ taught that mental adultery occurs when we cultivate the desire to have sex with a woman other than our wife. In other words, it's not only the *act* itself that is wrong but also the *intent* to sin.

What are you, as a Christian man, to do? You must look to Jesus to tame your sex drive. Yes, Jesus knows that you have strong impulses to be sexually intimate with the opposite gender. The issue is not the presence of the desire. Rather, it's the deliberate and repeated fantasizing of immoral sexual encounters.

Don't be ashamed that you might struggle in this area. And don't allow the realization of it to discourage you. Rather, depend completely on Christ to give you the power to say *no* to your impulses and *yes* to remaining virtuous. Remember, the Lord is always present to help you to behave in such a way that you will not bring pain to yourself or to others.

Let me offer this paraphrase of Matthew 5:28 "But I say to you that every man is to look at a woman respectfully as a sister in Christ. In so doing, he will never think about having sex with a woman who is not his wife, and consequently, never will."

Gracious Father, please help me to bring all of
my life under Your sovereign control. Amen.

MARK SUTTON

A Man and His Special Problems: Fear

FACING YOUR FEARS

Deuteronomy 1:17

Of what are you afraid? What can keep you awake at night and destroy any normal self-confidence? Right now, it's just you and God, so you can afford to be honest with yourself.

In every person's life is someone or something that gives them white knuckles, lifts their blood pressure, and causes their breathing to grow ragged. What is it for you? A failed business, kids who don't turn out right, a broken marriage, physical sickness that leads to death, or something else entirely? Whatever it is, you can be sure Satan knows about it, and he'll try to use it to keep you off balance and miserable.

So what can you do about it? Look carefully at Deuteronomy 1:17. It says that God knows what you're going through, who is harassing you, and what you need to make it safely through life. You need to let Him be your strength and shield. Believe me, He *will* come through, and at the proper time.

A Christian course titled "Adventure in Fathering" is for men and their children. During one of these courses, Robert, age six, wandered away from everyone else. He soon found himself at the edge of a great forest and realized that he was lost. Thankfully, the young boy had the presence of mind to remember what the course had taught him: "If you get lost, sit down and stay where you are." After a short while, the father came looking for Robert and found his son sitting on a log, waiting. When he saw his father, Robert said, "Dad, I wasn't worried, because I knew that if I was lost, you would come looking for me."[1]

Wherever you are as you read this devotional, whether on a log at the edge of a forest or on a sofa in your living room, you need to know that God is watching over you. Why not give your fears to Him and trust Him to deliver you?

Father, please take care of me, relieve me of my fears, and help me to rest in You. Amen.

SERVING GOD DESPITE YOUR FEARS

Numbers 14:3

The words in Numbers 14:3 came from the lips of a people who should have been grateful. A few years earlier, they had been slaves in Egypt. Families watched as their male babies were killed and their brothers and husbands were beaten at the slightest provocation. It's no wonder they longed for liberty. Then God answered their prayers miraculously. He not only brought the Israelites out of slavery but also promised to lead them into a wonderful land where they would be free.

As the descendants of Jacob made their way through the desert, they encountered a problem. Did they face it with courage? Did they trust in the God who had delivered them time and time again? Sadly, no. Instead, they were ready to go back into slavery to escape a temporary fear.

Does this sound familiar to you? When something doesn't go just right, are you sometimes tempted to throw up your hands and throw in the towel? Are you ready to quit living for Christ at the first sign of difficulty? Maybe you have the same problem as the Israelites. Perhaps you haven't surrendered total control of your life to God.

Not long ago, a doctor was driving from one hospital to another. He exceeded the speed limit to make up for lost time. Suddenly he heard a siren. Looking in his rearview mirror, he saw a police car with its flashing blue lights. His stethoscope was lying beside him in the seat, so he picked it up and frantically waved it at the policeman, hoping to impress the officer with his importance. But when he looked in his mirror again, he saw the policeman grinning and waving his own symbol of authority—a revolver!

Authority. Rights. Responsibility. These three words are frequently heard as we head toward a new millennium. We see individuals who are obsessed with shunning all authority and responsibility. Our culture says it's okay to grab your rights and keep them from anyone else. It is possible to become so caught up with ensuring your rights that you become a slave to the wrong kind of freedom.

I am eternally grateful that Jesus did not insist on His own rights. If he had, He would never have left heaven to die on a cruel, filthy cross for humankind. Because He took seriously the responsibility given Him by His heavenly Father, you have the privilege of becoming a child of God.

When you trust in Christ for salvation, you let Him become the Lord—the *Boss*—of your life. Or, to put it another way, Christ doesn't want to be just the *resident* of your life; He wants to be the *president* of your life.

When Jesus speaks, you should listen and obey. Listen, for the words come from someone who loves you. Obey, for the commands come from the One who died at Calvary for you. Don't go back into slavery. Don't let Satan and the fears he creates keep you from following Christ. Decide today that you'll live for God no matter what.

> *Dear God, please help me to go forward in my service for You, regardless of what might happen to me. Amen.*

DAY THREE

DESTROYING THE FEAR OF APPROVAL
Galatians 2:12

Peter needed a little help. Galatians 2:12 indicates that he changed his behavior according to the crowd he was with. Paul had to help him shift his focus from pleasing people to pleasing God.

Do you identify with Peter? Do you have one vocabulary at home, another at work, and still another at church? Do you change your behavior to fit your friends? In other words, are you so concerned about what others think that you allow the crowd, not Christ, determine your behavior?

A soldier in one of the Prussian regiments serving Frederick, czar of Russia, had a watch chain he wore continually. Being a poor man, he could not afford a watch. Instead, he had attached a bullet to the free end of the chain. While inspecting the troops one day, Frederick noticed this unusual ornament.

Deciding to have some fun at the soldier's expense, he took out his diamond-encrusted watch and said, "My watch tells me it is five o'clock; what time does yours tell?" The soldier gazed steadily at the czar and replied, "My watch does not tell me the hour, but it tells me every minute that it is my duty to die for Your Majesty." A moment of silence followed, then Frederick handed his own watch to the soldier. "Take this," he said kindly, "so that you may be able to tell the hour also."[2]

Perhaps you need something to remind you at all times of how you are to act. Maybe you need a symbol that helps you live for God and not for others, a token that will banish the fear of others and replace it with peace. The cross does for the believer what the bullet did for the soldier. It reminds us of whom we serve and how we are to live. The secret to successful living is successful dying. As we die to self daily, we give Christ first place in our lives. And with Christ filling our lives completely, there is no longer room for fear.

Lord, please help me to live for You, no matter where or with whom I find myself. Amen.

DAY FOUR

Overcoming the Fear of Standing in the Gap
Ezekiel 22:30

The English explorer Mallory was one of the world's great mountain climbers. It was his dream to climb and conquer that greatest of peaks, Mount Everest. He organized an expedition, but it failed. A second attempt also failed. A third expedition was begun, this time with the most extensive preparation possible. This assault, however, was the most tragic of all. Mallory and most of his team were killed in an avalanche.

The few survivors eventually straggled back to England. There, friends invited them to a banquet honoring Mallory and the other valiant members of their group. At the close of the banquet, one of the surviving members of the assault team stood to say a few words. He looked around the room at the pictures of Mallory and his comrades who had given their lives. Then, in tears, he turned to face a huge picture of Mount Everest that loomed behind the banquet table.

"I speak to you, Mount Everest," he said, "in the name of all living, brave people and those yet unborn. Mount Everest, you defeated us once, you defeated us twice, you defeated us three times. But Mount Everest, we shall someday defeat you, because *you can't get any bigger and we can!"*[3]

Man of God, remember that the outcome of the battle has been decided. Christ has already overcome Satan by way of the cross and the empty tomb. You should neither be afraid of Satan's power nor give in to it, for the Devil is a defeated foe awaiting certain doom.

Because you're assured of the victory, you need to be ready and willing to "stand in the gap" (Ezek. 22:30). By this I mean doing whatever you can to resist evil and make a difference for God in the world. Past failures are only stepping-stones to a stronger life in Christ. God's Word tells us that in Christ, we can only get spiritually stronger and stronger. Therefore, stand for Christ today. Resist evil and tell someone about the Lord!

> *Heavenly Father, help me to overcome any fear I might have of telling others about Christ. Amen.*

DAY FIVE

REMOVING THE FEAR OF DEATH

Proverbs 29:25

Proverbs 29:25 says, "Whoever trusts in the Lord shall be safe." Aren't those wonderful words? It means we don't have to fear anything this world can throw our way, not even death. So let's do a little experiment. Let's make sure you know that heaven is your destination when you die. Let's remove the fear of death for you *right now*.

A traveler in the Swiss Alps was having trouble finding the correct route to a small village. He saw a young boy standing beside the road and asked him whether he knew where the village was located. "I've never actually been there," the boy replied. Then he pointed at another road and said, "But I do know that people going to the village go by that road."[4]

Modern man is not alone in asking, "What is the correct route to heaven?" Almost 2,000 years ago a disciple named Thomas confessed that he neither knew where heaven was nor how to get there. Christ's response to him—and to all people—is noteworthy. He declared, "I am the way, the truth, and the life. No one comes to the Father except through Me" (John 14:6).

I've never been to heaven. But I know that people who go there go by a particular route—Jesus Christ. So let's help you get on that road right now. If you've never trusted in Christ, had your sins forgiven, and allowed Him to become the guiding influence in your life, you can do so right now. If the following prayer expresses the desire of your heart, say it (either silently or aloud) to God:

> Dear God, I confess that I've sinned against You. I want to turn away from my misdeeds right now. I understand that Your Son, Jesus Christ, died on the cross to pay for my sins and give me eternal life. In this moment, in the best way I know how, I put my trust in Him for salvation. Based on what Jesus did at Calvary, please cleanse me of my sins and make me right with You. And Lord, please help me to live for You. In Jesus' name, Amen.

If you used this prayer to turn away from your sinful past and to turn to Christ in faith for forgiveness, you no longer need to fear death. Jesus has paid the price for your sins so that you might have fellowship with God forever.

> *Lord, thank You for the salvation that You*
> *provide through faith in Your Son. Please help me*
> *to trust in Him for eternal life. Amen.*

DAY SIX

IGNORING THE FEAR OF THE UNKNOWN
Isaiah 51:12

The story is told of a first century battalion of Roman soldiers involved in a war. In the process of pursuing the enemy, they moved into what was then unknown territory. The mapmakers of that era designated the lands beyond their own journeys by drawing dragons and sea monsters in those areas. This showed that uncharted territories could be frightening and life-threatening. The commander of the battalion was unsure about whether to forge ahead into what might be danger or to turn back to what was familiar land, which would mean a retreat. So he sent a dispatch to Rome with the following urgent message: "Please send new orders. We have marched off the map."[5]

What kind of map are you following? As you live out your life, make daily decisions, and plan for the future, what kind of information do you have that will assure you success? Here are two even more important questions. Who drew the map you are following? And how do you know that it is accurate?

Isaiah 51:12 reminds us that if we follow God, the map will never be too small, for He is everywhere. This means that wherever you are, He has already been there and can lovingly guide you along the way. As a child of the Father, you can never "march off the map." So don't fear the unknown, and don't worry about tomorrow. God knows the future (as well as the present and the past) intimately. He also loves you deeply and will guide you unerringly.

Father, I know that whatever this day holds,
You are able to bring me through it safely.
Please help me to trust in You, especially when
I can't see what comes next. Amen.

DAY SEVEN

CRUSHING THE FEAR OF RECOGNITION
John 12:42

If you're a sports fan, you're probably aware of the "Blue Demons" of DePaul University. But why would a Catholic Institution like DePaul have a blue demon as its mascot?

DePaul was founded in 1898. Two years later, the institution began giving letters to players who had completed a year of varsity competition. At that time the university had no mascot. But when the students saw some of their own walking around campus with huge D's on their sweaters, they began calling them "D-Men." Over time, "D-Men" became "demon." Still later, the school chose to color its mascot blue, symbolizing loyalty. So today we have the "Blue Demons."[6]

If we're not careful, what we stand for can be eroded slowly until the message has been either erased or changed completely. Take, for instance, Christianity. Do those with whom you work know that you're a Christian? And do they know what you stand for? If your coworkers are unchurched, and if they're like most people, they don't even know what it really means to be a Christian. Church is a mystery to them, heaven a vague hope, and what they learn about God comes from scraps of conversation overheard in the bar after work.

This means that someone needs to explain the gospel to these people clearly and simply. But to do that, you've got to get over your "fear of recognition" (see John 12:42). You must let those around you know that you are, indeed, a Christian. When they finally realize this, the opportunities to share your faith will start coming your way as people ask questions about life.

Don't let what Christ stands for get lost in a fog of ignorance and apathy. Stand up and be recognized as one of His followers!

Heavenly Father, please help me not to be ashamed of Christ in the workplace, on the playing field, at school, or at home. Give me the strength to stand up for Him today. Amen.

Notes

1. Tim Hansel, *Through the Wilderness of Loneliness* (Chicago: David C. Cook, 1991), 143.
2. Clifton Fadiman, *The Little, Brown Book of Anecdotes* (Boston: Little, Brown and Co., 1985), 222.
3. *Soundings*, August 7, 1990, 1.
4. John Gilmore, *Probing Heaven: Key Questions on the Hereafter* (Grand Rapids: Baker Book House, 1989), 104.
5. *Homiletics*, April–June 1995, 24.
6. David Feldman, *What Are Hyenas Laughing At, Anyway?* (New York: G. P. Putnam's Sons, 1995), 76.

B R Y A N T   B A R N E S

A Man and His Special Problems: Forsaking God

DAY ONE

REMEMBER

Deuteronomy 4:9

In the history of the wars that the United States has fought, certain phrases have served as a rallying cry during the periods of battle. "Remember the Alamo!" was the cry during the fight for Texas' independence. "Remember the Maine!" led the U.S. into battle during the Spanish-American conflict. "Remember Pearl Harbor!" thrust America into World War II. In each war, the concept of remembrance served as a stirring inspiration to men and women called into battle. Remembrance is also vital in our walk with God. It keeps us on the trail of life.

Deuteronomy 4:9 charts two trails that we can follow. The first trail is possible if you "give heed to yourself, and keep your soul diligently." This trail makes an impact upon "our sons and grandsons" for good. This is a worthy goal with long-lasting results. The second trail leads to tragedy, especially as the things of God "depart from your heart all the days of your life." It is a backward glance upon a lost direction, a lost time, and a lost cause. What makes the difference? It is the presence of forgetfulness.

God's Word instructs us to remember holy days, His mighty deeds, and, as this verse says, "the things which your eyes have seen." Why is remembrance so important? Because it keeps us steady on the path of righteousness. Since God has proven His love to us in past days, we can depend on His continuing presence and grace for uncertain confusing times.

As you begin each week, why not adopt as your motto, "Remember the Lord." As you do, your life will benefit from the refreshing power of His Spirit.

Lord, right now I commit myself to building
upon the foundation of Your past work of grace
in my life. Amen.

DAY TWO

COMPLACENCY

Deuteronomy 6:10–12

The favored and reigning champion had lost, and now he was being interviewed by a ring of commentators, one of whom asked, "Can you explain what happened? Why did you lose the fight?" The one-time champ replied, "He wanted it more than I did. He was hungrier than I was. It's hard to stay on top when everyone is gunning for you."

Throughout the interview, the ex-champion repeatedly tried to explain the unexplainable. He concluded that it is tough to stay at the top, and desire is a fickle thing. The former champ had become complacent. Being surrounded by all the trappings of his title, wealth, and fame had caused him to lose his focus. What happened to the defeated champion can also happen to you as a man of God.

Deuteronomy 6:4 records a key biblical truth: "Hear, O Israel! The Lord is our God, the LORD is one." The Israelites were to remember, to teach, and to abide by this teaching. They faced a dangerous foe, however. That foe is complacency.

Verses 10 and 11 record a repetitive refrain concerning the things in the Israelite's new land. The people were to acquire cities, houses, hewn cisterns, vineyards, and olive trees with no effort. God had given them all these things. It was enough to make them proud and complacent. With two words in verse 12, Moses brought them to back to reality: "Watch out!" This is good advice for would-be champions of faith who might forget their God.

Lord, please help me to remember that my life
is devoted to serving You. Amen.

THE END OF THE ROAD

Psalm 9:17

The statement is true, "If it doesn't matter where you're going, any road will take you there." For the believer, the destination determines the present course. We do not live as others "who have no hope" (1 Thess. 4:13). Rather, because of our trust in Christ, we can live in hope everyday. God's presence sustains us, and we are assured that "He who began a good work in you will complete it" (Phil. 1:6). That's the good news about your life and future, if you're a Christian.

Psalm 9:17 approaches the subject of journeys and destinations from a different angle. David identified a certain group of people, and he lumped them together as one—the wicked. He then wrote about a strange place that awaits them—Sheol. The realm of the dead seems strange, mysterious, and unappealing.

Then, like a travel agent, David answered the inquirer's question: "How do we get there?" or, "How do we avoid such a place?" We learn that people get there by forgetting God. They pay no heed to the signs along the journey. They read no maps and seek no counsel. Wrong turns and loss of direction soon bring them where they feared most—the end of the road.

Perhaps as you look back on your own life, you can now see your folly. The road is littered with "ifs," "whys," and "laters." Perhaps the greatest tragedy is that when you reach the end of the road, there's no way to go back. Before it's too late, don't forget God. Keep your thoughts focused on Him, and He will safely guide you to your eternal home.

Dear God, as I journey along the path of life, please help me always to be mindful of You. Amen.

FACING OUR BULLIES

Isaiah 51:13

Bullies live down every street and inhabit every school yard. They mark out their territory and dare you to cross them. Most young boys have seen their shadow and cowered in fear. Even the sight of bullies causes our stomach to churn, our knees to knock, and our hands to tremble. They are a universal icon. We ask why they exist, but the asking is unimportant when we personally encounter them. We face the unavoidable test. Will it be fight or flight?

We measure our reaction. Bullies are always bigger than we are. If they aren't bigger than we are, then they talk tougher and they have a hard glare. Either we clench our fist and brace ourselves for the conflict, or we run while the cries of "momma's boy!" sting our ears.

Now the years have passed and only the harsh memories remain, but the specter of the bully raises its ugly head. Job responsibilities, family crises, unexpected illnesses, and the like make us feel the same way. They are "bullies" just the same. Is it fight or flight?

The Israelites faced a similar dilemma. Their enemies seemed bigger, and they sure talked tough. Israel wanted to run or at least make a deal with the bully. Then God spoke. He declared that He is "the Lord your Maker" (Isa. 51:13). The One who "laid the foundations of the earth" surely could protect His people from their oppressors.

Another way to face your bullies is to remember who is your Father. He created the universe and rules the galaxies. You are not a "momma's boy" but a child of the King. You can stand toe to toe and nose to nose with your bullies. Why? Because your Father owns the street, the block, and even your bully!

Dear God, please help me to face my "bullies"
in Your strength. Amen.

DAY FIVE

REGRET
Jeremiah 3:21

"Regret" is one of the most sorrowful words in the English language. It follows us to the last step in our life. How would you describe it? Consider the following thoughts.

- Regret is a backward glance over the wreckage of lost opportunity.
- Regret is always believing you have enough fuel to make it, then running out of gas in the middle of nowhere.

- Regret is realizing your children are now independent just when you need interdependence.
- Regret is finding the words "could," "would," and "should" dominating your vocabulary.

Jeremiah 3:21 paints a picture of deep regret. The Israelites wailed on the tops of the mountains, and the sound echoed from hill to hill down through the valley. It reminded everyone who heard it of past sins.

Did you know that there's a remedy for regret? Verses 22–25 reveal that God is our source of strength and relief. When we remember to put our trust in Him, our regret is transformed into hope and opportunity. Think about it! God calls us beyond our circumstances to find peace and renewal in Him.

Real Christian living minimizes regret. Why? Conviction begets conversion to Christ, and conversion begets commitment, and commitment begets spiritual transformation. "Regrets? Not anymore, for Jesus is helping me to give them up!"

Dear God, thank You for Your forgiveness and the hope that has replaced my regret. Amen.

DAY SIX

THE DANGER OF DAYDREAMING

Hebrews 2:1

There is a key and significant difference between dreaming and daydreaming. The Bible is full of people who had dreams—great people of faith such as Jacob, Joseph, and Peter. Young people, old people, and God's church need to have dreams. What is your dream for your life? Your family? Your church? Hold the dream close, commit it to God, and pursue it under the direction of His Spirit.

Daydreaming is another matter. It has the power to distract rather than to excite. Daydreams, though seemingly harmless, occur when life is moving forward at top speed. When one is operating a crane, driving a truck, or in any other position that demands attention, daydreaming is lethal.

Daydreaming might be put in the category of coveting. Cain daydreamed about offering an acceptable sacrifice to God; then he went and killed his brother, Abel. David daydreamed about

Bathsheba; then the king sent for her and had her husband, Uriah, murdered. Even now you may be daydreaming about an illicit relationship, criminal deed, or other sinful activity. Daydreams remove God from your thinking.

Hebrews 2:1 warned against daydreaming. The verse urged God's people to "pay attention," which means your mind is to be riveted on "the things you have heard," namely, the truth of God. Don't let your mind and soul drift away from God. Hold fast to Him and His limitless power.

Dear God, please help me to pay attention to You today. Amen.

DAY SEVEN

Mistaking Silence for Acceptance
Psalm 50:16–22

The problem of forgetting God seems easy to understand. He speaks to us through His Word. Men of faith, writing under the inspiration of the Holy Spirit, left a record of God's redemptive deeds. However, in our day of instantaneous news, e-mail, fax machines, and cellular phones, couldn't we get an update? A thundering voice? A sign in the heavens? Do we have to continue to depend upon *only* God's Word?

The answer is yes, for the Bible alone is "God-breathed" (2 Tim. 3:16). Of course, as we read Scripture, we discover that God is still active in the world today. He who created the earth and maintains its present existence will one day bring all things to a close. This means that God's Word is not a dead book but a living and powerful document (Heb. 4:12).

We have mistakenly believed that God's silence is a mark of acceptance. Psalm 50:16–22 speaks of wicked men engaging in evil deeds. Why did they continue to act sinfully? Asaph wrote, "You thought that I was just like you." When God was silent, these individuals thought He didn't care. We must not make that mistake in our lives.

Asaph spoke of a time of judgment upon sin. You might be thinking that you "got away with it" or that God "looked the other way." But you haven't escaped the presence of God or His final judgment. If you live with unconfessed sin, then acknowledge it, repent of it, and return to the Lord in faith (1 John 1:9). Remember, God will never be a party to sin in your life.

Dear God, please help me not to take Your silence as approval of sin in my life. Help me to live according to Your Word. Amen.

BRUCE HENNIGAN

A Man and His Special Problems: Unrestrained Passion

DON'T YOU KNOW WHO I AM?

1 Thessalonians 4:3–8

The businessman was livid, and his face reddened with anger. He had been waiting for his doctor to arrive to administer the treadmill test for his heart. During five calls to his office to reschedule appointments, he lashed out angrily at his secretary. Just as he decided to leave, his doctor arrived to administer the test. Only after verbally abusing the doctor and touting his own self-importance did the businessman climb on the treadmill.

As the telephone rang once again, the businessman began to walk. After only two minutes, he clutched his chest and fell to the floor, dead within seconds from a massive heart attack.

Anger. Lust. Debauchery. Gluttony. Greed. Power mongering. All are symptoms of our basic desire to throw off all moral restraints and indulge ourselves. First Thessalonians 4:3–8 clearly tells us the consequences of such lack of self-control. God calls us to be morally pure—or holy—in our behavior. The alternative is deadly.

Father, please help me today to seek Your
power to control the destructive passions that are
within me. Amen.

KILLER WHALES
Galatians 5:24–26

The ice-cold water hit me in the face and took my breath away. Incredibly, the killer whale had splashed water from his tank all the way up fourteen rows and into my lap. As I dried, I marveled at the relationship the human trainers had developed with each of their killer whales. The joy and happiness at working together was written all over their faces.

As I left at the end of the show, I noticed the largest whale far behind the stage in its own tank. Later, I learned this killer whale had suddenly turned on his trainer and killed him. I tried to imagine what would change the loving, passionate relationship I witnessed between trainer and animal into murder.

As men, we feel this sudden change of natures within us every day. It is like a lightning-fast ambush appearing out of nowhere. One moment, we are sane, civilized, Christian examples of manhood. The next moment, provoked by sometimes the most trivial event, we become raging, vicious animals.

Society tells us that we can be just a little bit bad. But, as Galatians 5:24–26 reveals, the dividing line between good and evil, between walking in the Spirit and walking in the flesh, is very fine. One minute we are working harmoniously with our God and the next we betray Him.

Father, please help me today to crucify the sinful nature and passions of my life and to live by the Spirit. Amen.

HEART'S DESIRES
Roman 8:5

I could not imagine hurting any worse than I did. The pain engulfed me, blinding me to logic and thought. Had I just been betrayed by my best friend? How could he have done this to me? I felt left out. Pushed out. Betrayed.

I sat in the darkness of the hospital chapel and wept. In the depths of my emotional pain, I sought for solace, for answers. In the months that followed, the pain dwelled just within my consciousness, always waiting to surface and strike again, pulling me down into despair and self-loathing. But always I sought God and His love and peace. In time, the pain began to decrease and the wounds began to heal. I placed my sight on God, not on my desire for revenge. I trusted that God would one day give back my friendship.

Almost a year had passed, and out of the blue my friend asked me to go to dinner with him and his wife. As we fellowshipped together, the pain and agony dimmed. Later, we found ourselves thrust together in church work, and I rejoiced as our friendship blossomed again. I had been faithful, and God had given me the desires of my heart (Rom. 8:5).

Lord, please help me to make the desires of Your Spirit the desires of my heart. Amen.

DAY FOUR

FRUITS OF DEATH

Roman 7:5

In life, my cousin and I had the same first name. In death, he bore a lifestyle foreign to me. His funeral was an odd combination of backwoods country and hard-shell Baptist mixed with uptown, street-wise, and flashy modern sensuality. I stood in the chapel while this strange and alien mixture of cultures brewed outside. I gazed on the feather boa and negligee intertwined in the leaves of a tree sitting next to the urn containing my cousin's ashes. I learned that the negligee was his favorite clothing.

In my mind, I saw a small, six-year-old boy struggling for acceptance from an estranged father and an absent mother. What had happened through the years? The answers were legion, built on a foundation of psychological babble and personal pain.

I sat by my wife during the funeral and listened to my cousin's gay and straight friends lament his passing, always pointing a finger of blame at that great, silent killer among us, AIDS. In the silence that followed, one of my country relatives, face reddened from the watermelon fields, stood shakily and cast a rueful eye on the assemblage.

"Weren't nothing that snuck up on him in the night that killed him. Were his lifestyle. It were his choice. Can't blame God for this one, folks. The fruit of his choices were death!" (see Rom. 7:5).

*Father, please help me to turn away from my
sinful nature to the fruits of Your Spirit. Amen.*

THE BEAST

Romans 7:15–20

Fear ruled our city. Somewhere on the darkened streets of one of the classiest parts of town, a predator roamed, breaking into women's homes at knife point. Much to our surprise, a local minister confessed to the crimes.

If a man of God cannot control this beast within, then where is our hope? Our hope lies not in logic or psychology, for they offer no permanent solutions to a side of our nature that is inborn from the dawn of Adam's disobedience. Our hope lies in Jesus Christ.

If we immerse ourselves daily in God through prayer, Bible reading, Christian family and friends, and church, then we give evidence of having this hope. Through faith in Christ, we can be confident that the beast of sin has been and will remain defeated (Rom. 7:15–20).

*Lord, please help me to seek Your will, Your
power, and Your grace so that I will not do what
I desire to do, but instead do what You want me
to do. Amen.*

RIGHT BEFORE OUR NOSES!

Galatians 5:19–21

My friend's breath reeked of alcohol, and it was only Monday morning. He rubbed the red from his eyes and slumped onto the couch in my office. Through the years, I had watched him get arrested for drunkenness, marijuana smoking, and other "minor indiscretions." I was amazed that he was still alive.

"That was some party last night. You should have come to the club and heard the band." He squinted in my direction. "I was in church last night," came my response.

My friend scrunched up his face in disgust and began a tirade against churchgoers. He rambled off a list of sins similar to the ones appearing in Galatians 5:19–21. "How can you expect me to go to church with hypocrites like that?" "How do you know they do those things if you don't go to church?" I asked. "All those Christians act that way. I should know because I am one," he responded.

Sinful passions are here, right in front of our noses. Sometimes, as men, we indulge in one or two "minor indiscretions" and point the finger of judgment at someone else. But God tells us that sin is sin. It's obvious to everyone, except sometimes to us!

Lord, please help me to see and abandon the
sinful passions in my life. Amen.

WHAT IS YOUR VALUE SYSTEM?
1 John 2:16

A doctor slammed the phone down in exasperation and rubbed his eyes. I asked him what was wrong. He glanced at me and recounted his financial woes. His huge home in an exclusive part of the city was costing far more than he had ever planned to spend. His children were costing a small fortune to send away to fine boarding schools across the country. His wife demanded a new, very expensive car. And the fee for membership in the newest country club in town had quadrupled.

When I suggested cutting back, he glared at me as if I were a leper. He then remarked, "The most important thing in my life is my house and my social standing. If I lose those things I might as well die! My life will have no meaning!" He did not see that the important values are from the Father (1 John 2:16).

It's sad that our society compels us to value our possessions, our social standing, and our automobiles over the value of our soul and the soul of our children. What is your value system? Is it shaped by the world and what society says is important? Or is your value system shaped by the Father and what He considers important?

Lord, please help me to see what is really of
value to me, namely, those things that are
of eternal significance. Amen.

MICHAEL DUDUIT

A Man and His Special Problems: Prosperity

DAY ONE

REAL RICHES
Revelation 3:17

Have you ever thought about what it would be like to be rich? Bill Gates and Michael Jordan rich? Every time I receive one of those Publishers Clearinghouse sweepstakes mailings, I can't help but think about what it would be like to have a few hundred million, or even a billion, stashed away. It's not hard to imagine spending winters in Waikiki and summers on a mountain lake! Most of us can enjoy the thought of being financially independent—even rich.

Yet, as Revelation 3:17 discloses, those who think their material wealth has brought satisfaction and self-sufficiency are merely fooling themselves. They might live in affluence and take pride in their accomplishments, but that materialistic pride blinds them to their own spiritual poverty. They are like the emperor who had no clothes, but foolishly convinced himself that he was arrayed in splendor.

The day is coming when all those precious trinkets we loved will end up as someone's bargain at an estate sale. As for us, we will stand before a holy and righteous God to answer for what we did in this life. That time of evaluation will reveal that the only true riches are found in the grace of God through faith in Christ.

Lord, please help me to recognize that Jesus is the only treasure that will last. Amen.

THE CONTEMPT THAT CORRUPTS

Deuteronomy 32:15

Imagine yourself as a gracious friend who reaches out to help a poor, helpless associate find a job in your company. No sooner does this man find a job—with your help—than he begins to criticize you to all the other employees and tries to get you fired from your own position! That kind of ingratitude is enough to make your blood boil!

Imagine, then, how God must have felt about Israel. Here is a people whom God had created and favored. Despite their inelegance, He blessed them and gave them a special place and identity among the nations of the world. Yet, in response to God's unconditional love and care, they acted toward God with utter contempt. The term Moses used for Israel ("Jeshurun") portrays the nation as an overfed farm animal, filling its belly on food provided by the owner, yet oblivious to him. Israel had been blessed by God, yet in the face of that blessing the nation had ignored Him (Deut. 32:15).

Contempt for God is a danger each of us faces. It is easy to enjoy His blessings in so many areas of life, and at the same time act as if He did not exist—or is, at most, a minor inconvenience. How sad that we can take God's gifts but treat Him with disdain.

Don't forget that the source of every blessing is found in our heavenly Father. And God wants us to experience the richest blessings that are possible only in a relationship with Him through faith in Christ.

Lord, thank You for the blessings You provide
—blessings that are undeserved, but which I
gratefully receive. Amen.

SITTING IN SHADE

Deuteronomy 8:11–18

All of us sit in the shade of trees we did not plant. We benefit from the sacrifices of others. Every person who has attended college has received the aid of others who came before them and made contributions to build buildings, endow professors, and create scholarships. The same is true throughout every aspect of life.

Moses was preparing the people of Israel to enter the Promised Land. He reminded them that they were about to receive a host of benefits that they did not create or deserve. All that they were about to receive was a gift of God. The nation's leader urged the people not to forget the Lord, Who was the ultimate source of their bounty (Deut. 8:11–18).

It's sometimes easy for us to forget that truth. We work hard to build businesses and careers, and to provide for our families and communities. We take pride in the results of our achievements. But it's important to remember that all we accomplish is ultimately a divine gift. It is God who has given us life and health and opportunity to prosper and achieve. Without Him, we would have nothing and be nothing.

Even as we sit in the shade of trees we did not plant, we should be thankful to those who planted them. We should also be thankful to the One who makes those trees grow. Most of all, we should be grateful for the eternal life that He makes available to us through faith in Christ.

Heavenly Father, thank You for all that You have provided and for all that You make possible day by day. Amen.

DAY FOUR

CARING FOR OTHERS
Ezekiel 16:49

One of the tragedies of contemporary American life is the continuing plague of poverty. Too many families live in want. Sometimes it may be the result of poor behavior, such as drug abuse. And sometimes it is the result of a cycle of poverty and dependence handed down from one generation to the next. Whatever the causes of poverty—and they are many—the result is that too many Americans feel hopeless and helpless.

It is interesting that in naming the sins of the ancient city of Sodom, Ezekiel focused on the fact that the relative affluence of the people had created a coldness and an indifference toward the poor and needy (Ezek. 16:49). The prosperity of the rich gave them time for idleness, which resulted in sexual immorality. (Undoubtedly, it would be easy for us to insert the name of our own communities where "Sodom" appears in the text.) Tragically, their abundance left no time for helping those in need. It's no wonder that God judged His people for their complacency and indifference.

God has blessed us with material prosperity. He expects us to share out of our abundance with those in need. That caring may take a variety of forms, from active participation in charitable causes to personal involvement with groups such as Habitat for Humanity. Whatever method is used, the principle is the same: part of our stewardship responsibility is sharing appropriately with others in need, even as God has blessed us.

Heavenly Father, You have blessed me by providing for my material needs. Please help me to share out of that abundance with others in need. Amen.

LIFE'S NOT FAIR!
Jeremiah 12:1

The teenage son was livid as he stormed through the back door. "It's not fair!" he declared. "I worked like a dog to write that paper for my English class. David didn't do any work, then bought a paper off the Internet. He got an A and I got a B-! That stinks!"

Dad looked up from his newspaper long enough to offer these profound words of wisdom: "Son, life's not fair, and the sooner you recognize that fact the happier you'll be."

Is that true? Is life really not fair? Jeremiah sure thought so. "Why is it that the wicked prosper and the cheaters seem to thrive?" he complained to God (Jer. 12:1). Many of us over the years have echoed the prophet's concern. All too often, the wicked do seem to get the best life has to offer whereas the faithful get what's left over. Did it ever seem that way in your life?

Remember two truths the next time you get the feeling that "life's not fair." First, God doesn't measure ultimate rewards by the twisted standards of the world. From His eternal perspective, the world and all that it achieves are transitory and passing away. Do the wicked prosper? Perhaps for a short while, but our righteous God will one day cause justice to prevail.

Second, thank God that life is not fair! If it were fair, God would punish us for the sin and rebellion in our life. Instead, God sent Christ to be an atoning sacrifice for our sins. He took on Himself the punishment that was rightfully ours. We ultimately don't want fairness. What we need is divine grace!

Lord, please help me to see things from Your perspective. And thank You for the grace that allows me to have a part in Your kingdom. Amen.

DAY SIX

FULL BARNS, EMPTY HEART
Luke 12:16–21

Every spring, the cartoon character Charlie Brown pulls out his kite and gives it another try. And every year, he ends up enmeshed in twine and branches as his "kite-eating tree" carries him to another misadventure. Charlie Brown only thinks he's the boss; it's really the kite that is calling the shots!

In Luke 12:16–21, Jesus described a man who thought he was calling the shots. He was the ultimate "positive thinker"—he thought positively about everything he did! Notice where his focus was: "my crops . . . my barns. . . my grain. . . my goods." This farmer/businessman thought he was in control, and his priorities reflected that tragic misperception. Then one night he discovered he was not an owner at all, but rather that he is owned by God. His life of efforts focused on worldly success were gone in an instant. No wonder the Lord called him a fool!

Possessions are not evil, but a life focused on their accumulation is a sad and foolish waste. Also, a life lived without a recognition of God's presence and claims upon us is an eternal tragedy. We are not guaranteed another day or hour. Whether you are to live another day, another decade, or much longer, live every moment with an attitude of thankfulness and service to Christ, who loves you and gave Himself for you on the cross.

Lord, please help me to so establish my priorities and my actions that my life will honor You each day. Amen.

FINDING BALANCE

Proverbs 30:8–9

One of my abject failures in life relates to learning to ski. I can put on all the attire, snap on the skis, ride the lift up the mountain, but from that point forward it is sheer disaster! I've come to the conclusion that I can't ski because it is a skill that requires balance—and I don't have any!

Skiing isn't the only area in life where balance is necessary. In Proverbs 30:8–9, the writer asked God for balance in his life in the area of material wealth. He did not want to be too rich, lest he be tempted to think he was self-sufficient. That is an ever-present danger for those whose affluence creates a pride of achievement that forgets that all they have is held in trust for the true owner, God. That temptation is why Jesus said it was so difficult for a rich person to enter the kingdom (Luke 18:25).

Yet the sage also didn't want to experience the other extreme—poverty. He recognized that material limitation brings with it other temptations, such as dishonoring God through stealing. It is interesting that while the Bible emphasizes the importance of caring for the poor and needy, the writer of Proverbs did not glorify being in a state of poverty.

Finding balance in life is a worthy goal. It is found in focusing on honoring God in every part of our lives. When that happens, we will be content in whatever level of material possessions we have, for we will have the greatest possession of all—a relationship with Christ.

Lord, please help me to keep my focus off my bank account and on serving You. Amen.

A Man and His Special Problems: Prejudice

THE SOURCE OF PREJUDICE

Acts 19:34

Fear breeds prejudice. Persons with a common enemy are quick to unite and give one another support against their foe. We see this at work at Ephesus, especially as a mob of people joined together in opposing the Christians and Jews and in praising Artemis (a fertility goddess; Acts 19:34).

This dynamic is also a key to understanding the bitterness that fueled the Civil War. The abolitionists of the North condemned the slavery of the South as inhumane and contradictory to the truth that all people are created equal. However, the elimination of slavery meant economic ruin for the plantations, which required a lot of cheap labor to continue operating profitably. The abolitionists further labeled slavery as unchristian, which was a profound threat to the religious self-esteem of the South.

The southern states responded against the "self-righteous Yankees" by uniting to form the Confederacy and seceding from the Union, all the while justifying slavery from the pulpit. Even today, racial prejudice is sustained and fueled by the perceived threat posed by people of one race to the economic and moral security of people of another race.

O Lord, please deliver me from the fear of
persons who differ from me. Teach me to
understand and to grow from my differences
with them. Amen.

THE UGLIEST PREJUDICE

ACTS 26:11

Paul declared to King Agrippa that he once had gone from synagogue to synagogue and city to city to find, arrest, and prosecute Christians (Acts 26:11). Such abhorrent bigotry has been seen throughout history (e.g., the burning of heretics at the stake during the Inquisition; the drowning of witches by Puritan communities; and the hanging of African-Americans by the "Christian" Klan).

Religious prejudice continues in our nation. The flames of bigotry are fanned by conservatives against liberals and liberals against conservatives over such issues as the interpretation of Scripture, the treatment of homosexuals, the role of women in ministry, the legalization of abortion, and the sanction of prayer in public schools.

God's Word stands opposed to all forms of racial and social prejudice. Rather than condemn people for the color of their skin or their economic status in life, believers should be sharing the gospel with them. Our energies and efforts should be devoted to tearing down barriers that exist between different communities and uniting them together through faith in Christ. In union with Him is true equality (Gal. 3:28).

Dear Lord, please help me to show Your love to
all people, regardless of their racial, social,
or economic status in life. Amen.

LOVE WITHOUT WALLS

JOHN 4:9

Why was the woman at Jacob's well surprised when Jesus asked her for a drink (John 4:9)? First, as a Samaritan, she was a member of a mixed race that the Jews hated. Second, she was known to be living in sin. Third, she was in a public place. Under such circumstances, a respectable Jewish man would not be talking to her. Thankfully, Jesus did talk to her, and through His sharing of the truth, He led her to believe in Him for eternal life.

In Ephesians 2:14, Paul noted that there was once a wall of hostility that separated Jews from Gentiles. The apostle also revealed that Christ broke down this wall and made peace between the two groups by making them all one people through faith in Him.

Did you know that walls of prejudice are still with us today as we enter the next century? Our "enlightened" society still prefers to shun the dying, the mentally ill, the illiterate, the poor, the sick, the homeless, and the aged because they somehow "disturb" our illusion of being in control. But the love of God will have none of it. His love calls us to break through these walls, to bring comfort to the lonely and the hurting, and to work for justice for all who remain oppressed.

O Lord, please give me the courage to break through the walls of prejudice and to carry compassion and hope to the forgotten people of my world. Amen.

DAY FOUR

LET GO OF HATRED
ACTS 10:28

I had dragged along the hatred of my father and myself like a ball and chain ever since I was seven years old. Now, I was a forty-year-old man ministering to the sick as a chaplain in a hospital renowned for its heart bypass surgery. One night in a vivid dream, I saw myself on a gurney outside the operating room. I heard a voice saying, "It is time." Then an orderly wheeled me into surgery, where I underwent a heart transplant. I understood this dream as God telling me that He was giving me the new, forgiving heart for which I had long prayed.

It was in this type of dramatic dream that Peter heard God telling him to let go of his prejudices against Gentiles as being common, or unclean, people and to accept them as brothers and sisters in Christ. The corresponding dream of the righteous Gentile, Cornelius, in which God told him to seek out Peter gave further weight to the apostle's own dream. This was a defining moment in not only the life of Peter but also the history of the early church, which was struggling to escape from prejudice.

Accepting a Gentile as a full brother in Christ without requiring the traditional Jewish elements of circumcision and dietary practices was a radical departure from Peter's religious roots. However, he clearly discerned that Christianity was meant for all people, regardless of their race, gender, social status, or economic condition (Acts 10:28).

O God of freedom and love, please shatter my
religious prejudices, which would hinder the
proclamation of the gospel. Amen.

CONSIGNED TO BEING AN OUTSIDER

Luke 18:9–12

I can still remember the searing pain of humiliation. I was so excited about playing Little League baseball that I hardly slept. Just as I had hoped, Saturday was a most beautiful day. Anticipation was in my every step as I walked toward the park. Then suddenly my memory fast forwarded so quickly that all I could remember was that same little seven-year-old boy running home with his glove and sobbing.

After years of replaying this unresolved event in my mind, I learned from my mother exactly what had occurred. She said that one of the Little League coaches required that I had to have my father or some other adult sign the registration form. But my parents had just recently divorced. Without a father, I felt utterly and hopelessly inadequate to be part of the team. I thus was consigned to being an outsider.

In Jesus' day, such people as tax collectors were despised by self-righteous Jews and thus consigned to be "outsiders" by the religious authorities. It's no wonder that the Pharisee in Jesus' parable looked at the tax collector with such disdain (Luke 18:9–12). But guess what? It was the humble and repentant tax collector, not the proud Pharisee, who returned home justified before God (vv. 13–14) because God sets Himself against the proud but shows favor to the humble (1 Peter 5:5).

Pride is at the heart of all prejudice. And humbling yourself under God's mighty hand is the first step in combating the prejudice in your heart (v. 6). After all, the humble person realizes that there is no basis for thinking of himself as better than someone else, for all have sinned and fall short of God's glory (Rom. 3:23). Likewise, all of us can be made right with God through faith in Christ (v. 25).

God's desire is that no one be barred from His kingdom just because of their race, gender, social standing, or economic status. All who repent and believe are saved. Now that's good news worth sharing!

Dear Father, please remove the cataract of prejudice from my eyes so that I might see with compassion the unsaved of the world. Amen.

DAY SIX

RELAPSES
Galatians 2:12

Experts describe alcoholism as a disease of relapse, meaning that people attempting to remain sober will have occasional periods during which they return to their former behavior. They typically take two steps forward and one step backward.

Galatians 2:12 suggests that Peter had a "relapse" of sorts when it came to fellowship with saved Gentiles. When the apostle first arrived at Syrian Antioch, he ate with non-Jewish believers. But afterward, when some legalistic Jews arrived, Peter refused to eat with his Gentile friends. He was afraid of what the legalists would say. Paul dealt with Peter's inconsistent behavior by publicly confronting Peter about his prejudice (vv. 14–16).

None of us is immune to such "relapses." We, too, can fail miserably at times by being prejudiced in our attitudes and actions. But God can graciously set us straight in our thinking and behavior. He can enable us to become men of integrity! Profound changes of the personality are achieved gradually, one day at a time. Despite our setbacks, God can rid us of our prejudices.

O Lord, please help me to conquer my prejudices. Amen.

DAY SEVEN

A DANGEROUS MEAL
Acts 11:3

Sharing a meal with another person can be dangerous to our prejudices. Eating together is an intimate act that signals acceptance and often leads to understanding and friendship. By eating with Gentiles, Peter broke the Jewish ceremonial law and sent a clear message to both Jews and Gentiles that he had embraced God's powerful directive to make no distinction among people, regardless of their gender, race, or economic or social status (Acts 11:3).

Former President Jimmy Carter fully understood the importance of getting enemies to eat together when he invited Anwar Sadat and Menachem Begin to Camp David to begin the Middle East peace talks. The sharing of unhurried moments of laughter and meals dissolved the walls of distrust and bitterness and allowed for communication that led to the eventual signing of the Middle East peace accord.

Walls of prejudice still abound in our society. Perhaps at times you think there's not much you can do about it. At first, Peter might have felt the same way, too. Yet his courageous act of associating with people of another race helped the early church to overcome its prejudices. Who knows what your efforts might do to help the church of our generation bridge barriers of prejudice so that the gospel might be proclaimed far and wide unhindered.

Lord, please help me to do whatever I can to
combat prejudice. Amen.

STEPHEN LIVESAY

A Man and His Special Problems: Self-indulgence

PREOCCUPATION WITH THE WORLD

Ecclesiastes 2:4−11

Satan has not improved much upon the basic material that he uses to pull men away from God. An examination of Ecclesiastes 2:4–11 indicates that the Devil used the great trilogy of temptations— lust of the flesh, the lust of the eyes, and the pride of life (1 John 2:16)— to distract Solomon. The king of Israel learned from experience that the fleeting pleasures of this fallen world have no eternal value.

Men today are just as easily captivated by the things Satan has to offer. One group craves physical pleasure. Another group is consumed by the desire to amass whatever they see. A third group is obsessed with the power that comes with being rich and famous. Regardless of the group one might identify, the Devil can use each form of lust to lead us away from God.

What's the solution? We must say *no* to our worldly aspirations and desires and *yes* to the will of God for our life. After all, friendship with the world makes us an enemy of God (James 4:4). Perhaps that is one reason why this world is fading away, along with everything it craves. But if we do the will of God, we will live forever in communion with Him (v. 17).

Lord, please help me to say yes to You and no to the things of this world. Amen.

PREOCCUPATION WITH WORK

Ecclesiastes 6:7

How is it that "all man's efforts are for his mouth, yet his appetite is never satisfied?" (Eccl. 6:7). The answer is that men have greatly misunderstood God's intent for work. Labor is not an end in itself, and it can never satisfy the eternal longings of their heart. Tragically, Satan has duped many to believe his lies and has thereby driven them away from God.

The Devil gets other men to think, "OK, if work can't be my god, I'll reject it altogether!" But this way of thinking is just as erroneous as the previous mind-set. The work that God gives us to do is not meaningless or trivial. It was His original intent that we, like Him, be engaged in productive pursuits. You glorify God when you use your talents and gifts for the betterment of mankind. But when you serve only yourself through your work, that work has lost its meaning and value.

Remember, allowing yourself to be preoccupied with work is not the will of God. But neither is being lazy and unproductive. The balance comes when you see your work as an opportunity to serve God and your fellow humans. If this is your way of thinking, you can be enthusiastic about the work the Lord has given you to do, for ultimately nothing that you do for Him is ever useless (1 Cor. 15:58).

Lord, may You be well-pleased with my offering of work today. Amen.

PREOCCUPATION WITH FOOD

Isaiah 55:1–2

Most of us have heard stories of people who were so overweight that the most they could do was lie in bed and eat. Their preoccupation with food was like a cruel taskmaster that kept them enslaved. The more they ate, the more they wanted to consume. Eventually their fixation on food killed them.

Isaiah 55:2 asks why we are so preoccupied with food, especially when it lasts for only a short time and meets only our physical needs. Wouldn't it make more sense to be concerned with the spiritual condition of our souls? Verse 1 urges us to come to God in faith and receive what He freely offers.

This sentiment parallels what Jesus said in Matthew 6:25–34. It's so easy for us to worry about whether we will have enough food and drink. And yet this mind-set is foolish, for God cares immensely for us and will supply all of our needs from His eternal riches in Christ (Phil. 4:19). It's no wonder that Jesus said He is the bread of life (John 6:35). Therefore, rather than be preoccupied with food, which is of no long-term value, we should focus our minds and hearts on Jesus, Who is eager to satisfy our eternal longings.

Lord, please enable me to look to Christ, the bread of life, to meet my deepest needs. Amen.

DAY FOUR

PREOCCUPATION WITH ACHIEVEMENT
Proverbs 27:1

Perhaps the most insidious of Satan's lies is the message that our achievement today will give us a secure tomorrow. This notion contradicts the teaching of Proverbs 27:1. Those who are preoccupied with their achievements fail to realize that they have no control over the future and that their accomplishments can be undone in the blink of an eye.

The words of the sage are echoed by James 4:13–17, where we read about the overly confident person who thinks that he can do whatever he desires. But such optimism is shortsighted, for it arrogantly assumes that he knows what will happen tomorrow. The man who is preoccupied with achievement doesn't realize that his life is like the morning fog. It's here for a little while, and then it's gone.

How then should we, as men of God, think about the present and the future? It's better for us to say, "If God desires, He will permit me to accomplish this task or finish that project." Otherwise, we will be guilty of boasting about our own plans, which we have made independently of God. As James declares, all such boasting is evil.

Lord, please help me to see that my hope for tomorrow rests in my relationship with You, not in my achievements today. Amen.

PREOCCUPATION WITH DESIRE

Proverbs 23:1–3

What is the point of Proverbs 23:1–3? It's a warning that we should be careful when eating with an important or influential person who is seeking to bribe us. No good will come from such a meal, so we are wise to curb our desire for his delicacies.

This passage is also a fitting warning against preoccupation with desire. Consider the person who is so focused on getting what he wants that he becomes the unwitting stooge for some sinister mind. All of us are susceptible to this temptation. For some, the desire to climb the corporate ladder of success might cause us to sacrifice time with our family. For others, the desire to have a new house or car can prevent us from giving faithfully to the work of the Lord.

To the undiscerning, the things of this world look very appealing. But disaster always awaits those who bite at the bait of unchecked greed. Preoccupation with desire can become so enslaving that it prevents us from following our Lord's will and walking in obedience to Him. Only as we abide in God's truth and heed His wise counsel can we be truly free (John 8:32–36).

Father, please liberate me from my unwholesome
desires so that I can be free to do Your will.
Amen.

PREOCCUPATION WITH PRIDE

Philippians 3:4–11

What is pride? It's inordinate self-esteem. Synonyms might include conceit and haughtiness. Arrogance was the sin that eventually led to the downfall of Satan (Ezek. 28:12–19), and it is the Achilles' heel for many would-be church leaders (1 Tim. 3:6). It's also the one sin that plagued the life of Paul before he got saved.

In Philippians 3:4–11, the apostle related that as far as unsaved religious people go, he stood head and shoulders above his peers. His family heritage, Jewish training, and strict obedience to the law were the envy of many. His preoccupation with pride was so great that he harshly persecuted the church.

But then Paul met Christ on the road to Damascus. After that life-changing encounter, Paul no longer valued the things that were the foundation of his pride. The apostle declared that he considered these worldly trappings to be worthless because of what Jesus had done for him. In fact, everything else in the world—including his pride—couldn't compare in value to knowing the Lord.

Perhaps you're a talented, intelligent, and confident guy. If so, you can especially identify with the way Paul was before he met Christ. Deep down inside you know what it is to be preoccupied with pride. And after considering this passage, you also realize how pointless it is to think this way. Why not take a cue from Paul? Give up your pride, humble yourself in God's presence, and make knowing the risen Lord you consuming desire. You won't regret doing so!

Lord, please help me to exchange my preoccupation with pride for knowing Christ intimately and personally. Amen.

DAY SEVEN

PREOCCUPATION WITH SINFUL HABITS
Colossians 3:5–15

All of us struggle with sinful habits. For some, it's a preoccupation with unwholesome thoughts. For others, it's being enslaved to ungodly actions. Regardless of the ingrained sinful behavior, we know that it is like a ball and chain that spiritually weighs us down.

Paul knew all about the disaster associated with sinful habits. In fact, he wrote extensively about this subject in his church letters. For example, in Colossians 3:5–15, the apostle described two ways of living. One way was characterized by such vices as lust, impurity, sexual sin, and shameful desires. The other way was known for its kindness, gentleness, patience, and humility.

How can you, as a man of God, end your preoccupation with sinful habits? Paul had the answer. He said you should strip off the garment of your old evil nature along with its wicked deeds. In its place, you should put on the garment of the brand-new nature, which is continually being renewed after the image of Christ.

What the apostle wrote is crucial to understand. If you want to conquer those sinful habits in your life, you must not only jettison them but also replace them with godly habits. So, instead of being hot tempered, malicious, and foul in your behavior, let the power of Christ help you to be tenderhearted, merciful, and thankful. When you do, the peace of Christ will rule your heart and set you free from any and all preoccupation with sinful habits.

Lord, please help me to develop the godly habit of using my mind, body, and tongue as instruments of righteousness. Amen.

THAD MOORE

A Man and His Special Problems: Trouble

ARE YOU GETTING BITTER OR BETTER?

Acts 5:40−41

Bitterness is an ugly disease that can infect anyone. Older people can easily become bitter about past experiences. Committed Christians can also fall into the trap of bitterness. At first, they might think that serving Christ will exempt them from all harm, but they soon discover otherwise and eventually become ill-natured from their harsh experiences.

Acts 5:40 says that the religious leaders had the apostles flogged for sharing the gospel. Jesus' followers could have protested such mistreatment. They also could have recanted, or blamed God for the beating. Instead, they rejoiced, for they knew that the Lord had counted them worthy to suffer dishonor for the name of Jesus (v. 41). They weren't flustered by their afflictions, for they realized that nothing was more fulfilling than sharing the gospel and seeing people come to know Christ.

How do you respond when troubles come your way and when others question your faith? Do you see these experiences as obstacles or as opportunities? Your attitude will make all the difference. You can choose to be filled with gratitude or with bitterness. The choice is entirely in your hands.

The thankful attitude of the apostles gave them the courage to continue sharing the gospel. They were aware of the danger in witnessing, but the joy of Christ chased away their bitterness. Let your devotion to Christ so fill you with joy that is serves as a shield against bitterness.

Lord, please help me to guard against bitterness
and resentment. Amen.

ARE YOU ENDURING OR ENJOYING?

2 Corinthians 6:10

A young challenger in a boxing match was asked how he defeated a well-known and respected champion. He replied, "I just kept getting up for one more round."

This attitude reflects that of Paul when it came to suffering for the cause of Christ. Despite poverty, insults, heartaches, and setbacks, he never gave up. Instead, he always had joy, and this kept him going (2 Cor. 6:10).

Paul realized that there was a greater purpose in life than just being financially secure. Seeing the gospel proclaimed throughout the world was the more noble goal. Therefore, he was willing to take delight in hardships because they gave him an opportunity to show others his love for Christ.

What is your attitude about serving Jesus and possibly encountering hardship for His sake? Are you merely enduring, or are you rejoicing in the midst of your suffering? Admittedly, finding joy in your trials is never easy, but it is possible. Consider your troubles as an opportunity to become more Christ-like. If that results, then you truly have reason for joy!

Lord, please help me to find joy in becoming more Christlike through the hardships of life. Amen.

FAITH THAT OVERCOMES TROUBLES

Habakkuk 3:17−18

Have you ever felt like the writer of the old song, "Nobody Knows The Trouble I've Seen"? At first, Habakkuk seemed to feel that way. He did not understand why evil people prospered and good people suffered. He longed to see God punish the wicked for their crimes.

God dealt graciously and patiently with Habakkuk's complaints. The Lord told the prophet that in His eternal plan and timetable, justice would prevail. But even when life seemed unfair, the just were to live by their faith (Hab. 2:4). In other words, the righteous were to trust God, Who is infinitely wise and good, to direct all things according to His purposes.

Thankfully, Habakkuk learned this important lesson. He declared that even though Judah's crops might fail and the nation's livestock might die, he would still rejoice in the Lord. The prophet's feelings were not controlled by the circumstances of life but by his faith in God (3:17–18).

How about you? Does nothing in life right now make sense? Do your troubles seem overwhelming? Why not take your eyes off your difficulties and turn to the Lord in faith? Remember, He is the God of your salvation. By trusting in Him, you can receive strength to weather the harshest experiences.

Father, I trust in You to give me the strength
I need to overcome my troubles. Amen.

DAY FOUR

HOPE THAT OVERCOMES TROUBLES
Hebrews 10:34

Someone once said, "You can live for forty days without food, three days without water, and four minutes without oxygen. But you cannot live one second without hope!" Hebrews 10:34 confirms this adage. Despite the troubles they faced, the original readers of this letter were able to thrive spiritually in the midst of their problems because their hope was in Christ.

The hope of the early church was not based on some cheap optimism or some fleeting promise of the world. Their confident assurance was based on the person and work of Christ. They knew that He would never turn His back on them. He was their strength in time of weakness and their joy in time of sorrow.

Where is your hope? Is it in your home, family, money, or job? You could loose all of those things. Yet, no one can take away your salvation in Christ. The forgiveness and joy you have in Him are sure (John 10:28–29; Rom. 8:39; 1 Peter 1:4–5). People and fads come and go, but Christ is your solid rock for all situations. He will never disappoint you.

Lord, thank You that my hope is in Christ, who
will never disappoint me. Amen.

SURPRISED AT SUFFERING?

1 Peter 4:12–13

You've put your faith in Christ. You love Him and serve Him devotedly. Why, then, does He allow you to suffer? Are you surprised that He doesn't prevent messy things from happening to you?

Peter wrote to a group of believers who were suffering for the cause of Christ. Apparently, they were shocked that others would persecute them for their faith. The apostle encouraged them not to be surprised because even their Lord was not immune from experiencing hardships. Instead, Peter urged them to rejoice in the midst of their fiery trials because their difficulties made them partners with Christ in His suffering (1 Peter 4:12–13).

Are you taken aback by Peter's words? Perhaps you always assumed that serving Christ would be easy and free from suffering. Guess again! If Jesus, your Lord, experienced hardship as He served the Father, you can expect to encounter the same hardship.

When persecution strikes, consider it an opportunity to show others the reality of your faith in Christ. Let them see through your actions that Christ's power works best in your weakness (2 Cor. 12:9). Remember, it is when you realize your own mortality and limitations that Jesus' sovereignty and greatness are most evident (v. 10).

Dear Lord, please help me to rejoice in You, despite any sufferings I might be experiencing. Amen.

THE HOPE OF HEAVEN

Revelation 7:15–17

Did you ever have an accident as a child and run to your mother for help? Perhaps she held you in her arms and wiped away your tears. As wonderful as those experiences might have been, they cannot compare to our Lord's wiping away every tear from our eyes (Rev. 7:15–17).

The promise of heaven is one of our greatest assurances as we face troubles. Christ is Lord over all, and His pledge to bring us to our eternal home is guaranteed. In light of this promise, our troubles do not seem so overwhelming.

What should be your response to problems? You don't want to give up, even when the world seems overrun with wickedness and injustice. Yes, at times the forces of darkness seem to be overwhelming. But Jesus is infinitely more powerful than any foe you might have (1 John 4:4).

Are you troubled? You shouldn't be, for Christ—who conquered Satan, sin, and death—is in heaven right now preparing a place for you. When everything is ready, He will come and get you so that you will be with Him always (John 14:1–3). What a fantastic promise! What a wonderful Lord!

Lord, thank You for the hope of heaven. Amen.

DAY SEVEN

ARE YOU FREE OR IMPRISONED?

ACTS 16:23–34

What constitutes incarceration? Do you have to be behind bars to be a prisoner? We learn from Acts 16:23–34 that Paul and Silas were imprisoned and guarded by a jailer. But who was really free?

The world would assert that the jailer was free and that the two missionaries were imprisoned. But take a closer look at the passage. Yes, Paul and Silas were sitting in an inner dungeon and had their feet clamped in stocks. But their souls were free because they had trusted in Christ.

In contrast, the jailer was not physically bound, but he had no assurance of salvation. In fact, the thought that some prisoners might escape during his watch convinced him that he should commit suicide. Only the quick thinking of Paul prevented such a tragedy. God used him and Silas to lead the troubled jailer and his family to salvation in Christ.

Today, many people are imprisoned by worry, greed, or lust for power. They think that freedom is defined by having a lot of money and prestige. But that's a warped viewpoint because Jesus said that everyone who sins is a slave to sin (John 8:34). Remember, true freedom comes only through faith in Christ (Gal. 5:1).

Lord, thank You for setting me free when I trusted in Christ for salvation. Amen.

KEN CORR

A Man and His Body: Physical Fitness

LOVING GOD BY BEING HEALTHY

Mark 12:29–30

Recently, I was asked to speak to a class in our church on how to pray for our congregation. I asked the group to pray that we would be not only a growing church but also a healthy church. One member in the class asked, "What does a healthy congregation look like?"

I honestly was not prepared to answer that question. But as I reflected later, I began to think about the issue in personal terms, and then the words of Jesus in Mark 12:29–30 gave me fresh insight. A healthy Christian is growing in his love for God emotionally, mentally, spiritually, and physically. This means that I must be committed to a balanced and wholesome lifestyle.

In recent years, we have heard that we need to eat well and exercise regularly so that we will live longer, feel better, and look more attractive. But we seldom hear that we need to do these things because we love God. Maybe that is the reason why so many of our efforts at diet and exercise fail. Perhaps we would do better if we saw our efforts as a way of worshiping and glorifying the Lord.

Dear God, please help me to be healthy as a way of not only feeling better and looking more attractive but also offering my love to You. Amen.

MY BODY, GOD'S TEMPLE

1 Corinthians 6:19–20

Growing up in east Alabama, I was taught that my body was God's temple, which meant that I was not to use alcohol, drugs, or tobacco, or to have premarital sex. However, as I grew older, I began to realize that 1 Corinthians 6:19–20 taught more than that.

This passage encourages us not only to avoid things that are harmful to our body but also to do things that will keep it healthy. The neglect and abuse of our body is a spiritual matter. Similarly, the exercise of and care for our body is also of concern to God. How could deliberately letting our body deteriorate be honoring to God?

A few years ago, my cholesterol level was at 358 and rising. Because my family has a history of heart disease, I was concerned. But my efforts at diet and exercise were perfunctory. I told myself that one day I would have to get this condition under control. But then I realized that the issue was more than a health problem; it was also a spiritual problem. Only then did I begin to make important lifestyle changes.

Your body is God's temple and is to be used for His glory. Ask yourself whether you need to make some changes to offer God a healthier, more Christ-honoring body.

Lord, please help me to be responsible with the way I treat my body, for I know that it belongs to You. Amen.

DAY THREE

GOD'S ATHLETES
1 Corinthians 9:24–27

Our family was watching ice skating on television, admiring the grace and skill of the athletes, when my wife asked, "Do you think I could learn to skate like that?" I responded, "Are you willing to work eight hours a day for years?"

World-class athletes make their sport look easy. But what we don't see are the years of disciplined training required to develop the level of skill that makes the activity "look" easy.

Paul admired the dedication of athletes and believed that the same level of commitment was required of Christians in matters of faith. The apostle practiced what he preached. He disciplined not only his mind, his spirit, and his time but also his body. He realized that spiritual growth required him to control his physical appetites.

If this was true for Paul, how much more is it true for you? If you're like me, it's easy to ignore your body in pursuit of spiritual things. But your spiritual progress requires both a disciplined body and a disciplined soul. As we learn from 1 Corinthians 9:24–27, God's athletes must be in shape.

Lord, please help me to control my appetites better so that I might present to You a body that is ready to serve You. Amen.

Holistic Spirituality
Exodus 15:26

I visited in the hospital room of my friend, who had just been diagnosed with cancer. The initial shock and grief were accompanied by the question that is asked so often at times like this, "What did I do to deserve this?"

Exodus 15:26 seems to make the promise that if we keep God's commandments and live faithfully, we will not get sick. We know too much today about the spread of viruses and bacterial infections to believe that all disease is a result of disobedience. But the text clearly points to a relationship between bodily health and the spiritual life. When we are in spiritual distress, our physical health suffers. When we ignore our physical health, our spiritual lives suffer.

Modern medicine is beginning to recognize that we can't separate the body and the spirit. Holistic medicine seeks to treat the whole person—body, soul, and spirit.

I do not believe that all disease points to a spiritual problem, but I do believe that wellness requires us to take care of our bodies and our spirits. A holistic spirituality will give attention to both spiritual health and physical health, because the two cannot be separated.

God, I know that You want me to be healthy. I confess that sometimes it is easier for me to be committed to my spiritual disciplines than to my physical disciplines. Help me to see the changes I need to make in order to be well in every area of my life. Amen.

DAY FIVE

An Avenue of Prayer
1 Thessalonians 5:17

My legs, back, and lungs were aching as I finished the second mile of my daily jog. Suddenly, I asked myself, "Why am I doing this?" I often ask myself that question in the mornings when I would rather be doing anything else but strenuous exercise. The answer is simple: "I am offering my daily prayer to God."

I was raised in the southern, evangelical, Baptist tradition, in which prayer is primarily thought of as special moments of intercession and thanksgiving with heads bowed and eyes closed. A Catholic woman helped me begin to enlarge my understanding of prayer when she said, "My work is my prayer."

When any activity is surrendered to God for giving Him glory, that activity is prayer. Thus working, playing, and exercising can be avenues of prayer to God. In light of this, 1 Thessalonians 5:17 makes a lot more sense. Now, when I begin my morning jog, I remind myself that I am not exercising simply for my health. I am primarily doing it as an avenue of prayer to God.

Father, please help me to make even my daily
exercise routine an avenue of prayer to You. Amen.

DAY SIX

The Spirituality of Eating
Daniel 1:8–16

Throughout the Bible, a close relationship exists between spirituality and eating. Even a cursory reading of the Bible reveals this intimate connection. For example, the first sin involved the act of eating. The law of Israel contained many dietary restrictions. Abstaining from certain foods was a form of ritual purity. Fasting, as a form of repentance and devotion, was encouraged. Jesus used a meal as the abiding symbol of His sacrifice. And the joy of heaven is compared to a banquet feast.

The account of Daniel's and his companions' refusal to eat the king's food is another example of the interrelationship between spirituality and eating. Commentaries discuss at length the reasons for Daniel's refusal to eat the king's food. Although there may have been many reasons for his refusal, there was only one outcome: "At the end of ten days their appearance seemed better and they were fatter than all the youths who had been eating the king's choice food" (Dan. 1:15). The account is a reminder that maintaining a healthy diet is one way of honoring God.

This is a truth that we need to hear today. We give little thought to the spirituality of eating, and our diets reflect it. The relationship between our spirit and our body should not be underestimated. We would do well to consider our diets and begin to make some changes not only for our health but also as a way of honoring God.

God, please help me not to sin against You
in my eating. Amen.

DAY SEVEN

DISCIPLINED APPETITES
Philippians 3:17–21

I was raised in a church that practices baptism by immersion, and I was baptized at the age of eight. As I stepped into the baptismal waters, I had little understanding of the vow that I was taking. I did not realize that baptism is symbolic of death to my former life controlled by sin and of resurrection to a new life controlled by God. All that I knew was that I had trusted in Christ for salvation.

Through the years, I have learned more about the demands of that baptismal vow. For example, I now know that it is not always easy to fulfill. And the appetites of life are just as real for Christians as they are for unbelievers. But the memory of that ceremony is a reminder that my allegiance and loyalty, my citizenship and devotion, belong to God.

In Philippians 3:17–21, Paul drew a sharp contrast between those who are believers and those who are the enemies of Christ. The latter give their allegiance to their appetite. It is a picture of someone who is undisciplined and ruled by his physical desires.

But Christians are to be different. We are called to discipline our appetites, or our bodily desires, for we have a higher calling. As citizens of heaven, every aspect of our life—including our physical cravings—must come under the lordship of Christ. There is no exception to this truth.

God, please help me to live as a citizen of heaven
and to serve You in all that I do. Amen.

MARVIN DOUGLASS

A Man and His Body: Sexuality

WE ARE MAN

Genesis 1:26—27

We are man. We are told that we are "fearfully and wonderfully made" (Ps. 139:14) and that our bodies are temples of the Spirit (1 Cor. 3:16) and the dwelling place of Christ (Col. 1:27). Yet, we are warned that the "flesh sets its desire against the Spirit, and the Spirit against the flesh" (Gal. 5:17). How can this contrast be? Are we vessels to bring forth bitter as well as sweet water, sometimes simultaneously? Yes! We are a reflection of both the creation and the Creator.

We are man, instructed to rule over all God's creation (Gen. 1:26–27). But, first, we are to rule ourselves, for we, too, are God's creation, and are to bring discipline and balance to our human vessels. Self is not easy to rule, however, and it is even more difficult to lead. But self-discipline is a learned behavior and is the price of our appointment to leadership.

Therefore, the first duty of a godly ruler is to rule himself. This task is accomplished by studying the way of those who have gone before us and by marking a trail for those who will come after us. We are both the sculptor and the stone, both the teacher and the student. We are man.

Father, please help me to be the man
You intended. Amen.

CLOSER THAN BLOOD KIN

Genesis 2:24

Man is a social creature. He enjoys community, both giving and receiving friendship and love. He counts friends as assets and his family as treasures, and he takes great pride in his progeny. He carefully guards his reputation in the community, and he subtly solicits the praise of his peers.

But when a man is tired, alone, and overcome with the lusty urge for intimacy, he turns for solace not to the community or even to his children, but to his wife. She is the source of satisfaction for this primal drive. To no other person can a man be as closely related as to this one with whom he becomes intimately united in both soul and body (Gen. 2:24).

When a man is hungry after he has finished his meal, he will turn to his wife for the nurture that only she can provide. This nurture dwells in her body and is released in response to the signal of his need. And then he sleeps, lying, like a satisfied child, captured and exclusive, in her arms.

Father, please help me to find intimacy and companionship with the wife You have given to me. Amen.

THINKING, FEELING, DOING

2 Corinthians 10:5

The largest number of sins, if tallied, would be not of the body but of the mind. We have learned behavioral constraints as a result of self-imposed social restrictions. We do not act out our imaginations or give uncensored vent to our desires. Still rampant, however, are our thoughts, over which society has no control. Laws do not police the mind. We are accountable to no person for our thoughts, which are one of the few remaining vestiges of unregulated freedom.

We are accountable only to God and to ourselves for our thoughts. Our tendency is to allow free thinking, with little or no mental discipline. The mind is the ultimate privacy where we can let down any facade and be, without apology, whoever we are.

Behaviorists say that sexual thoughts are the most prevalent of our mental patterns. The average person, males particularly, experience sexual thoughts every minute when the mind is allowed to wander aimlessly. The time between thoughts may vary with individuals, but the sexual content is consistent and, for many men, unwanted. How do we deal with unwanted thoughts?

Thought control is a learned function. Unless you are experiencing a mental or personality disorder, you can control your thinking. Paul wrote that we are to "bring every thought into subjection" and to "take captive every thought and make it obedient" (2 Cor. 10:5). The prerequisite is desire, and when we control our minds, we automatically decrease sinful behavior.

Lord, please help me to control my behavior by the controlling of my thoughts. Amen.

THE REDEMPTION OF SUFFERING

1 Peter 4:1–4

Early church father Origen allegedly had himself castrated in an effort to reduce his lustful desires. We do not know how effective this extreme measure was, but we can identify with the struggle. The motivation for this mutilation was a desire to live a life for God alone, and to separate from mundane, earthy things. But only a few men have been called to celibacy.

The Christian man's calling is to be active in his world. To do this, he must be among those who are physical and mundane and unspiritual. Many such people live their lives to gratify their evil human desires. The Christian man is not blind to their behavior, and he is not immune to the temptation to mimic their behavior because he, too, is human. But what can he do to overcome enticements to sin?

In 1 Peter 4:1–4, we learn that "he who has suffered in his body is done with sin." And, as a result of this suffering, a man will live for the will of God rather than for "evil human desires." What, then, can a Christian man do to achieve spiritual victory over mental and physical temptation? Should he castrate himself? Certainly not!

Celibacy is not an adequate, practical answer. Rather, he must surrender completely and without qualification to the will of God, for only in spiritual union with Christ is victory possible.

Lord, please help me to resist my evil human desires and thereby draw closer to You. Amen.

RITE OF PASSAGE
2 Timothy 2:22

Spring, some people say, is "when a young man's fancy turns to love." Dormant hormones stir and cry for release. The boy is awakened and stumbles clumsily toward manhood. He feels the fever of carnal awareness. New and confusing thoughts crowd in as intruders. They seem frightening, foreboding, and forbidden. All he has been taught and teased to avoid now tantalizes him, drawing him toward the heat of an unseen, unexplained sexual fire.

Older men laugh at the young man's torment. They joke and ask questions, which for them were answered long ago. The boy is driven, like salmon, to pursue relentlessly his quest for the historic breeding grounds. The search will consummate in explosive release for the boy and assurance of posterity for the future.

After breeding, salmon die, but men do not. They live on and pray for wisdom and strength to subdue this self-perpetuating passion. What begins, however, as the rite of passage into majority, if abused, can become the passage to moral failure. The body and the mind mature and attempt to realize equilibrium, for the passion remains a source of exhilaration and exasperation.

In time, the fire weakens, and an older man is lured by a sense of false security. He thinks that he is beyond the fire of sexual passion. But proceed with caution, for this fiery steed has teeth of steel, which can bite the bit and run, uncontrolled, into mayhem. No wonder Paul wrote, "Flee the evil desires of youth" (2 Tim. 2:22).

Father, please give me the courage to seek a pure heart. Amen.

GOD'S BEHAVIORAL
MODIFICATION PROGRAM

1 Corinthians 5:3—5

First Corinthians 5:3–5 presents a distressing thought. Paul commanded that a member of the church who was guilty of gross immorality be turned over to Satan for the destruction of the "flesh," the instrument of his sin. The apostle further wrote that this destruction, in turn, would "save the spirit."

At first, this terrifying idea conjures a picture of punishment imposed with an inquisitional thumb screw. More terrifying still, these punishments, or any others, would be meted out by the archenemy, Satan.

But such isn't an accurate understanding of the passage. Paul's ultimate goal was remedial, not punitive. The apostle reasoned (and hoped) that after the offender was separated from the spiritual protection of the church, he would recognize his sin, repent, and return to the Lord and the fellowship of His people. Ultimately, all church discipline has as its goal spiritual restoration.

The good news is that even deviant sexual behavior can be changed. The Lord can enable you to conquer and control your passions. I'm not saying that this will be easy. But it can be done. In fact, it must be done, if God is to be glorified.

*Father, please protect me from myself by helping
me conquer and control my sexual desires. Amen.*

THE CALL OF THE WILD

Proverbs 9:13—18

Humans are sexual beings, so created by God's design. The sexual nature is both the assurance of procreation and the unique relationship between male and female. Sexual intimacy is a dominant drive and culminating experience. Sexual pursuits have many faces. Pyramids and skyscrapers, art and architecture, are often defined as subtle, veiled expressions of sexuality.

The powerful, sexual expressions of human nature are strongest in the young. The rituals allure the victim until they are successfully enchanted and subdued. However, the fine movements of human intimacy are perfected over time only with practice. Perfection of love comes as each participant seeks out the particular needs of his or her mate and takes pleasure in the provision.

Since the dawn of time, people have struggled with the desire to gratify their sexual urges incorrectly. The Christian man is not immune to this temptation. It's easy for him to gaze across the valley to the plush, green fields of new grain. He can become entranced by the brilliant color, the waving stalks, and the alluring shimmer. But if he fails to heed the warnings of Scripture, he will soon discover rocks beneath the grain. By the time he sees the adder, he will have already felt the deadly sting of its bite (Prov. 9:13–18).

Father, please help me to give my sexual love
only to my wife. Amen.

K E N   W A L K E R

A Man and His Finances: Money

RUNNING AFTER WHAT?

Ecclesiastes 5:10

S. Truett Cathy, founder of the Chick-fil-A fast-food chain, has taught Sunday school to eighth-grade boys for more than 40 years. Many of his students think that inheriting a million dollars would solve all of their families' problems. They also think that a nice home, clothes, vacations, and cars will buy lasting happiness.

But, Cathy says, "Money's not going to solve our problems. It only adds to the problem. Seeing business people having over and above what they need—often, it creates problems. Material things are not going to be the solution to our problems in our homes."

Cathy's comments reflect the truth that Solomon outlined in Ecclesiastes 5:10. Many other examples abound in our society. Some professional athletes, corporate executives, and movie stars earn more money than most of us will see in a lifetime. Yet many of them search desperately for elusive fulfillment and happiness.

But some stories are closer to the "average" person, too. Take, for example, the man who won $16.8 million in the Pennsylvania lottery in 1988, only to be embroiled later in lawsuits, criminal charges, and marital woes. His brother went to prison for trying to murder him.

Each of us must ask ourselves, *For what am I striving in life? Do I run after promotions, pay increases, and prestige, all the while thinking that church membership makes me "okay"? What is the focus of my heart? If it's money, I am doomed never to find the answer.*

Lord, please help me to see that true riches can never be found in the world's goods. Help me to set my sights today on Your calling. Amen.

THE SOURCE

Deuteronomy 8:18

Although I remember it like yesterday, more than a decade has passed since the October 1987 stock market crash wiped out my public relations business. A psychology of fear dried up financing and led many companies to pull in their horns. One client on a healthy retainer canceled within a month. Three companies who owed me substantial sums of money went bankrupt. By the end of the year, I didn't know how we would survive.

Recovery was slow and painful. I kept waiting for that "magic" check to fall from the sky and wipe out our debts. I thought that would be only fitting. If it weren't for the companies who had never paid me, I wouldn't have had any debt. But the check never came.

A few years passed. One afternoon I scanned my accounts receivable. Although things had improved, times were still tough. Losing my temper, I growled, "God, where are You? I don't see any miraculous provision. We tithe, but I don't see any special blessings. Everything in this file is something I've worked for."

Suddenly, a thought shot through my mind. Gently yet forcefully, it asked, "Where do you think the work came from?" I felt as though I had been slapped in the face—kindly.

I have never forgotten that lesson. If you are tempted to think that your good fortunes are a result of your brilliance, read Deuteronomy 8:18 and ask yourself, *"From where did it come?"*

Lord, please help me to see You as the source of everything I have, whether the blessings I appreciate or the adversity that helps me to grow. Amen.

THE POWER

1 Chronicles 29:12

I've interviewed some pretty famous people, including professional athletes Reggie White, Mark Brunell, and A. C. Green; NASCAR driver Darrell Waltrip; comedian Mark Lowry; Charles Colson, whose Watergate-era conversion led him to start Prison

Fellowship; and singers such as Ricky Skaggs, Larnelle Harris, and "Butterfly Kisses" father Bob Carlisle.

What is the outstanding quality of these men? It's humility. Of course, Christian faith helps them to recognize that their accomplishments come from a source greater than themselves. Still, basking in the monetary rewards and the glow of an adoring public can make it easy for them to forget what caused their success.

The headlines of the past decade are littered with names, great and small, of those who couldn't handle the stress and temptations of affluence. How easy it is for us to judge them without recognizing our own cravings. Given the right circumstances, any of us could also fall. We continually need strength (1 Chron. 29:12).

Instead of striving for personal and monetary gain, pause to thank God for wherever you are today. Remember that the Lord has chosen to place you where you live, in this era, for a special purpose. If He chooses to elevate you, He will. What you do for God today doesn't depend on your renown or wealth. Follow the One who knows when you can be trusted to handle the pressures that accompany great achievement.

Lord, You have chosen the place where I am and the job that I do so that I can live for Your glory. Please help me to fulfill that destiny. Amen.

DAY FOUR

A JOB WELL DONE
Ecclesiastes 5:19

Do you ever get giddy over your work? The joy derived from a job well done carries more meaningful rewards than a paycheck. Many men know the pleasure of crafting things with their hands. They measure, hammer, plane, and shape raw wood into objects, whether as complex as a housing development or as simple as a walking stick.

However, that isn't my story. I never learned such skills as a boy. What one lacks in his youth is tough to grasp later in life. Yet I know the joy of sharing the gospel through writing hundreds of testimonies, stories of mission trips, and relating miracles that God performs in our world.

One of my most enjoyable tasks came from writing a book that has never been published. It tells the story of two brothers who smuggled food, supplies, and Bibles into Eastern Europe before the fall of Communism. Both of them tried to help others escape from Romania. One succeeded.

The two brothers hoped to let Americans know about their fellow Christians' suffering and to raise additional funds to help persecuted believers. For various reasons, publication of the book was delayed and then halted when the Romanian dictator was overthrown.

Although I made little money working on that manuscript, I will always remember the pleasure of writing it. I was thrilled to help relate this dramatic story of God's miraculous protection and intervention behind the Iron Curtain. It remains a highlight of my career.

Such a feeling is a gift of God. The same gift is available to every man who toils in His name.

God, thank You for the rewards of work. Amen.

DAY FIVE

FISHING WITHOUT BAIT

Matthew 4:19

Surveys show that the average American church member gives two to three percent of his income to his place of worship. Although that amount is twice as much as non-churchgoers give to charity, contrast it with the words of Malachi 3:10: "Bring all the tithes into the storehouse, that there may be food in my house" (NKJV).

Some people would argue that New Testament believers don't have to tithe because we're not under the law. But check out the parable of the widow's mite in Mark 12:42–44. Jesus commended a woman who gave 100 percent. Christ raised the bar far above a legalistic standard. He give His life. In return, He deserves our all, whether it's money, time, or devotion.

The sad truth is that giving by church members has dropped over the last three decades with a corresponding rise in personal indebtedness for personal luxuries. And at what cost? The ability of the church to spread the gospel has diminished greatly.

Imagine what your church could do with nearly triple its current income (assuming that some members *do* tithe). What new ministries could be started? Poor people fed? Missions outposts established? Tracts and gospel literature distributed in your neighborhood?

Many church members dislike lessons or sermons about giving, saying that giving is a personal matter between them and God. If that is so, can you honestly say that the Lord is pleased with your giving to His church—one about which He cared so much that His Son died for it? Like the disciples, we are called to be fishers of men (Matt. 4:19), but fishing requires money. Think how successful you would be on the lake if you couldn't afford any bait.

Lord, please show me ways that I can live on less so that I can give more to Your work. Amen.

DAY SIX

LIFE'S REWARDS

Psalm 62:10

One of the strangest news stories I ever saw concerned a small-town merchant who was robbed and murdered on his way home from work. The reporter concluded, "Fortunately for the deceased, he had dropped his money in the night depository before he was murdered, and the only thing that was lost was his life."

You may laugh at that awkward choice of words. But how many Christians measure their worth by the world's values? They equate God's blessings with fine homes, fashionable clothes, new cars, and other "executive privileges," as if things could somehow buy happiness.

As financial counselor and author Howard Dayton notes, the Scriptures address the topic of money more than any other single subject. God's Word is clear that we are to be good stewards of our money. However, the Bible also teaches that material possessions do not bring eternal life.

Psalm 62:10 reminds me of Paul's message in Philippians 4:11–12, where he said that he had learned to be content in all circumstances, whether in plenty or in want. We often focus on the hurdle of having too little while forgetting the equally tough challenge of having too much.

As middle age advances, I have become more aware of the things that can't be bought: a good marriage, healthy family relationships, close friends, faithful prayer partners, and fulfillment through God. True, we all have bills to pay. Money is part of living in this world. But if you focus on eternal matters, love far outranks money.

*Father, please help me to appreciate the riches in life
that have nothing to do with my bank account. Amen.*

PURCHASING EVIL

Hosea 2:8

Christian men have a problem with pornography. That fact was documented several years ago in a study by Dr. Archibald Hart, dean of the Graduate School of Psychology at Fuller Theological Seminary. In a survey of six hundred married men (mostly Christians), he learned that 91 percent of those from Christian homes had been exposed to pornography within two years of puberty; 71 percent said that pornography was destructive to their sexuality.

Promise Keepers has also surveyed men at their huge stadium rallies. More than half of the respondents admitted struggling with pornography, which is often the gateway to more serious problems (such as having affairs or patronizing prostitutes).

From personal experience, I know how tough it is to over-come the influence of this God-forsaken material. If there is one thing I wish I had never done before I was saved, it is that I watched X-rated movies.

Pornography is such a stronghold of evil that men have written many books addressing it. Although I can't offer easy solutions in a short devotional, I must point out that sampling pornography is identical to Israel's giving offerings to idols.

The Bible is clear that we are only stewards of God's posses-sions. Psalm 50:10 says He owns "the cattle on a thousand hills." To use His money to purchase or participate in any way with illicit sexual material is like taking God's money and giving it to the Devil. Christian brothers, this ought not to be (Hos. 2:8).

*Lord, please help me to use wisely Your
resources so that my actions will glorify You. Amen.*

BOB HARTSELL

A Man and His Finances: Investments

THE PRUDENCE OF PROVIDING

Proverbs 6:6–11

"Knowledge is the possession of information; wisdom is the ability to apply it."

That's the answer one of my professors gave to a student's question. Most people that I, as a family finances consultant, have counseled knew that they wouldn't have enough money to retire, but they weren't doing anything about it. Their common explanation was that today's expenses don't leave anything for tomorrow's investments.

Consider the wisdom of the ant mentioned in Proverbs 6:6–11. Without anyone standing over it, the ant acts on what it knows. The first lesson from the ant is that current industry avoids want; even ants are wise enough not to allow laziness to lead them into poverty and starvation.

A popular humorist recently offered the following advice for today's youth: "Pull up your pants. Turn your hat around. Go to work." I think Solomon would endorse that advice—and not just for young people.

The second lesson from the ant is that prudent investing provides for the future. No one can guarantee the future, but if most of us exercised the ant's wisdom, we'd have little need to worry whether the Social Security fund will expire before we do or whether we'll become dependent upon our families or society in old age.

The ant balances the needs of the present and the future. Should men be less wise? Most men know better, but many of them don't do better. A. L. Williams popularized a slogan, later made famous by a shoe manufacturer: "Do it!" This is a keen observation that is also relevant to investing.

God, please give me wisdom to apply the knowledge You've provided about finances and investing. Amen.

THE REQUIREMENT OF RESPONSIBILITY
1 Timothy 5:8

Occasionally, a student in my Family Assets Management class will express the notion that investing is optional. The typical line of reasoning is that if something happened to him, the government would take care of him or his family. His goal was to enjoy life now, not to build a retirement portfolio.

God's message, however, is that we have a moral and spiritual obligation to provide for ourselves and our families. Evidently, Paul took this injunction very seriously, for he stated, "This we commanded you, that if any would not work, neither should he eat" (2 Thess. 3:10). The admonition to provide for our own families lest we deny the faith and become worse than infidels is a judgment from Scripture (1 Tim. 5:8).

As I was discussing with one client life insurance as a means of providing for his family in the event of his premature death, he responded, "That won't matter to me. One second after I'm dead, I won't care about my family." I couldn't dispute his logic, but I was appalled at his crassness. He had an unemployed wife and children who were too young to provide for themselves. Yet he felt that his responsibility terminated at death.

The atheist or the infidel might conclude that he has no obligation to those dependent upon him, but that conclusion is unsuitable for a Christian. If we choose to have a family, we assume the responsibility of providing for them—in both the present and the future. Thus, investing is not optional!

Gracious Lord, please give me the courage and the discipline to provide for my loved ones. Amen.

THE DANGER OF DELAY

James 4:13–15

In our twenties, we say, "I'm barely making enough to live on. I don't have any money to invest." In our thirties, we say, "I want to enjoy boating, camping, and vacations with my wife and children while we're young. We have plenty of time to invest." In our forties, we say, "I have to pay for my kids' college education. I can't afford to invest." In our fifties, we say, "Investments couldn't grow fast enough for me to retire on them." In our sixties, we say, "It's too late! Why didn't I have sense enough to start when I was young?!"

Excuses don't buy groceries! With a 12 percent return, to have $100,000 at age sixty-five takes only $10.21 a month starting at age twenty-five. But we need $32.46 at age thirty-five, $108.71 at age forty-five, and $446.36 at age fifty-five. Or $2000 invested annually in a 12 percent IRA during ages twenty-two to twenty-seven (six years—$12,000) and left alone until age sixty will produce $683,000, while starting at age twenty-eight it takes $2000 *every year* ($64,000) to match that return. Left until age sixty-five, it would top $1.3 million.

True, we have no assurance that we will live long enough for our investments to mature to full capacity. But it is equally true that we have no assurance we will live five or ten years to start investing for our family's future.

James gives us a truth from life. We don't know what tomorrow will bring, or whether we will have a tomorrow (James 4:13–15). Preparing for a tomorrow we might not have seems to be a better choice than having a tomorrow for which we didn't prepare.

Dear God, please keep me from procrastination and help me to act wisely today. Amen.

THE HAZARD OF HASTE

Proverbs 28:20

You've probably heard the following adages.
"Haste makes waste."

"Fools rush in where angels fear to tread."
"No need to do today what can be put off until tomorrow."
"Moderation in all things—especially moderation."

So what do you do to avoid both the danger of delay and the hazard of haste? Make a commitment to the practice of investing now and developing a money management plan that puts tithing first and investing second before any other spending. Get started on the activity now.

But don't rush into any specific investment as if it were the only opportunity available and will expire at midnight. Good investments are always available! Avoid get-rich-quick schemes (Prov. 28:20). Occasionally, someone becomes a millionaire overnight. But don't bet your future on it happening to you.

Two rules of sound investment are time and consistency. Start now (you'll never be younger!) and invest at least a base amount each week or month—more whenever you can.

"Where do I get the money to start?" I taught a class the goal of which was to help a family stop wasting $2000 a year in needless spending so that they could put the money into an IRA. Most people increase regular spending or splurge when they get a raise, bonus, or birthday gift. Don't do that! Instead, add those dollars to your regular investments. Start now, but invest patiently.

*Loving Father, may greed and desire for success
never stampede me into foolish action concerning
investments. Amen.*

DAY FIVE

THE REALITY OF RISK
Luke 14:28

I was almost fifty years old before I developed a theology of risk. Having been a minister or professor all of my adult life, and believing implicitly in institutional security, I was declared surplus and released from my position at an age, rank, and salary that made me essentially unemployable. Immediately, I understood that life offers only apparent—not actual—security.

Then I took a new look at the biblical record. I found risk from the start. From God's creation of man and entrusting him with a garden through His work with the patriarchs, Moses, the kings, and the prophets to the incarnation and ministry of Jesus, God risked redemption on people who wouldn't accept it. And Jesus risked dying for people who would reject Him.

So I wasn't surprised that there was no sure thing in investments, or that return is directly related to risk. The safest, government-insured investments produce the lowest returns, seldom keeping pace with inflation. Investments offering higher returns offer no guarantees. But if you don't play, you can't win. Only those who risk losing have the opportunity of winning. The fans in the stands never wear a championship ring!

Consider the insight from experience stated by Jesus in Luke 14:28. It is wise to think about the possibilities before committing resources. In other words, make a calculated risk.

Nothing is risk-free. But that's no excuse for either avoiding a venture or walking into it blindly, impetuously, or stupidly. "Counting the cost" is a prudent, scriptural practice. The only successful investors are those who count the cost and then take the risks.

God, please give me wisdom as I calculate the cost
of each investment I make. Amen.

THE DOMAIN OF DOLLARS
I Timothy 6:7

Occasionally, in problem solving, I suddenly see a solution sitting right in front of my face that is waiting for me to discover it. My wife calls this "a blinding flash of the obvious." Today's youth are more inclined to say, "Duh!"

Maybe that's the way you feel about Paul's reminder to Timothy that people bring nothing into the world and they carry nothing out of it (1 Tim. 6:7). This verse suggests that whatever resources God entrusts to our care in this life are intended to produce results while we are on earth. For example, money belongs to the physical domain. Since we can't take any with us, it seems wise to use it to the best advantage while we're here. That means maximizing its return.

In his charming and insightful little book *The Richest Man in Babylon,* George S. Clason tells how Arkad learned from Algamish to reinvest his profits (compound his interest) instead of consuming them.

"And what do you do with the rental [interest]?"

"I do have a great feast with honey and fine wine and spiced cake. Also I have bought me a scarlet tunic."

"You do eat the children of your savings. Then how do you expect them to work for you? And how can they have children that will work for you? First get thee an army of golden slaves and then many a rich banquet may you enjoy without regret."

Ten thousand dollars invested at 8 percent for thirty years will produce $109,357—if you don't "eat your golden slaves."

Heavenly Father, please help me to use wisely the money You have entrusted to my care. Amen.

THE ACCOUNTABILITY FOR ASSETS

Matthew 25:14–30

The most distressing attitude among people I have counseled on family assets management was this: "It's my money, I can do with it as I please!" That's just enough truth to be misleading. Yes, God generally leaves us alone to do as we please with our material wealth, as did the master in the parable recorded in Matthew 25:14–30. But that shouldn't blind us to the story's eternal principle: God holds us accountable for our actions.

A careful reading of this parable will reveal the following additional truths:

- The servants and the goods belonged to the master.
- The goods matched the stewards' abilities.
- Two servants doubled their master's assets, but one was afraid to try.
- The master assumed the risk because the goods were his, not the servants'.
- I need not envy another person who has greater resources than I because God has entrusted me with all that I'm capable of handling.

- Others' successes need not make me feel guilty or a failure, for God knows that not all people have the same ability.
- I need not fear risking failure with the resources God has entrusted to me. I need fear only failing to risk.
- The servant who was upbraided was not one of the two who risked failure, but the one who failed to risk.

Lord, please help me be a courageous and faithful steward of the resources You've entrusted to me. Amen.

DAVID FARR

A Man and His Finances: Stewardship

OTHERS OR YOURSELF?

Proverbs 11:25

Joe questioned his friend Dennis, "How will I survive if I need to consider others before myself? Twice a month I give a tithe to the church and every spring I give to the local shelter after cleaning out the garage. If I did much more, I believe my family would begin to feel the effects and suffer." Dennis responded, "Actually, the opposite happens. When you give spontaneously, joyously in an effort to address a person's needs, God will bless you spiritually."

At first, the seeming contradiction confused Joe. But then he realized that God's Word does not contain contradictions. Instead, apparent discrepancies are a reflection of how the Lord interacts with His children. God owns everything, and we are just stewards of what He gives us. If the Lord commands us to help those who have needs, He will provide for our needs (though not for our greeds).

At that moment, Joe remembered his neighbor, who recently had lost his job and was struggling to meet his family's needs. Joe asked Dennis to meet him next week to work on a project. When Dennis returned the following week, he discovered Joe at work in his neighbor's garage, fixing different household items. Joe's neighbor asked Dennis why Joe was giving so much when they barely knew one another. Dennis smiled and said, "Joe likes to share his time and talent, for he knows that God is looking out for him."

Lord, please help me to honor You with all that I have. Amen.

SPIRITUAL ECONOMICS
2 Corinthians 9:6−7

Max worked at a local engineering firm for thirty years and was very careful with his money. His motto was "buy skeptically, sell grudgingly." His thirty years of service was marked with frugality. In fact, Max would save the used calculator tape by using a large clip. When the first side of the calculator tape had been exhausted, Max would invert the tape and use the other side. If Max ever purchased a new item, he was filled with buyer's remorse.

One day, a Christian service organization asked businessmen to participate in fixing a local shelter for women in crisis. At first Max was reluctant, but after their plea, he felt he should take time to work with the other men. When Max arrived, he discovered many of his colleagues toiling on the project. He saw their smiles in the midst of the dust, sweat, and noise of heavy labor. As the men gathered, Max and one other man were the last to receive an assignment. The project manager's finger pointed to a broken toilet in a small bathroom with leaky plumbing.

Max began to wonder why he did not give them a few dollars and forget the whole thing. Jim, an elder at a local church, was Max's assistant. As the afternoon passed, Max became frustrated with his assignment. In contrast, Jim enjoyed the work. At the end of the day, Max asked Jim why he was so happy. Jim replied, "I've been out of work for two months. This is the first time I could do something for someone else." Max was perplexed. "Why isn't Jim looking for a job?" he thought. Then Jim told Max how God loves a cheerful giver (2 Cor. 9:6–7). Jim believed that God would provide for all of his needs.

Lord, please give me a cheerful heart so that I might know Your joy. Amen.

SEEING GOD'S WAY
Isaiah 58:10

Carl was an investment banker living on the West Coast, and his work dictated an early start. Adding to the morning routine, the forty-five-minute drive to work was monotonous. As Carl mentally reviewed the day's duties, he remembered a biblical principal discussed in his men's Bible study earlier that week. The men were challenging one another to give to the hungry, poor, and oppressed whenever they saw the opportunity (see Isa. 58:10).

As Carl stopped at the traffic light on the familiar intersection, he noticed a homeless man standing on the corner. He was elderly, and his face was weathered by the sun, wind, and rain. His clothes hung on him, threadbare and stained. Just then, an ambulance roared by, delaying the traffic and sustaining the red traffic light.

Carl thought, "That homeless man could be the next potential patient for an ambulance." As the traffic crawled, Carl's BMW stopped in line with the homeless man on the corner. Carl rolled down his car window and motioned for the homeless man. Carl shook his hand, while placing a twenty-dollar bill in the palm of his hand. As the traffic cleared, the homeless man unraveled the twenty-dollar bill to reveal Carl's business card. On the back of the card, Carl wrote, "Give me a call. I want to help."

Lord, thank You that Jesus is the Light of the world. Please let His light shine forth in me. Amen.

DAY FOUR

SHARING
Matthew 5:42

Billy asked, "Why should I give Jenny half of my doughnut?" His dad, John, peered over the newspaper to see the six-year-old boy waiting at the breakfast table for an answer. Like most boys, Billy found it hard to get along with his younger sister, Jenny. In fact, if you asked Billy's parents, they would admit that it was also difficult for *them* to get along with Jenny because she tended to be a bit precocious and a know-it-all. However, John believed Billy needed to understand what it meant to share. John remembered a preacher who once said, "We are to give to everyone who asks, not give everything to him that asks" (see Matt. 5:42).

"Billy, why did Jenny ask you for half of your doughnut?" John queried.

Billy's frustration began to increase as Jenny continued to demand half. "But dad, she has a bowl of cereal. Why should I give her half of my doughnut?" Billy questioned his father.

"Is that the last doughnut?" asked John.

Looking at his sister, Billy said begrudgingly, "Yes."

"Then why don't you give her half of your doughnut? God has given us everything we need and has provided our meals. What does God ask us to do when we see someone in need?"

Billy thought about what his father was asking and remembered what he had learned in a Sunday school lesson. Since Billy had not taken a bite out of his doughnut, he decided to give it to his sister.

Father, please forgive me when I'm not as generous as I ought to be to others, especially those in need. Amen.

DAY FIVE

REAL LOVE
Luke 6:38

For many years, Clarence forgot his wedding anniversary. Well, at least he would remember at the last minute and scurry to a nearby florist and purchase a half dozen roses. One day, Clarence noticed a colleague who appeared to have a happy marriage. Roger's wife called her husband at work, they engaged in romantic conversation, and ended the conversations with mutual greetings of love. In the back of Clarence's mind, he thought of Roger's intermittent, romantic telephone calls as frivolous. But he saw how Roger loved his wife, and that love was returned in the same measure.

Clarence realized that his generosity should be shown in return for the immense goodness of God. He called his wife and asked whether she had any dinner plans. His wife, Gail, surprised by the question, prepared for a lovely evening. The night went by quickly, and Clarence discovered the joy of giving more and receiving the same in return (see Luke 6:38).

Lord, please help me to discover the joy of giving to others. Amen.

TRUST GOD WITH EVERYTHING

Luke 12:33

Kevin came from a family who doubted the integrity of others. In fact, trust was difficult to obtain in family discussions. Nonetheless, Kevin strove to fan the flames of his new faith in Christ. The greatest form of anxiety in Kevin's family was money. He began to question his wife's purchases and the need to give over and above their tithe. Kevin's wife, Nancy, responded to his inquiry by reminding him of his faith in Jesus.

Nancy said, "Those who have placed their trust in God and their hope in His kingdom are commanded to have a new attitude about their earthly possessions" (see Luke 12:33). Kevin suddenly realized that he needed to depend more on God, who provided for all of his needs, than on material goods. He admitted his weakness and asked for his wife's forgiveness. From that point, Kevin ceased to trust in material things and placed his trust exclusively in God.

Father, please help me to place my trust
exclusively in You. Amen.

CARRY ON!

Acts 20:35

Pastor Larry has ministered to a small community for more than nine years and planted several other ministries based on his encouragement of others. When people meet and speak with Pastor Larry, they can't help feeling better about themselves. Encouragement is definitely one of Larry's spiritual gifts and is evidenced both at work and at home. Because of Larry's encouraging words and constant urge to improve, his wife and children believe they are better people (see Acts 20:35).

However, the surrounding community has deteriorated as a result of an economic shift in market demands. Many individuals left the community for better jobs and were replaced by transient families with lower skills and abilities. Schools, stores, and various businesses seemed to change overnight. Larry, an African-American pastor, felt alienated in a community that once embraced his encouragement. Larry was ready to throw in the towel.

Then, an elderly lady named Pearl visited Pastor Larry's office. "I've watched you for nearly ten years, consoling, shepherding, and ministering to this community. You have been an encouragement to everyone." The pastor leaned forward in his chair and said, "Then why are so many people leaving and being replaced by individuals with animosity to God's Word?" Pearl said, "God has brought them for you to grow in your ministry. In fact, I believe God gifted you with an encouraging heart for such a time as this."

Larry paused, thanked Pearl for her honesty, and then excused himself to go home. As he approached his house, a family of three greeted him. "Thank you, Pastor," said the family's father. "We have been to three other cities and we never felt at home until we arrived here."

Lord, please give me the strength and wisdom to encourage others. Amen.

JIM SNEAD JR.

A Man and His Finances: Savings

THE BEGINNING AND THE END OF LIFE

1 Timothy 6:7

The birth of a baby is a most exciting event in human life. In previous generations, the birthing process was done behind closed, sterile doors. Sadly, this made the arrival of the infant seem distant and detached for extended family members. But now, because physicians allow family members to have some part in the blessed event, it is an awesome experience for everyone involved.

Every birth has one characteristic in common: the infant comes into the world with nothing. Over the newborn's lifetime, he will begin to acquire a host of possessions. This certainly has proven true with me. The places where I have space to store my belongings are running over with no room to spare. I sometimes wonder how I got all this stuff!

But here's a sobering thought: Just as we brought nothing into this world, so we will not carry any of our earthly possessions with us when we die (1 Tim. 6:7). Seminary president Maxie Dunnam once said, "You never see a U-Haul® trailer following the funeral car!" Nevertheless, we can leave a bit of ourselves in the lives of the people we touch. For example, we can pass on to our children and grandchildren the knowledge and love of God that we have learned throughout our lifetime. Now that's a wonderful heritage!

O Lord, please help me to leave to my children
and grandchildren an awareness of Your love
and truth. Amen.

WHAT ONE PERSON CAN DO!

Genesis 41:35−36

The people who lived in Egypt during the reign of Pharaoh had to have confidence in the government and in the God of Joseph (Gen. 41:35–36). But today we lack confidence in our government, and many people don't even give lip service to God. And in our personal lives, debt is pulling many families under. Moreover, society does not tell us that we need to prepare for the rainy days that are bound to come.

What can one person do? I was moved by the story of media mogul Ted Turner's pledging $1 billion to create a new foundation to benefit United Nations causes, such as helping refugees, fighting disease, and cleaning up land mines. Turner readily gave up some of his vast wealth to help others in need.

So what can you do? Consider Joseph. Yes, he was just one person. Yet God used him to save many people from starvation. The Lord might not make you the prime minister of a powerful nation, but He can enable you to do much good for the kingdom through the money you save and use wisely. Who knows how many lost people might be converted to Christianity through your tithe or how many struggling believers might be encouraged in their faith because you gave to the work of the Lord?

Father, please help me to be wise in saving money so that I can use it to do as much good as possible for Your kingdom. Amen.

DON'T LET IT GO TO WASTE!

Proverbs 12:27

The lazy man mentioned in Proverbs 12:27 is a paradox. He is willing to do work, but only to a certain extent. For example, he is able to expend enough effort to catch some game. But then, for whatever reason, he stops. Although he has a successful hunt, he refuses to cook the animal he catches so that he can eat it.

What's the difference between the lazy man and the wise man? Diligence. Diligence is the characteristic of a person who not only starts something but also finishes it. He makes wise use of his possessions and resources and follows through to the end. In contrast, the lazy man not only squanders what he has but also makes wastefulness a way of life. Clearly, this is poor stewardship.

What resources has God given you? Perhaps it's money that you've acquired and saved over the years. What are you doing with it? If you are wise, you will not only value it but also make good use of it. For example, you will use the possessions and resources at your disposal to start and finish jobs you know God wants you to do, thus both advancing the work of His kingdom and bringing glory to Him.

Father, please help me to make wise use of my possessions and resources. Amen.

DAY FOUR

NAÏVETÉ VERSES PRUDENCE
Proverbs 14:15

What does Proverbs 14:15 mean by the phrase "the simple person?" Scholars uniformly agree that it means someone who is naive and gullible. A good synonym for it might be a "simpleton." It refers to someone who is untrained intellectually and morally.

The wise person stands in sharp contrast to the simple person. The prudent man can discriminate between right and wrong and ponders, rather than readily accepts, every word he hears. He is not only mature but also skilled in acting temperately and judiciously.

When it comes to savings, the simple person probably would be an easy target for get-rich-quick schemes. At the drop of a hat, he might indiscriminately give away his money to some shady deal, never suspecting that anything is wrong. That would hardly be true of the wise man. He would discern every step he takes in spending his hard-earned savings. And he would use his keenly trained sense of right and wrong to detect whether someone is trying to swindle him.

Which type of person do you tend to be with your savings? Are you an easy target for con artists or someone who avoids being taken in by the bogus claims of others? Take a few moments to search your heart, and resolve today to use the wisdom of God to avoid being gullible.

*Lord, please help me to have the discernment to
avoid being swindled by others. Amen.*

DAY FIVE

Our Most Precious Treasure

Proverbs 21:20

As I consider Proverbs 21:20, my mind goes to a statement made by Colin Powell: "Clearly, the future of our country lies in the success of our children and the value that we, as adults, ensure they receive."

Our most precious treasure today is our children. They are like clay—ready to be molded into vessels and filled with God's knowledge.

The wisdom of Scripture can be wasted if we do not work to pass it on to our children and grandchildren. Role modeling, or mentoring, is necessary if our loved ones are to drink deeply from God's fountain of saving truth.

The fool, sadly, fails to see the importance of passing on any spiritual heritage to his loved ones. Instead, he selfishly hoards whatever knowledge, understanding, and material goods he gets, never imagining that he is acting irresponsibly.

The wise person is much more godly in his actions. He is eager to share his material and spiritual resources with his loved ones. He knows that this is his God-given opportunity to make a lasting difference in the lives of others. He does not mind the necessary sacrifice of time and energy because he realizes that he is helping to create a better future for them and for all of the people they touch with their lives. Wouldn't you like this to be true of you?

*Lord, help me to do what I can to invest in my
most precious treasure—my loved ones. Amen.*

WEALTH AND RICHES
Psalm 112:3

Psalm 112:3 contains a lot of horse sense. The wise man values the material and spiritual blessings of God, whereas the fool wastes and misuses whatever he has.

Consider the materialistic society in which we live. The availability of easy loans has put many people on the edge of bankruptcy. We are living in a time when purchasing and buying gives some people a great sense of power. Credit cards extend that sense of power even more.

Potential savings fly out the window as the desire to keep up appearances and to accumulate more drives the prodigal to spend every penny he earns. As he stretches his credit to the limit, he eventually discovers that he is spending more than he can realistically afford. The prudent man is far wiser. He realizes that it is good for him to put money aside for hard times. He also knows that God is pleased with such foresight and restraint.

Are you like the wise man or the foolish man in your spending habits? As you examine your lifestyle, consider whether your spending is intended to please merely yourself or to please the Lord.

Father, help me to be God-pleasing, not merely
self-pleasing, in the use of my hard-earned
savings. Amen.

A RECYCLING STORY
John 6:12

Every bit of information that we read in the Bible surges with life's instructions. For example, John 6:12 gives us a picture of a frugal Lord. An unexpected emergency had occurred; a large crowd of five thousand men (not counting women and children) were listening to Christ, and He decided to feed them (Mark 6:44).

When everyone had eaten as much as they wanted, Jesus commanded His disciples to gather up the leftovers, so that nothing would be wasted. When they did, they were able to fill twelve baskets from the pieces of bread the people did not eat. Undoubtedly, Jesus' followers were amazed at this result!

We should be, too, for it reminds us that God gives in abundance. Perhaps that spare change in your pocket might not seem like very much. But consider how much you could save over a period of time if you decided to set aside, rather than immediately spend, your "extra" money? And imagine what God could possibly do with it to further His kingdom.

Remember, God can take whatever money you have to offer— even your loose pocket change—and use it effectively beyond your wildest expectations. So what are you waiting for? Start saving!

God, please help me to be thrifty with whatever resources You provide so that it can be used to further Your work. Amen.

Biographical Information
of Contributors

Z. Allen Abbott, who wrote Week 11, is the Executive Director of American Baptist Men, USA, in Valley Forge, Pennsylvania. He previously worked at radio, television, and cable stations in both the United States and Canada. Allen has written for a wide variety of publications, including *The American Baptist Quarterly* and *The Journal of the American Academy of Ministry*. He received his education at Northern Kentucky University and The Southern Baptist Theological Seminary. He is married to Conda and loves sports (especially hockey and golf), travel, telecommunications, and computers. He can be reached at P.O. Box 851, Valley Forge, PA 19482-0851.

Leonard Albert, who wrote Week 14, is Executive Director of Church of God Lay Ministries in Cleveland, Tennessee. He travels extensively throughout the United States and the rest of the world, speaking on evangelism, apologetics, and cults. He is also a conference leader, and he has written five books, including *Evangelism Breakthrough*. Leonard received his education from Lee University. He can be reached at P.O. Box 2430, Cleveland, TN 37320-24301.

Guenter Apsel, who wrote Week 16, is a retired minister living half the year in his native Germany and the other half in the United States. He is the President of the European Forum of Christian Men and has served as a minister for men in the Evangelical Church of Westphalia in Germany. Guenter has written for many publications, including yearly devotional booklets titled *Ein Weggeleit*. He was educated at Bethel Theological College, the University of Heidelberg, the University of Basel, and the University of Muenster. Guenter is married and has one daughter. He can be reached at 1114 Lake Willisara Circle, Orlando, FL 32806-5581.

Don M. Aycock, the editor of this book, wrote the outline and topics, selected the Scripture passages, and wrote Weeks 7, 21, and 32. He is pastor of the First Baptist Church in Palatka, Florida. He also leads "Legacy Builders" men's conferences around the country. Don has written dozens of articles and fifteen books, including *Eight Days That Changed the World, Walking Straight in a Crooked World, The Christian Writer's Book* (with Len Goss), *Apathy in the Pew, Prayer 101,* and *Be Still and Know: How to Have a Conversation with God.* Don received his education at Louisiana College, Southern Baptist Theological Seminary, and New Orleans Baptist Theological Seminary, from which he has the Th.D. degree. He and his wife, Carla, have twin teenage sons, Chris and Ryan. Don enjoys traveling, playing the guitar, and fishing. He can be reached at 501 Oak Street, Palatka, FL 32177, or donaycock@usa.net.

Bryant Barnes, who wrote Week 41, is pastor of the Calvary Baptist Church in Tupelo, Mississippi. He received his education from William Cary College and New Orleans Baptist Theological Seminary, from which he received the Th.D. degree. Bryant is married to Cheryl. They have one son, Colin. Bryant enjoys golf, tennis, and reading. He can be reached at P.O. Box 1008, Tupelo, MS 38820.

Rick Brand, who wrote Week 26, is pastor of the First Presbyterian Church in Henderson, North Carolina. He has written for many publications, including *The Ministers Manual, The Abingdon Preaching Annual, Expository Times,* and *The Clergy Journal.* Rick received his education at Davidson College and Princeton Theological Seminary. He is married to Betty, and they have two children, Vic and Jeff. Rick enjoys bookbinding, woodworking, racquetball, and restoring his 1941 Ford. He can be reached at P.O. Box 726, Henderson, NC 27536.

Michael B. Brown, who wrote Week 1, is Senior Minister of Centenary United Methodist Church, in Winston-Salem, North Carolina. He chaired the commission that created "Vision 2000" and has preached on "The Protestant Hour." He is the author of many publications, including *Ordinary Sins, It Works for Us!* and *Be All That You Can Be.* Michael was educated at High Point University, Duke University, and Drew Theological Seminary (where he earned a D.Min.). Michael is married to Carolyn. They have two children, Adam and Zachary. Michael can be reached at P.O. Box 658, Winston-Salem, NC 27102.

Harold Bryson, who wrote Week 30, is Professor of Christian Studies at Mississippi College in Clinton, Mississippi. His numerous publications include *How Faith Works, Increasing the Joy, Portraits of God, Building Sermons to Meet People's Needs,* and *Expository Preaching.* Harold was educated at Mississippi College and New Orleans Baptist Seminary (where he earned the Th.D. degree). He is the father of two grown sons, William and Thomas. When he is not working, Harold can be found fishing. He can be reached at P.O. Box 4013, Clinton, MS 39058.

Jim Burton, who wrote Week 3, is Director of Volunteer Mobilization for the North American Mission Board in Alpharetta, Georgia. He was previously with the Baptist Brotherhood Commission. He leads "Legacy Builders" men's conferences around the country. Jim is the author of many articles and the book *Legacy Builders*. He is also a widely published photographer. Jim received his education at Western Kentucky University and Southwestern Baptist Theological Seminary. He and his wife, Kim, have two sons, Jim and Jacob. Jim (the father) enjoys sports, reading, writing, and photography. He can be reached at 7130 Titchfield Place, Cumming, GA 30041-8374.

James Carter, who wrote Week 9, is Director, Division of Church-Minister Relations of the Louisiana Baptist Convention in Alexandria, Louisiana. He has also been the pastor of five churches. James is a prolific author with many books to his credit, including *Ministerial Ethics* (with Joe Trull), *Facing the Final Foe, Help for the Evangelistic Preacher,* and *Christ and the Crowds.* He received his education at Louisiana College and has M.Div. and Ph.D. degrees from Southwestern Baptist Theological Seminary. James is married to Carole, and they have three grown children, James, Edward, and Chyrisse Ann. James (the father) can be reached at P.O. Box 311, Alexandria, LA 71309.

Stephen Clark, who wrote Week 12, operates his own communications development, management, and consulting business in Indianapolis, Indiana. He has also served as an editor at several publishing houses, including Bridge Publishing. He has written many articles and books, including *Cry of the Innocents* and *All They Want Is the Truth.* He is working on a soon-to-be-published book on spiritual warfare. Stephen received his education at Evangel College. He lives with his cat, Jiniwin, and is an active member of his church. He can be reached at 5287 Crestview Avenue, Indianapolis, IN 46220-3216.

Ken Corr, who wrote Week 47, is pastor of the First Baptist Church of Memphis, Tennessee. He has written for *The Book of Daily Prayer,* among other publications. Ken has degrees from Auburn University and Southwestern Baptist Theological Seminary, from which he received the D.Min. degree. He is married to Denise, and they have four children, Zachary, Rachel, Caroline, and Charlotte. Ken enjoys reading, coaching basketball, and jogging. He can be reached at 200 E. Parkway, Memphis, TN 38112.

Randy Davis, who wrote Week 38, is the pastor of the Trinity Baptist Church in Hammond, Louisiana, and he is an adjunct faculty member of New Orleans Baptist Theological Seminary. He is the author of *Pray for Your Family,* and he has also written for *Missions Today* and other publications. Randy received his education at Union University and New Orleans Baptist Theological Seminary, from which he received the Th.D. degree. Randy is married to Barbara, and they have two children, Jessica and Daniel. Randy enjoys cooking, computers, and weight lifting. He can be reached at 42062 Pumpkin Center Road, Hammond, LA 70403.

Marvin Douglass, who wrote Week 48, is in private practice as a Christian counselor in Lake Charles, Louisiana. He has written for publications such as *The Theological Educator*. Marvin has three earned degrees, including the Ph.D. degree from New Orleans Baptist Theological Seminary. He is married to Karen. They have five children and twelve grandchildren. He enjoys motorcycles and sailing. He can be reached at P.O. Box 5384, Lake Charles, LA 70606.

Michael Duduit, who wrote Week 43, is Executive Vice President of Union University in Jackson, Tennessee. He is also active in church and academic life and hosts a national preaching conference each year. Michael is the author of numerous books, including *Communicate with Power, Joy in Ministry,* and *Handbook of Contemporary Preaching.* He is the editor of the *Abingdon Preaching Annual.* He is also editor of *Preaching* magazine. Michael has degrees from Stetson University, Southern Baptist Theological Seminary, and Florida State University (Ph.D.). He and his wife, Laura, have one son, James Robert. Michael can be reached at Union University, 1050 Union University Drive, Jackson, TN 38305-3697.

Terry Etter, who wrote Week 33, is Director of Men's Life in Grand Rapids, Michigan. He has written for various publications, including *New Man* magazine. Terry was educated at DePauw University and received a doctorate from the University of Illinois. He is married to Rosemary, and they have two children, Lisa and Rachel. Terry loves skiing, running, golfing, and encouraging men to pursue their faith with passion. He can be reached at 2850 Kalamazoo Avenue, SE, Grand Rapids, MI 49560.

David Farr, who wrote Week 51, is acting Director of Development for Promise Keepers in Denver, Colorado. He is in the process of being ordained by the Evangelical Church Alliance. David was educated at Colorado State University, the University of Colorado, and Denver Theological Seminary. He has written for *Focal Point* magazine, among other publications. He is married to Diane, and they have one son, Peter Isaac David. David (the father) enjoys reading, writing, running, aerobics, and racquetball. He can be reached at P.O. Box 103001, Denver, CO 80250-3001.

C. W. Fogleman, who wrote Week 36, is a retired professor of sociology living in Lake Charles, Louisiana. He has written for publications such as *Social Forces*. Among his degrees, he has the Ph.D. degree from Louisiana State University. C. W. is married to LeVerane. They have three daughters and several grandchildren. C. W. loves traveling and deep-sea fishing. He can be reached at 1009 Fair Oaks Lane, Lake Charles, LA 70605.

Leonard Goss, who wrote Week 24, is Senior Acquisitions and Development Editor for Broadman & Holman Publishers in Nashville, Tennessee. He has been involved in Christian publishing for many years. Len received his education from Phoenix College, Arizona State University, the University of Windsor, and Trinity Evangelical Divinity School. He has published widely, including writing (with Don Aycock) *The Christian Writer's Book* and *Writing Religiously*. Together, they also edited *Inside Religious Publishing*. Len has also written *The Crossway Stylebook*. Len is married to Carolyn, and they have two sons, Joseph and David. Len enjoys golfing, walking, reading, and playing the guitar. He can be reached at 127 Ninth Avenue, N., Nashville, TN 37234.

John Harris, who wrote Week 39, is a retired pastor from Pineville, Louisiana. He has written for many publications, including *Home Life* and *Church Administration*. John was educated at Mercer University and the Southern Baptist Theological Seminary. John is married to Ruth, and they have two daughters, Emily and Johnita, and three grandchildren. John enjoys camping and working on his 1953 Chrysler Windsor. He is also deeply involved in Habitat for Humanity. He can be reached at 106 Ivy Lane, Pineville, LA 71360.

Bob Hartsell, who wrote Week 50, is President of Hartsell & Associates Worldwide Funding in Hot Springs, Arkansas. He has had career experience as a local-church minister, university/seminary professor, private consultant/trainer, and substance abuse counselor. Bob received his education at Ouachita Baptist University, New Orleans Baptist Theological Seminary, Kansas State University, and Louisiana State University, where he received his Ph.D. degree. He enjoys flying, photography, canoeing, and fishing. Bob is married to Elinor, and they have two daughters, Nikki and Lynaire, and a son, Bruce. They also brag about their six grandchildren. Bob can be reached at 2 Oliete Lane, Suite 100, Hot Springs, AR 71909.

Doug Haugen, who wrote Week 22, is Director of Lutheran Men in Mission, a men's ministry of the Evangelical Lutheran Church in America in Chicago, Illinois. He is also the President of the North American Conference of Church Men's Staff, who cooperated in

331

putting together this book. Doug was educated at the Lutheran Bible Institute and Moorhead State University. He wrote a weekly newspaper column for twelve years, and has written various Bible study materials. Doug is married to Doris, and they have two children, Derek and Dawn. Doug enjoys travel, softball, and other sports. He can be reached at 8765 West Higgins Road, Chicago, IL 60631.

Harold Hawkins, who wrote Week 23, was President of the Brotherhood of St. Andrew, an Episcopal/Anglican community. He wrote a regular "President's Message" for the quarterly *Cross* magazine. Harold was educated at North Central College. He was married and the father of four daughters and was committed to the work of ministry to men. Harold enjoyed gardening, golf, and volunteer work. He died while this book was in preparation. His widow can be reached at 2603 Woodland, Park Ridge, IL 60068.

Bruce Hennigan, who wrote Week 42, is a physician from Shreveport, Louisiana. He is a published playwright whose works include *The Adventures of Montana Holmes*. Bruce is a graduate of Louisiana State University (LSU), Shreveport, and LSUMC, Shreveport. Bruce is married to Sherry, and they have two children, Sean and Casey. Bruce enjoys theater, snow skiing, writing, and collectibles. He can be reached at 2003 Chase Crossing, Shreveport, LA 71118.

Dennis Hillman, who wrote Week 25, is Publisher of Kregel Publications in Grand Rapids, Michigan. He received his education at Southern Methodist University and Dallas Theological Seminary. He also served as a pastor for fourteen years before taking his current position. Dennis is married and is the father of five children. His hobbies include water sports and "home repair." Dennis can be reached at 937 W. Main, Middleville, MI 49333.

C. Thomas Hilton, who wrote Week 4, is the pastor of Amelia Plantation Chapel in Amelia Island, Florida. He has written for many publications and is the author of *Be My Guest* and *Ripe Life*. Thomas received his education from Macalester College, Princeton Theological Seminary, and Drew University Theological Seminary, where he received the D.Min. degree. Thomas is married to Janet, and they have four children and eight grandchildren. He enjoys reading and writing. He can be reached at P.O. Box 8014, Amelia Island, FL 32034.

Robert Leslie Holmes, who wrote Week 5, is the pastor of the First Presbyterian Church of Pittsburgh, Pennsylvania. He received his education at the University of Mobile, Reformed Theological Seminary, and Columbia Theological Seminary. Robert is the author of *Don't*

Try to Stop on a Mountain and the coeditor of *Come to the Banquet*. He and his wife, Barbara, have two grown children and two grandchildren. Robert's hobbies include photography, writing, reading, and travel. He can be reached at 320 Sixth Avenue, Pittsburgh, PA 15222.

Fisher Humphreys, who wrote Week 15, is Professor of Theology at the Beeson Divinity School at Samford University in Birmingham, Alabama. He is the author of numerous books, including *Thinking About God, The Heart of Prayer, The Death of Christ,* and *The Nature of God*. He was educated at Mississippi College, Loyola University, Oxford University, and New Orleans Baptist Theological Seminary. Fisher is married to Caroline, and they have two grown children. He enjoys travel, novels, and movies. He can be reached at 800 Lakeshore Drive, Birmingham, AL 35229-2252.

Heinz Janzen, who wrote Week 27, was a consultant with Mennonite Men before his retirement. He was the pastor of three churches and served as the General Secretary of the General Conference Mennonite Church from 1969–1980. Heinz has written for *The Minister's Manual, Bible Study Guides,* and *The Mennonite*. He received his education at Bethel College and Biblical Theological Seminary of New York. He and his wife, Dotty, have three grown children and four grandchildren. Heinz enjoys reading history, gardening, walking, and refreshing his German language skills. He can be reached at 722 Main Street, Newton, KS 67114-0347.

Joe Johnson, who wrote Week 20, is President of Johnson Literary and Talent Services in Antioch, Tennessee. He has written three books and more than thirteen hundred articles, and he was a producer and editor for Broadman & Holman Publishers. Joe received his education from Mississippi College and New Orleans Baptist Theological Seminary. He is married to Mary Sue, and they have three grown sons. Joe enjoys music, research, and freelance writing. He can be reached at 2915 Walnut Crest Drive, Antioch, TN 37013.

Mark Johnson, who wrote Week 19, is the managing editor of *Preaching* magazine in Jackson, Tennessee. He has written for various publications, including the *Abingdon Preaching Annual*. Mark received his education at Wake Forest University, Southwestern Baptist Seminary, and Southern Baptist Seminary, from which he earned the Ph.D. degree. Mark is single and loves photography and working out. He can be reached at 28 Collinwood Cove, Jackson, TN 38305.

Gary Kunz, who wrote Week 44, is a patent examiner in the U.S. Patent and Trademark Office in Washington, D.C. His specialty is anticancer and antiviral drugs. Gary received his education from the University of Illinois, Southern Baptist Theological Seminary, and the University of Louisville (where he earned a Ph.D. degree). Gary has written numerous scientific articles. He is married to Margaret and loves reading, tennis, and hunting for mushrooms. He can be reached at 100 Summit Hall Road, Gaithersburg, MD 20877.

Stephen Livesay, who wrote Week 45, is Vice President for Institutional Advancement at Belhaven College in Jackson, Mississippi. He is the author of many publications, such as articles in *Ready Reference: Ethics* and various book reviews. Stephen received his education at Bob Jones University, Oakland University, and the University of Michigan (where he earned a Ph.D. degree). He is married to Corinne, and they have three children, Brent, Kara, and Katie. Stephen enjoys photography, travel, and watching auto racing. He can be reached at 117 Lake Forest Lane, Clinton, MS 39056.

David McCracken, who wrote Week 28, is Senior Associate in the Office of Disciples Men in Indianapolis, Indiana. He was educated at Manchester College, Purdue University, and Christian Theological Seminary. David has written numerous articles for publications such as *The Disciple*. He and his wife, Carolyn, have five sons. David enjoys singing in men's quartets and gospel groups. His passion is hands-on men's mission work. He can be reached at 130 E. Washington Street, Indianapolis, IN 46204.

Curtis Miller, who wrote Week 29, is Associate for Men's Ministry for the Presbyterian Church (USA) in Louisville, Kentucky. He was educated at Ohio State University and Louisville Presbyterian Seminary, from which he received the D.Min. degree. Curtis is single and enjoys golf, music composition, and collecting vintage guitars. He can be reached at 100 Witherspoon Street, Room 1613, Louisville, KY 40202.

Thad Moore, who wrote Week 46, is the pastor of the First Baptist Church of Holly Springs, Mississippi. He has written for a wide variety of publications, including the Mississippi State Baptist paper and the Annuity Board of the Southern Baptist Convention. Thad has degrees from Mississippi College, Midwestern Baptist Theological Seminary, and New Orleans Baptist Theological Seminary. He is married to Kim, and they have two children, Lydia and Shaw. Thad enjoys sports and reading. He can be reached at 265 Chulahoma, Holly Springs, MS 38635.

Jim Neal, who wrote Week 2, is President of Dad, The Family Shepherd, in Little Rock, Arkansas. He has written for publications such as *Artists in Ministry*. Jim received his education at Cornerstone

College. He is on the teaching faculty of Promise Keepers and is also a professional golfer. His hobbies include computers. Jim and his wife, Ruth, have four children and eight grandchildren. He can be reached at 50 Blue Mountain Dr., Maumelle, AR 72113.

H. Ray Newman, who wrote Week 6, is a specialist in Men's Ministries with the Georgia Baptist Convention in Atlanta, Georgia. He is a former pastor of six different churches. Ray was educated at Columbus State University and Southwestern Baptist Theological Seminary. He and his wife, Gwen, have one son, Rusty, one granddaughter, and 3 grandsons. Ray enjoys reading, especially when he is not traveling throughout Georgia for his work. He can be reached at 2930 Flowers Road South, Atlanta, GA 30341.

Will Pollard, who wrote Week 13, is Director of Media and Men's Ministries for the State Convention of Baptists in Ohio. He received his education at East Texas Baptist University and Southwestern Baptist Theological Seminary. Will is married to Peggy, and they have one son and two grandchildren. He has written for many publications including *Leadership* Magazine. Will enjoys golf, yard work, and home remodeling. He can be reached at 1680 E. Broad, Columbus, OH 43203.

Donald Rock, who wrote Week 31, is the pastor of the St. Paul's United Church of Christ in Woodsfield, Ohio. He has written for both national and local publications, including newspapers. Donald received his education at Heidelberg College, Terra Tech, and Methodist Theological Seminary. He is married to Shirley, and they have five grown children, David, Glenn, Carol, Susan, and Steven. Donald enjoys woodworking and wood refinishing. He can be reached at 307 South Main, Woodsfield, OH 43793.

Al Saunders, who wrote Week 35, is National Director of Adult Ministries for the Pentecostal Assemblies of Canada. His publications include *Except They Be Agreed, Positive Parenting,* and *Putting the Pieces Back Together*. Al is a graduate of Eastern Pentecostal Bible College and is a Certified Pastoral Counselor. He is married to Audrey, and they have three children and two grandchildren. Al enjoys bicycling, rollerblading, walking, and cross-country skiing. He can be reached at 6745 Century Avenue, Mississauga, Ontario, Canada L5N 6P7.

Ed Scott, who wrote Weeks 10, 17, and 34, is pastor of the First Baptist Church of Many, Louisiana. He is the author of *Pray for Your Pastor: A 40-Day Intercessory Prayer Plan*. He received his education at Pensacola Junior College, Baptist Bible College, and New Orleans Baptist Theological Seminary, where he earned the Th.D. degree. Ed is married to Leatrix,

and they have two children, Megan and Ross. Ed enjoys golf, ham radio, and computers. He can be reached at P.O. Box 239, Many, LA 71449.

Scott Shaver, who wrote Week 37, is the pastor of the First Baptist Church of Natchitoches, Louisiana. He also serves on various boards, including the Executive Board of the Louisiana Baptist Convention. He was educated at East Texas Baptist University and has the D.Min. degree from New Orleans Baptist Theological Seminary. Scott is married to Linda, and they have two daughters, Katy and Claire. Scott enjoys hunting and camping. He can be reached at 1414 E. 5th Street, Natchitoches, LA 71457.

Harold Ivan Smith, who wrote Week 8, is a death educator and consultant in Kansas City, Missouri. He also leads grief groups at St. Luke's Hospital. (These groups are based on storytelling.) Harold has written many books, including *Holy! Me?*, *Singles Ask*, *On Grieving the Death of a Father,* and *Grieving the Death of a Friend.* He received his education at Scarriett College, Vanderbilt University, Luther Rice Seminary, and Asbury Seminary (where he earned a D.Min. degree). Harold enjoys reading, antiques, and cemeteries. He can be reached at P.O. Box 24688, Kansas City, MO 64131.

Jim Snead Jr., who wrote Week 52, is Executive Director of United Methodist Men Foundation in Nashville, Tennessee. He has 35 years of experience working with men and boys. He is also the chairman of the 1999 World Forum of Christian Men in Jerusalem. Jim has written *More Prayers for Men,* and he has penned more than 2,000 articles for national publications. His education is from the University of Georgia and the 243rd National Training for Scout Executives. Jim is married to Ann, and they have three daughters and four grandchildren. Jim can be reached at 504 General George Patton Road, Nashville, TN 37221-2448.

Mark Sutton, who wrote Week 40, is pastor of the Brookwood Baptist Church in Shreveport, Louisiana. He has written hundreds of articles for various publications and is the author of *Thirty Days to a Better Marriage.* Mark received his education at Louisiana College and Southwestern Baptist Seminary. He is married to Susan, and they have three daughters. Mark enjoys playing his guitar and leading "Rekindle the Flame" marriage seminars, which are based on his book. Mark can be reached at 8900 Kingston Road, Shreveport, LA 71118.

Ken Walker, who wrote Week 49, is a freelance writer from Louisville, Kentucky. He is the coauthor of *Ultimate Warriors* and the lead editor of *Manpower.* Ken has also written more than 750 magazine and newspaper articles. He says of himself, "I write about what God is doing in the world." He received his education from Ohio University. Ken is married to Janet and has four stepchildren and seven grandchildren. Ken enjoys basketball, reading, and golf. He can be reached at 3630-A Brownsboro Road, #272, Louisville, KY 40207.

Ross West, who wrote Week 18, is President of Positive Difference Communications in Rome, Georgia. He is a seminar leader on the areas of work, time management, job satisfaction, and faith in the workplace. Ross is the author of two books titled *Go to Work and Take Your Faith Too!* and *How to Be Happier in the Job You Sometimes Can't Stand.* He received his education at Louisiana Tech University, Southern Baptist Theological Seminary, and New Orleans Baptist Theological Seminary. Ross is married to Martha, and they have one son and two grandchildren. Ross enjoys reading, travel, photography, and hiking in the woods. He can be reached at 100 Martha Drive, Rome, GA 30165-4138.